THE
DIABETIC
Goodie
COOKBOOK

THE
DIABETIC
Goodie
COOKBOOK

Classic Desserts and Baked Goods to Satisfy Your Sweet Tooth

KATHY KOCHAN

PHOTOGRAPHY BY ANNA JONES
Food Styling by Melissa Mileto

THE EXPERIMENT

NEW YORK

The Experiment, LLC | 220 East 23rd Street, Suite 600 | New York, NY 10010-4658
theexperimentpublishing.com

This book contains the opinions and ideas of its author. It is intended to provide helpful and informative material on the subjects addressed in the book. It is sold with the understanding that the author and publisher are not engaged in rendering medical, health, or any other kind of personal professional services in the book. The author and publisher specifically disclaim all responsibility for any liability, loss, or risk—personal or otherwise—that is incurred as a consequence, directly or indirectly, of the use and application of any of the contents of this book.

THE EXPERIMENT and its colophon are registered trademarks of The Experiment, LLC. Many of the designations used by manufacturers and sellers to distinguish their products are claimed as trademarks. Where those designations appear in this book and The Experiment was aware of a trademark claim, the designations have been capitalized.

The Experiment's books are available at special discounts when purchased in bulk for premiums and sales promotions as well as for fund-raising or educational use. For details, contact us at info@theexperimentpublishing.com.

Library of Congress Cataloging-in-Publication Data

Names: Kochan, Kathy, author.
Title: The diabetic goodie cookbook : classic desserts and baked goods to
    satisfy your sweet tooth-over 190 easy, blood-sugar-friendly recipes
    with no artificial sweeteners / Kathy Kochan.
Other titles: Diabetic goodie book
Description: New York, NY : The Experiment, LLC, 2021. | Originally
    published: Diabetic goodie book. 1996.
Identifiers: LCCN 2021028124 (print) | LCCN 2021028125 (ebook) | ISBN
    9781615197682 (paperback) | ISBN 9781615197699 (ebook)
Subjects: LCSH: Diabetes--Diet therapy--Recipes. | Desserts. | Low-fat
    diet--Recipes.
Classification: LCC RC662 .K625 2021 (print) | LCC RC662 (ebook) | DDC
    641.5/6314--dc23
LC record available at https://lccn.loc.gov/2021028124
LC ebook record available at https://lccn.loc.gov/2021028125

ISBN 978-1-61519-768-2
Ebook ISBN 978-1-61519-769-9

Cover and text design by Beth Bugler

Manufactured in China

First printing November 2021
10 9 8 7 6 5 4 3 2 1

I wish to dedicate this, my first cookbook, to the men in my life: My husband, Hank, and my sons, David and Marc. Without their love, support, patience, and willingness to try anything once, this book would never have been created.

CONTENTS

Cheesecakes 94

Yogurt Cheese 96

No-Bake Peachy Ricotta
  Cheesecake 97

No-Bake Swirl Cheesecake 98

Creamy Ricotta Cheesecake 100

Chocolate Cheesecake 101

Berry Buttermilk
  Cheesecake 103

Fruity Cheesecake 104

Pineapple Cheese Pie 105

Pumpkin Swirl Cheesecake 106

Black and White
  Cheesecake 108

Apple Cheesecake 109

Light Cheesecake 110

Cheesy Jam Squares 111

Layered Cheesecake
  Squares 113

Pineapple Cheesecake
  Squares 114

Coffee Cakes & Scones 116

Apple Crumb Coffee Cake 118

Banana-Date Crumb Coffee
  Cake 120

Berry Coffee Cake 121

Buttermilk Spice
  Coffee Cake 122

Nutty Raspberry
  Coffee Cake 123

Streusel Coffee Cake 125

Pineapple Coffee Cake 126

Speedy Chocolate
  Coffee Cake 127

Mixed Berry Coffee Cake 128

Blueberry Cornmeal Scones 130

Chocolate Chip Scones 131

Date Scones 132

Ginger Scones 133

Strawberry Scones 135

Fruit Desserts 136

Microwave Applesauce 138

Simple Baked Apples 139

Apple-Berry Yogurt Dessert 140

Apple-Nut Torte 142

Fruit with Yogurt Cream 143

Speedy Fruit Crisp 145

Blueberry-Nectarine Crisp 146

Peach Snowcaps 147

Peach Melba Parfait 148

Strawberry-Rhubarb
  Dessert 150

Baked Meringue Pears 151

Berry Baked Pears 153

Pineapple Sherbet 154

Peachy Ice Cream 155

Strawberry Sorbet 156

Frozen Yogurt Pops 159

Light and Fruity Shake 160

Homemade Dried Fruit 160

Ambrosia Bars 161

Muffins 162

Maple Apple Muffins 164

Apple Spice Muffins 165

Banana—Poppy Seed Muffins 166

Blueberry Muffins 168

Chocolate Chip Muffins 169

Corn Muffins 170

Fruity Bran Muffins 171

Cranberry Muffins 173

Honey Bran Muffins 174

Pineapple-Orange Muffins 175

Raspberry Muffins 176

Maple Nut Muffins 177

Peanut Butter and
  Jelly Muffins 178

Pumpkin Muffins 180

Raspberry Jam Muffins 181

Strawberry Muffins 182

Spicy Ginger Muffins 183

Zucchini Muffins 184

Poppy Seed Muffins 186

Pies, Tarts & Cobblers 188

Puddings 228

Quick Breads 246

ҒOREWORD

by Linda Hachfeld, MPH, RDN

· · · · · · · · · · · · · ·

What a delight to work with such varied recipes as are found in *The Diabetic Goodie Cookbook*. Who doesn't look forward to a dessert after a meal? Or a midafternoon snack reminiscent of a childhood memory, such as your mother's chocolate chip cookies? With recipes like Sesame Tea Bread (page 271), Pumpkin Swirl Cheesecake (page 106), Blueberry-Nectarine Crisp (page 146), and Strawberry Shortcake (page 72), you'll find something here for any time of day. Get excited to try a fresh new recipe, and you may discover that it becomes a family favorite.

Dessert is often thought of as a guilty pleasure, because desserts traditionally come loaded with sugar, saturated fat, and calories, which don't align well with any healthy eating plan. The current Dietary Guidelines for Americans (DGA) advise limiting added sugars to 7 to 10 percent of calories per day and limiting saturated fats to less than 10 percent of total calorie intake.

Kathy's recipes meet this challenge head on and offer more. They . . .

» are nutrient dense. These recipes contribute dietary fiber (using whole grains), health-enhancing antioxidants and phytonutrients (found in whole fruits and vegetables), a variety of high-quality proteins (nuts, seeds, eggs, reduced-fat dairy), and healthy fats* (olive oil).

» help meet healthy food group recommendations. The recipes count as vegetable, fruit, starch, protein (very lean meat), or dairy.

» contain small amounts of sugar, without the use of artificial (low- or no-calorie) sweeteners. Just enough sugar is used to get the right browning effect, body, texture, and taste.

» offer controlled portions. Everyone benefits from eating healthy food in reasonable amounts—doing so helps to maintain or achieve a healthy weight and to manage blood sugar levels.

One last piece of good news: Kathy has managed to do all the above so successfully that most of the recipes in this book are only *1 carb choice* per serving.

Enjoy moving inward to the recipes. Make something that appeals to your taste, because I can assure you that Kathy considered your health to be so important, she's made every bite count.

LINDA HACHFELD, MPH, RDN, is the award-winning author of *Cooking à la Heart* and a lifelong community advocate for heart-healthy living.

*As of June 2018, partially hydrogenated oils (PHOs), the major source of artificial trans fat in the food supply, are no longer Generally Recognized as Safe (GRAS). Trans fats are associated with a number of negative health effects. Although they were banned by the FDA, they are still found in some products, such as fried or baked foods and nondairy coffee creamers, due to certain exemptions. Be sure to read labels and check ingredients lists for partially hydrogenated oil.

ꝯHANDY ꝷIPS from ꝀATHY'S ꝀITCHEN

FOODS

» If your baked goods aren't rising, check the freshness of your baking powder. Mix 1 teaspoon with ⅓ cup (80 ml) hot water. If the mixture doesn't foam, the powder is stale and should be discarded.

» If your brown sugar is rock hard, add a slice of soft bread to the package and close it tightly. In a few hours, the sugar will be soft again. Remove the bread and store the sugar in an airtight container.

» To soften butter, unwrap it, cut it into pieces, place it on a plate, and microwave it on high for 10 to 15 seconds.

» To determine if your eggs are fresh or stale, place a whole egg into a glass of cold water. A fresh egg will sit horizontally at the bottom; an egg that sits vertically is stale (unsuitable for baking), and an egg that floats should be disposed of carefully.

» Use a small funnel to separate the yolks and whites from cold eggs. Crack the egg over the funnel; the white will run through, and the yolk will remain in the funnel.

» When beating egg whites, separate the whites from the eggs as soon as you remove them from the refrigerator. Let them stand at room temperature for at least half an hour before attempting to beat. Be sure the beaters and bowl don't contain any fat, which will inhibit the whites from foaming and becoming stiff. Rinse them with some white vinegar first and let air-dry. Don't use plastic bowls, which are impossible to get completely clean once fat has touched them.

» When using fresh fruit in a recipe, choose only ripe fruits. They will be more flavorful because of their natural sugar. The riper they are, the sweeter they usually taste. To ripen fruit, place it in a paper bag, close it loosely, and store it at room temperature. Fruit is ripe when it gives gently to pressure and smells sweet. Refrigerate until needed.

» Don't wash berries until just before using. Hull strawberries after they are washed and drained.

» It's best not to peel fruit, since fruit skins are high in natural fiber. If you prefer to peel, fruits such as peaches and apricots can be plunged into a pot of boiling water for 30 seconds, drained, and run under cold water. The peel should slide off.

» Extra-ripe bananas can be peeled and frozen in plastic bags. Thaw them before using in baking.

» Dried lemon and orange peels can be purchased in the spice section of the grocery store. Read the label and be sure to purchase unsweetened peels.

» When you have time, chop walnuts, pecans, or other nuts and store them in a plastic bag or container in the refrigerator. They will keep indefinitely. Nuts can also be frozen.

» To lower the amount of fat in traditional recipes containing nuts, decrease the amount of chopped nuts by toasting them. Toasted nuts have more flavor, so you can use less. To toast nuts, place chopped nuts in a baking pan and bake for 3 to 5 minutes in a preheated 350°F (180°C) oven. Cool before stirring into a batter. You can also toast nuts and store them in a covered container or plastic bag until ready to use.

» Chill pie crust pastry for at least 1 hour before rolling so it can be rolled extra thin. Save excess dough in the freezer.

» To make Yogurt Cheese (page 96): Place yogurt in two coffee filters or a triple layer of cheesecloth placed in a strainer or colander over a sturdy measuring cup or bowl, cover, and refrigerate. Allow to drain for 2 hours to achieve Greek yogurt; drain yogurt overnight for 12 hours or longer to get the consistency of a firm yogurt cheese. Save the high-protein whey (drained liquid) to use in smoothies, recipes such as the Featherweight Sponge Cake (page 62) or the

Nutty Maple Chiffon Cake (page 59), or other recipes that require water, such as soups or stews. Cover and store yogurt cheese in the refrigerator. The whey may continue releasing; just pour off any accumulated liquid before using.

PREPARATION

» Spray your measuring cup or spoons with cooking spray before measuring molasses or honey.

» Snip dates or dried apricots with kitchen scissors. Wet the scissors or spray them with cooking spray before snipping.

» Use an ice cream scoop to fill cupcake liners without spilling.

SAFETY AND CLEANLINESS

» Keep a damp cloth close at hand for quick cleanup. Wipe off the counter, stovetop, and microwave each time you use them.

» Use a damp cloth to wipe off cans before opening the tops. Wipe the blade on your can opener after each use.

» Wash utensils as you work.

» Wash unpeeled fruit before using.

» Use sharp knives to prevent injuries.

» Wrap foods in an airtight resealable plastic bag or freezer-safe container. Label and date items before placing in the freezer. Use oldest items first. See page 15 for freezer storage times.

MEASURING INGREDIENTS

» Baking powder, baking soda, cream of tartar, and spices: Dip and fill a measuring spoon, then level it off with a small metal spatula or table knife.

» Brown sugar: Spoon into a dry measuring cup and pack down firmly, then level it off with a metal spatula.

» Granulated sugar: Spoon into a dry measuring cup, then level it off with a metal spatula.

» Fat-free evaporated milk and egg substitute: Always shake the can or carton before measuring in a glass liquid measure.

» All-purpose and whole wheat flours: Stir to aerate the flour, spoon it into a dry measuring cup, then level it off with a metal spatula. Cake flour: Spoon lightly into a dry measuring cup, then level off with a metal spatula.

» Liquids: Pour into a liquid measuring cup, place on the counter, and check measurements at eye level.

EQUIVALENT MEASURES

MEASURE	EQUIVALENT	METRIC EQUIVALENT (LIQUID)
Dash	Few drops (liquid) Less than ⅛ teaspoon (dry)	
½ tablespoon	1½ teaspoons	8 ml
1 tablespoon	3 teaspoons	15 ml
4 tablespoons	¼ cup	60 ml
5 tablespoons + 1 teaspoon	⅓ cup	80 ml
8 tablespoons	½ cup	120 ml
10 tablespoons + 2 teaspoons	⅔ cup	160 ml
12 tablespoons	¾ cup	180 ml
16 tablespoons	1 cup	240 ml
2 cups	1 pint	480 ml
4 cups	1 quart	980 ml
4 quarts (liquid)	1 gallon	4 L
1 fluid ounce	2 tablespoons	30 ml
8 fluid ounces	1 cup	240 ml
16 fluid ounces	1 pint	480 ml
32 fluid ounces	1 quart	980 ml

COMMON FOOD EQUIVALENTS

INGREDIENT	AMOUNT	APPROXIMATE MEASURE	METRIC EQUIVALENT
Dairy			
Butter	1 stick 2 sticks 1 pound, 4 sticks	½ cup 1 cup 2 cups	113 g 227 g 454 g
Cream cheese	3-ounce package 8-ounce package	⅓ cup 1 cup	85 g 227 g
Cottage cheese	8-ounce container	1 cup	227 g
Ricotta	1 pound	2 cups	454 g
Eggs			
Eggs	4 large 7 to 15 whites 14 to 16 yolks	1 cup 1 cup 1 cup	200 g 245 g 245 g
Dried egg whites	2 teaspoons dried + 2 tablespoons warm water	1 white	35 g
Instant meringue mix	6 tablespoons mix + ⅓ cup cold water	1 ounce sweetened meringue (3 egg whites)	30 g

INGREDIENT	AMOUNT	APPROXIMATE MEASURE	METRIC EQUIVALENT
Fruit (fresh, unless otherwise specified)			
Apples	1 pound	3 medium (3 cups sliced)	454 g
Bananas	1 pound 1 medium	3 small (2 cups sliced) ½ cup mashed	454 g 112 g
Blueberries	1 pound	3 cups	454 g
Dates	1 pound	2¾ cups pitted and chopped	454 g
Lemons	1 medium	2 to 3 tablespoons juice; 1 tablespoon grated zest	85 g
Limes	1 medium	1 tablespoon juice; 1½ to 2 teaspoons grated zest	65 g
Oranges	1 medium	⅓ cup juice; 1 to 2 tablespoons grated zest	140 g
Peaches	1 pound	3 to 4 medium; 2½ cups sliced	454 g
Plums	1 pound	6 to 8, depending on variety; 2½ cups chopped	454 g
Raisins	6-ounce package 15.5-ounce package	1 cup 2½ cups	170 g 439 g
Rhubarb	1 pound	4 to 8 trimmed stalks; 2 cups cooked	454 g
Strawberries	1 pound	3 cups whole; 2¾ cups sliced	454 g
Milk			
Buttermilk	1 quart	4 cups	1 L
SACO buttermilk powder	1 tablespoon powder + ¼ cup water	¼ cup liquid buttermilk	60 ml liquid buttermilk
Fat-free evaporated milk	5-ounce can 12-ounce can	⅔ cup 1½ cups	147 ml 354 ml
Instant nonfat milk powder	about 1 tablespoon powder + ¼ cup water	¼ cup liquid milk	60 ml liquid milk
Nuts (shelled)			
Almonds, whole	1 pound	3 cups	454 g
Almonds, slivered	1 pound	4 cups	454 g
Pecans, halves	1 pound	4 cups; 3¾ cups chopped	454 g
Walnuts, halves	1 pound	4½ cups; 3½ cups chopped	454 g

INGREDIENT	AMOUNT	APPROXIMATE MEASURE	METRIC EQUIVALENT
Miscellaneous			
Carrots, whole	1 pound	5 to 6 medium; 3½ cups shredded	454 g
Carrots, baby	1 pound	2 to 3 cups; 12 to 15 carrots per cup	454 g
Graham crackers	15 crackers 13.5-ounce box crumbs	1 cup fine crumbs 3¾ cups; enough for three 8- or 9-inch pie crusts	102 g 383 g
Peanut butter	18-ounce jar	2 cups	510 g
Tapioca, quick-cooking	8-ounce box	1½ cups; 3¾ cups cooked	226 g
Vanilla and other extracts	1 ounce	2 tablespoons	30 ml

INGREDIENT SUBSTITUTIONS

Buttermilk: Commercial buttermilk powder can be substituted for liquid buttermilk. Use 1 tablespoon of dry buttermilk powder and ¼ cup (60 ml) water for each ¼ cup (60 ml) of liquid buttermilk a recipe requires. Mix the buttermilk powder with the dry ingredients and add the required amount of water with the wet ingredients. Cover and store opened containers of buttermilk powder in the refrigerator. Buttermilk powder, such as the SACO brand, can be found in the same baking aisle as flour and sugar in most grocery stores.

If buttermilk is not available, use regular, plain nonfat yogurt or sour milk. To make sour milk, add lemon juice or white vinegar to a glass measuring cup. (See measurements below.) Add enough nonfat milk to equal the amount of sour milk required and stir. Wait about 3 minutes for the milk to curdle, then stir again.

TO MAKE:	USE:
1 cup (240 ml) or ¾ cup (180 ml) sour milk	2 tablespoons lemon juice or white vinegar
½ cup (120 ml) sour milk	1 tablespoon lemon juice or white vinegar
⅓ cup (80 ml) sour milk	1½ teaspoons lemon juice or white vinegar

Egg substitute: Several brands of egg substitute can be found in the freezer or refrigerator section at the grocery store. If you choose to use whole eggs or egg whites, use this substitution guideline:

» ¼ cup (60 ml) egg substitute = 1 whole egg = 2 egg whites

Shelf-stable dried egg whites: These are necessary when the recipe requiring eggs or egg whites is not cooked or baked, as in many pudding, unbaked cheesecake, and meringue recipes. When using commercial products, use these substitution guidelines:

» For 1 egg white, use 2 teaspoons (4 g) of dried egg whites (such as Just Whites), and 2 tablespoons warm water.

» Dried egg white powder can be added to the dry ingredients in any recipe calling for egg whites; remember to also add 2 tablespoons of liquid in any form (like water, juice, or milk) to the wet ingredients.

» If you are using instant meringue mix, 6 tablespoons are the equivalent of 3 egg whites, and should be mixed with 1/3 cup (80 ml) cold water.

Olive oil or canola oil: Use extra-light or light olive oil. It has a subtle hint of olive oil flavor, which intensifies but doesn't overpower other ingredients. Olive and canola oil are high in monounsaturated fats and low in saturated fats, which research suggests has a protective impact on HDL cholesterol levels, a desirable trait for the prevention of heart disease. Other liquid vegetable oils are sources of polyunsaturated fats and can be exchanged for the same amount of olive oil.

Flour: Use white whole wheat flour or whole wheat pastry flour in place of whole wheat flour for a baked good that is lighter in color and texture.

NUTRITION INFORMATION

The recipes in this book are both calorie and carbohydrate controlled. They are sensitive to the type of fat used and encourage the use of monounsaturated fats such as canola or olive oil. (The recipes call for light or extra-light oil because of the taste, not because extra-light has any fewer calories, which it doesn't.) Some recipes call for butter (always about half the amount found in traditional recipes), because light margarines and tub margarines are made with a high percentage of water, which will produce a product that's undesirable in taste and appearance. Stick margarines contain partially hydrogenated fat, which is more harmful to our health than saturated fat.

With this in mind, each recipe provides a nutrient profile giving the total calories, carbohydrates, protein, fat, cholesterol, sodium, and fiber found in a single serving. If an ingredient is listed as optional, its nutrient value is *not* calculated in the nutrient profile or food exchanges.

GROUPS/LISTS	CARBS (G)	PROTEIN (G)	FAT (G)	CALORIES
Carbohydrates				
Starch	15	0 to 3	0 to 1	80
Fruit	15	0	0	60
Milk	12	8	0–8	Varies
Nonfat, 1%	12	8	0–3	100
Reduced fat, 2%	12	8	5	120
Whole	12	8	8	160
Other CHOs	15	Varies	Varies	Varies
Non-starchy vegetables	5	2	0	25
Meat and Meat Substitutes				
Plant-based protein	Varies	7	Varies	Varies
Lean	0	7	0 to 3	100
Medium-fat	0	7	4 to 7	130
High-fat	0	7	8+	150
Fat	0	0	5	45

For more information on meal planning, exchange list food groups, carbohydrate counting, and nutritional recommendations for diabetes management, visit the Academy of Nutrition and Dietetics at eatright.org or the American Diabetes Association at diabetes.org.

CARBOHYDRATE CALCULATOR

When managing diabetes, weight loss, or metabolic syndrome, it's important to know your foods' carbohydrate content. Budgeting your carbohydrate intake is important for controlling blood sugar (glucose) levels and discouraging insulin resistance. The recipes in this book provide both the total amount of carbohydrate (found in the Analysis); and the Carb Choices (immediately following the Exchanges). The carb choices are based on the following equation:

1 carb choice = 15 grams of carbohydrate = 1 starch, 1 fruit, *or* 1 milk exchange

We used the ranges that follow to determine equivalent carbohydrate servings or carb choices for *The Diabetic Goodie Cookbook*'s recipes.

CARBOHYDRATE CONVERSION CHART	
Carbohydrate (grams)	*Carb Choices*
0 to 5	0
6 to 10	½
11 to 20	1
21 to 25	1½
26 to 35	2
36 to 40	2½
41 to 50	3

Use the Nutrition Facts panel when selecting packaged foods to help guide your food choices. Below, you'll find the definitions of various nutrition claims used on food packages.

NUTRITION CLAIM DEFINITIONS

Manufacturers use eye-catching claims such as "light/lite," "free," "low," "reduced," "less," and "high" to give their products a competitive edge. Here are key nutrition terms and their meanings as defined by the federal government.

Calorie-free: Less than 5 calories per serving.

Low-calorie: Less than 40 calories per serving.

Reduced-calorie/fewer calories: Calories per serving reduced by 25 percent or more, compared to a similar product.

Light/lite/lightly: At least one-third fewer calories or 50 percent less fat than similar products. When describing color, texture, or taste, the particular characteristic *must* be identified. For example, an olive oil bottle must state that it is "light in color" since no oil is truly light in calories or fat.

Fat-free/no-fat/nonfat: Less than 0.5 grams of fat per serving.

Low-fat: Less than 3 grams of fat per serving. Milk percentages such as 1% and 2% describe the fat volume, not the fat calories. Inspect milk labels carefully for fat content, as they are highly variable. For instance, 2% low-fat milk has 5 grams of fat per cup, while 1% drops to 2.5 grams per 8-ounce cup.

Reduced-fat/less fat: At least 25 percent less fat than similar products.

Saturated fat-free: Less than 0.5 grams of saturated fat and less than 0.5 grams of trans fatty acids per serving.

Low in saturated fat: Less than 1 gram of saturated fat per serving and not more than 15 percent of calories from saturated fat.

Reduced/less saturated fat: At least

25 percent less saturated fat than similar products.

Cholesterol-free: Less than 2 milligrams of cholesterol and 2 grams or less of saturated fat per serving. Other analogous terms are "no cholesterol" and "zero cholesterol."

Low-cholesterol/low in cholesterol: No more than 20 milligrams of cholesterol and 2 grams or less of saturated fat per serving.

Reduced-cholesterol/less cholesterol: At least 25 percent less cholesterol than similar products.

Lean/extra-lean: Refers to meat, poultry, and seafood. "Lean" describes products with no more than 10 grams of fat, 4.5 grams of saturated fat, and 95 milligrams of cholesterol per 100 grams of cooked weight (about 3½ ounces). Extra-lean meat contains less than 5 grams of fat, less than 2 grams of saturated fat, and less than 95 milligrams of cholesterol per 100 grams of cooked weight.

Sugar-free: Less than 0.5 grams of total sugar per serving.

Reduced-sugar/less sugar: At least 25 percent less sugar than similar products.

Sodium-free/salt-free: Less than 5 milligrams of sodium per serving, and no sodium chloride (table salt).

Low sodium: Less than 140 milligrams of sodium per serving.

Very low/low-sodium: Less than 35 milligrams of sodium per serving.

Reduced-sodium/less sodium: At least 25 percent less sodium than similar products.

Light/lite in sodium: At least 50 percent less sodium than similar products.

More/fortified/enriched/added: Contains at least 10 percent more of the Daily Value for vitamins, minerals, protein, dietary fiber, or potassium than a similar product.

Refer to the following agencies for more information on nutrition labels, or for answers to food and nutrition questions:

Academy of Nutrition and Dietetics: eatright.org

USDA Food and Nutrition Information Center: nal.usda.gov/fnic

REASONS FOR IMPERFECT COOKIES

Irregular in size and shape	Improperly dropped or overbaked
Dark and crusty edges	Baking sheet too large for oven
Dry and hard	Overbaked
Doughy	Underbaked
Excessive spreading	Dough too warm Baking sheet too hot Oven temperature incorrect Dry ingredients undermeasured

WHAT HAPPENED TO MY CAKE?

	BUTTER CAKE	SPONGE-TYPE CAKE
Coarse grain	Used all-purpose flour instead of cake flour Excess leavening Not enough creaming Undermixing Baking temperature too low	Used all-purpose flour instead of cake flour Excess leavening Not enough creaming Undermixing
Too heavy or compact	Excess liquid, butter, or eggs Not enough flour or leavening Overmixing Baking temperature too high	Underbeaten egg yolks or overbeaten egg whites Overmixing
Heavy, soggy bottom layer	Excess liquid Butter too soft Underbeaten eggs Undermixing Baking time too short	Excess eggs or egg yolks Underbeaten egg yolks Failure to bake batter properly after turning into pan
Hard top crust	Baking temperature too high Baking time too long	Baking temperature too high Baking time too long
Cracked or humped top	Excess flour Not enough liquid Overmixing Uneven spreading of batter Baking temperature too high	Excess flour or sugar Baking temperature too high
Sticky top crust	Excess sugar Baking time too short	Excess sugar Baking time too short
Falling	Excess sugar, liquid, leavening, or shortening Overbeaten egg whites	Excess sugar Incomplete mixing
Tough crumb	Not enough sugar or butter Excess flour or eggs Baking temperature too high Overmixing	Not enough sugar Underbeaten egg yolks or egg whites Omission of cream of tartar (Angel Food Cake) Excess eggs Baking temperature too high Baking time too long
Crumbling or falling apart	Excess sugar, leavening, or butter Undermixing Incorrect preparation of pan Incorrect cooling	
One side higher than the other	Uneven spreading of batter Pan warped Range or oven rack not level Pan too close to wall of oven Uneven oven heat	Pan warped Range or oven rack not level
Pale top crust	Baking temperature too low Not enough sugar or butter Excess flour Overmixing	Baking temperature too low Overbeaten egg whites Baking time too long Pan too large

Some cakes may not be successful because of the failure to beat and add egg whites and egg yolks separately as the recipe directs. Follow each recipe's directions precisely and carefully. Adding whole eggs, no matter how thoroughly beaten, may produce different results.

FREEZER HINTS AND STORAGE TIMES

Custard or cream pies: Do not freeze.

Unbaked pies: Prepare according to the recipe. Do not cut vents in the top crust until ready to bake. Wrap, label, and freeze. To bake, unwrap the unthawed pie, make slits in the top crust, place it in a preheated oven (at the temperature specified in the recipe), and bake, allowing 10 to 15 minutes longer than the recipe time.

Baked pies: Prepare according to the recipe. Cool completely. Wrap, label, and freeze. Thaw and warm at 375°F (190°C) for 30 to 40 minutes.

Chiffon pies: Prepare according to the recipe. Wrap, label, and freeze. Thaw in the refrigerator.

Unbaked cobblers or tarts: Prepare according to the recipe. Wrap, label, and freeze. Place unthawed in preheated oven (at the temperature specified in the recipe) and bake, allowing 10 to 15 minutes longer than the recipe time.

Baked cobblers or tarts: Prepare according to the recipe. Cool completely. Wrap, label, and freeze. Thaw and warm at 375°F (190°C) for 30 to 40 minutes.

Cookies: Bake and cool according to the recipe. Place wax paper between layers of cookies to store. Freeze in an airtight, labeled container. Thaw at room temperature.

Refrigerated dough: Form unbaked dough into rolls and wrap securely in labeled aluminum foil; seal in freezer bags. Thaw in the refrigerator and bake according to the recipe.

Cheesecakes: Prepare and bake according to the recipe. Cool completely. Wrap securely, label, and freeze. Place in the refrigerator to thaw; do not thaw at room temperature.

Cakes: Prepare and bake according to the recipe. Cool completely. Wrap securely, label, and freeze. Thaw at room temperature.

Coffee Cakes: Prepare and bake according to the recipe. Cool completely. Wrap securely or seal in a freezer bag; label and freeze. Thaw at room temperature or in the refrigerator. Heat individual slices in the microwave for 30 to 90 seconds. Can be reheated in preheated 350°F (180°C) oven for 5 to 10 minutes. Best served warm.

Scones: Prepare and bake according to the recipe. Cool completely. Wrap securely or seal in a freezer bag; label and freeze. Thaw at room temperature or place on a paper plate and defrost in the microwave for 30 to 90 seconds, until thawed and/or warm. Can be thawed and reheated in a 350°F (180°C) oven for 5 to 10 minutes, or toasted in the toaster oven. Serve warm.

Muffins: Prepare and bake according to the recipe. Cool completely. Wrap securely or seal in a freezer bag; label and freeze. Thaw at room temperature or place on a paper plate and defrost in the microwave for 1 to 2 minutes, depending upon the number of muffins, until thawed and/or warm.

If desired, split and toast. Defrost individual muffins in the microwave for 30 seconds.

Quick Breads: Prepare and bake according to the recipe. Cool completely. Wrap securely or seal in a freezer bag; label and freeze. Thaw at room temperature or place on a paper plate and defrost in the microwave for about 8 minutes, until thawed and/or warm. Can be reheated in a preheated 350°F (180°C) oven for 5 to 10 minutes, and thawed, sliced, and toasted.

When preparing food for freezer storage, make sure to remove all air from the wrap, container, or freezer bag to prevent freezer burn. Securely wrapped, food will better retain its original fresh flavor and texture when thawed.

FREEZER GUIDE FOR BAKED GOODS		
Cakes	Butter-type	4 months
	Angel food	6 to 8 months
	Sponge	6 to 8 months
	With fruit	6 months
Cheesecakes	Baked	3 months
Cookies and bars	Baked	12 months
Cobblers and tarts	Baked	6 months
	Unbaked	6 months
Coffee cakes	Baked	3 months
Muffins	Baked	3 months
Pies	Unbaked	6 months
	Baked	6 months
	Chiffon	2 months
Quick breads	Baked	3 months
Scones	Baked	3 months

Cookies & Bars

Tips & Tricks

» For evenly browned cookies, use bright, shiny baking sheets at least 2 inches (5 cm) narrower and shorter than your oven. Discard old, darkened baking sheets and purchase new ones if cookies do not bake correctly.

» Try working with three or four baking sheets so you can fill and bake at the same time.

» Lining baking sheets with parchment paper will make cleanup easier. But line the pan with parchment paper or spray it with cooking spray only if the recipe directs you to do so.

» Always place dough on a cool baking sheet; it will spread too much on a hot one.

» To mold cookies, roll the dough between the palms of your hands. Make sure the dough is smooth so the cookies brown and have the correct texture.

» Cookies should be removed from the baking sheet with a metal spatula and placed on wire racks until they cool completely (about 10 minutes) before being stored in a tightly covered container.

» If cookies don't bake well, check that your oven temperature is correct. If the oven is too hot or too cool, your cookies will not bake evenly. Use an oven thermometer to determine if your oven is gauged correctly.

» When you want fresh-baked cookies in a flash, whip up a recipe for bar or square cookies. These cookies take less time to make, since you just mix and pat them into a pan. Many bars and squares require only one bowl for mixing and bake in about 30 minutes. After about 10 minutes of cooling, you can cut them into squares or 2 x 1-inch (5 x 2.5 cm) bars and serve. Most bars or squares are moist and should be stored tightly covered. Since they're cut into individual pieces, they don't retain their freshness as long as most cookies.

» Quick-fix bars include Apple-Raisin Bars (page 33), Chocolate Jam Squares (page 43), Simple Banana-Nut Bars (page 38), Banana–Poppy Seed Bars (page 166), Chewy Coconut Squares (page 45), Devilish Chocolate Bars (page 42), Mix-in-the-Pan Date Bars (page 46), Date Chews (page 47), and Raspberry Bars (page 50).

» Refer to page 12 for reasons for imperfect cookies and pages 14 and 15 for storage tips to help freeze cookies and bars.

Chocolate Chip Cookies

Prep time: 15 minutes ◆ Bake time: 8 minutes

¾ cup (90 g) all-purpose flour

¾ cup (90 g) whole wheat flour

½ cup (45 g) old-fashioned rolled oats

½ teaspoon baking soda

½ cup (1 stick/113 g) butter, softened

¼ cup (48 g) packed brown sugar

2 tablespoons granulated sugar

1 large egg

1 tablespoon nonfat milk

1 teaspoon vanilla extract

½ cup (80 g) mini semisweet or dark chocolate morsels

Cooking spray

1. Preheat the oven to 375°F (190°C). Line baking sheets with parchment paper.

2. Stir together the flours, oats, and baking soda in a medium bowl.

3. Use an electric mixer at medium speed to cream the butter and sugars in a large bowl until light and fluffy; scrape down the sides of the bowl as needed. Beat in the egg, milk, and vanilla and scrape down the sides of the bowl.

4. Use a rubber spatula to stir the dry ingredients into the creamed mixture just until well blended; stir in the chocolate morsels.

5. Drop the batter by teaspoonfuls onto the lined baking sheets, spacing them about 2 inches (5 cm) apart. Spray the flat bottom of a 2-inch (5 cm) glass with cooking spray and use it to flatten each cookie, respraying the glass as necessary.

6. Bake for 8 to 10 minutes, until lightly browned. Use a metal spatula to transfer the cookies to wire racks to cool completely. Store tightly covered. Freeze for up to 12 months.

> **Variation:** *To make bar cookies, add 1 tablespoon orange juice to the batter and spread the batter into a 13 x 9 x 2-inch (33 x 23 x 5 cm) pan that has been sprayed with cooking spray. Bake for about 12 minutes, until browned. Cool for about 10 minutes before cutting into 32 bars.*

Makes 4 dozen cookies; 24 servings

Per serving (2 cookies): 99 Calories, 12 g Carbohydrate, 2 g Protein, 5 g Fat, 17 mg Cholesterol, 60 mg Sodium, 1 g Fiber
Exchanges: 1 Starch, 1 Fat (1 Carb Choice)

Oatmeal Cookies

Prep time: 10 minutes • Bake time: 8 minutes

⅓ cup (43 g) chopped nuts

1 cup (120 g) whole wheat flour

⅓ cup (23 g) nonfat milk powder

¼ cup (15 g) wheat bran

¼ cup (28 g) wheat germ

1 teaspoon baking powder

1 teaspoon baking soda

1 teaspoon ground cinnamon

½ teaspoon ground nutmeg

¼ teaspoon ground cloves

½ cup (122 g) unsweetened applesauce

½ cup (96 g) packed brown sugar

½ cup (1 stick/113 g) butter, softened

2 large eggs

2 cups (180 g) old-fashioned rolled oats

¼ cup (43 g) raisins

Cooking spray

1. Preheat the oven to 350°F (180°C). Line baking sheets with parchment paper.

2. Place the nuts in a small baking pan and bake for 3 to 5 minutes, until toasted; set aside.

3. Whisk together the flour, milk powder, bran, wheat germ, baking powder, baking soda, cinnamon, nutmeg, and cloves in a medium bowl; set aside.

4. Use an electric mixer at medium speed to beat the applesauce, brown sugar, and butter in a large bowl until light and fluffy. Add the eggs and beat at medium speed until well mixed, scraping down the sides of the bowl as needed. Gradually beat in the flour mixture at low speed until blended, scraping the bowl after each addition. Stir in the oats, toasted nuts, and raisins until well blended.

5. Drop the batter by rounded teaspoonfuls about 2 inches (5 cm) apart on the lined baking sheets. If desired, spray the flat bottom of a 2-inch (5 cm) glass with cooking spray and use it to flatten each cookie, respraying the glass as necessary.

6. Bake for 8 to 10 minutes or until lightly browned. Use a metal spatula to transfer the cookies to wire racks to cool completely. Store tightly covered. Freeze for up to 12 months.

Makes 6 dozen cookies; 24 servings

Per serving (3 cookies): 126 Calories, 16 g Carbohydrate, 3 g Protein, 6 g Fat, 25 mg Cholesterol, 94 mg Sodium, 2 g Fiber
Exchanges: 1 Starch, 1 Fat (1 Carb Choice)

Spice Cookies

Prep time: 15 minutes ✦ Bake time: 7 minutes

1 cup (120 g) all-purpose flour

¾ cup (90 g) whole wheat flour

2 teaspoons baking soda

1 teaspoon ground cinnamon

½ teaspoon ground ginger

½ teaspoon ground cloves

½ cup (120 ml) canola or extra-light olive oil

¼ cup (80 g) molasses

2 tablespoons sugar, plus more for dipping

1 large egg

2 tablespoons reduced-fat milk

1 teaspoon butter extract (optional)

Cooking spray

1. Preheat the oven to 375°F (190°C). Line baking sheets with parchment paper.

2. Whisk together the flours, baking powder, baking soda, cinnamon, ginger, and cloves in a medium bowl.

3. Use an electric mixer at medium speed to beat the oil, molasses, sugar, egg, milk, and butter extract, if desired, in a large bowl until well blended.

4. Gradually add the dry ingredients to the molasses mixture and beat at medium speed until well blended, scraping the bowl after each addition.

5. Form the dough into 1-inch (2.5 cm) balls, spacing them about 2 inches (5 cm) apart on the lined baking sheets. Spray the flat bottom of a 2-inch (5 cm) glass with cooking spray, dip it in sugar, then use it to flatten each cookie. Respray the glass as necessary and dip it in sugar for each cookie until all are flattened.

6. Bake for 7 to 10 minutes or until browned. Use a metal spatula to transfer the cookies to wire racks to cool completely. Store tightly covered. Freeze for up to 12 months.

Makes 4 dozen cookies; 24 servings

Per serving (2 cookies): 89 Calories, 10 g Carbohydrate, 1 g Protein, 5 g Fat, 8 mg Cholesterol, 110 mg Sodium, 1 g Fiber
Exchanges: ½ Starch, 1 Fat (½ Carb Choice)

Chocolate Jam Thumbprints

Prep time: 20 minutes ◆ Bake time: 10 minutes ◆ Chilling time: 1 hour

1 cup (120 g) all-purpose flour

½ cup (60 g) whole wheat flour

¼ cup (20 g) unsweetened cocoa powder

½ teaspoon baking soda

¼ teaspoon salt

½ cup (1 stick/113 g) butter, softened

½ cup (96 g) sugar

2 large eggs

1 tablespoon vanilla extract

½ cup (160 g) plus 2 tablespoons no-sugar-added berry jam of your choice

1. Preheat the oven to 350°F (180°C). Line two baking sheets with parchment paper.

2. Mix the flours, cocoa powder, baking soda, and salt in a small bowl.

3. Cream the butter in a medium bowl. Gradually beat in the sugar and the eggs, until the mixture is light and fluffy. Add the vanilla and gently stir the flour mixture into the creamed mixture until the flours are incorporated and the mixture is well blended.

4. Chill the dough for at least 1 hour. For each cookie, use your hands to roll about 1 tablespoon of dough into a ball. Place the balls about 2 inches (5 cm) apart on the lined baking sheets. Use your thumb to press a deep indentation into the center of each cookie. Each cookie should spread to about 1½ inches (4 cm).

5. Bake for about 6 minutes, remove baking sheet from the oven and spoon about ½ teaspoon of jam into each cookie's indentation. Return the cookies to the oven and bake 3 to 4 minutes more, until the cookies are firm and the jam has congealed. The jam should firmly fill the indentation, and a little jam may spill down the side.

6. Immediately use a metal spatula to transfer the cookies to wire racks to cool. When the cookies are cool, place them in a container with wax paper between the layers. Store tightly covered in the refrigerator or freeze.

Variation: *For vanilla thumbprints, omit the cocoa powder and increase the all-purpose flour from 1 cup (120 g) to 1¼ cups (150 g). Proceed with the recipe as directed.*

Makes 40 cookies; 20 servings

Per serving (2 cookies): 114 Calories, 18 g Carbohydrate, 2 g Protein, 5 g Fat, 30 mg Cholesterol, 103 mg Sodium, 1 g Fiber
Exchanges: 1 Starch (1 Carb Choice)

Fruity Nut Cookies

Prep time: 30 minutes • Chilling time: 1 hour • Bake time: 15 minutes

½ cup (60 g) all-purpose flour, plus more for dipping

½ cup (60 g) whole wheat flour

1 teaspoon baking powder

¼ teaspoon salt

½ cup (1 stick/113 g) butter, softened

1 cup (71 g) unsweetened shredded coconut

1 cup (130 g) chopped nuts, toasted

½ cup (83 g) chopped pitted dates

1 large egg

¼ cup (43 g) raisins

2 teaspoons brandy, bourbon, or orange juice

1. Stir together the flours, baking powder, and salt in a large bowl. Use a pastry blender to cut in the butter until the mixture forms pea-size crumbs.

2. Stir in the coconut, toasted nuts, dates, egg, raisins, and brandy, and mix with a wooden spoon or by hand until a dough forms. Cover and refrigerate for 1 hour.

3. Preheat the oven to 350°F (180°C). Line baking sheets with parchment paper.

4. Shape the dough into 1-inch (2.5 cm) balls and place them about 2 inches (5 cm) apart on the lined baking sheets. Put 1 to 2 tablespoons all-purpose flour in a small bowl. Dip the tines of a fork in flour, then flatten the balls, making a crisscross design, occasionally dipping the tines in the flour to avoid the fork sticking to the dough.

5. Bake for about 15 minutes or until lightly brown. Use a metal spatula to transfer the cookies to wire racks to cool completely. Store tightly covered. Freeze for up to 12 months.

Makes 4 dozen cookies; 16 servings

Per serving (3 cookies): 203 Calories, 14 g Carbohydrate, 3 g Protein, 16 g Fat, 26 mg Cholesterol, 89 mg Sodium, 3 g Fiber
Exchanges: ½ Starch, ½ Fruit, 3 Fat (1 Carb Choice)

Peanut Butter Cookies

Prep time: 20 minutes ◆ Bake time: 10 minutes

1 cup (120 g) all-purpose flour

¾ cup (90 g) whole wheat flour, plus 1 to 2 tablespoons extra, for shaping cookies

1 teaspoon baking powder

¾ teaspoon baking soda

¼ teaspoon salt

¾ cup (192 g) natural peanut butter

½ cup (1 stick/113 g) butter, softened

⅓ cup (64 g) packed brown sugar

¼ cup (48 g) plus 3 tablespoons granulated sugar

2 large eggs, at room temperature

3 tablespoons nonfat milk

1 tablespoon vanilla extract

1. Preheat the oven to 350°F (180°C). Line two baking sheets with parchment paper.

2. Stir together the flour, baking powder, baking soda, and salt in a medium bowl.

3. Use an electric mixer at medium speed to beat the peanut butter, butter, brown sugar, and the ¼ cup granulated sugar in a large bowl until smooth; scrape down the sides as needed. Beat in the eggs, milk, and vanilla until blended. Gradually add the dry ingredients and beat at medium speed until well blended.

4. Put the remaining 3 tablespoons granulated sugar in a shallow rimmed plate or bowl. Put 1 to 2 tablespoons whole wheat flour in a separate small bowl or cup. Using a tablespoonful of dough per cookie, shape the dough into 1-inch (2.5 cm) balls, roll in the sugar, and place them 2 inches (5 cm) apart on a lined baking sheet. Flatten the cookies with the tines of a fork, making a crisscross design, dipping the tines occasionally in the whole wheat flour to avoid the fork sticking to the dough.

5. Bake for 10 minutes, switching the baking sheets from top to bottom racks, until lightly browned. Use a metal spatula to transfer the cookies to wire racks to cool completely. Store tightly covered. Freeze for up to 12 months.

Makes 4 dozen cookies; 48 servings

Per serving (1 cookie): 75 Calories, 8 g Carbohydrate, 2 g Protein, 5 g Fat, 13 mg Cholesterol, 66 mg Sodium, 1 g Fiber
Exchanges: ½ Starch, 1 Fat (½ Carb Choice)

Orange Butter Cookies

Prep time: 15 minutes ◆ Bake time: 8 minutes

1 cup (120 g) all-purpose flour

¾ cup (90 g) whole wheat flour

2 teaspoons baking powder

¼ teaspoon salt

½ cup (1 stick/113 g) butter, softened

⅓ cup (64 g) granulated sugar

1 large egg, at room temperature

1 tablespoon grated orange zest

3 tablespoons fresh orange juice

1 tablespoon vanilla extract

Cooking spray

Granulated or colored sugar, for dipping

1. Preheat the oven to 350°F (180°C). Line two baking sheets with parchment paper.

2. Stir together the flours, baking powder, and salt in a small bowl.

3. Use an electric mixer on medium speed to cream the butter in a medium bowl, scraping down the sides occasionally. Add the sugar and beat until light and fluffy, scraping the bowl occasionally. Add the egg and orange zest; beat well.

4. Combine the orange juice and vanilla in a small bowl. With the mixer at low speed, add the dry ingredients to the butter-sugar mixture alternately with the juice mixture, beating until the mixture is thoroughly blended into a dough.

5. Using a tablespoon of dough per cookie, shape the dough into balls and place them 2 inches (5 cm) apart on the lined baking sheets. Spray the flat bottom of a 2-inch (5 cm) glass with cooking spray, dip it in sugar, then use it to flatten each cookie. Respray the glass as necessary and dip it in sugar for each cookie until all are flattened. Or after flattening the cookie, sprinkle sugar over each.

6. Bake for about 8 minutes, switching the baking sheets from top to bottom racks, until the cookies are lightly browned around the edges. Use a metal spatula to transfer the cookies to wire racks to cool completely. Store tightly covered. Freeze for up to 12 months.

Makes 3 dozen cookies; 18 servings

Per serving (2 cookies): 109 Calories, 13 g Carbohydrate, 2 g Protein, 6 g Fat,
24 mg Cholesterol, 77 mg Sodium, 1 g Fiber
Exchanges: 1 Starch, 1 Fat (1 Carb Choice)

Anise Biscotti

Prep time: 30 minutes • Bake time: 40 minutes

2 cups (240 g) all-purpose flour, plus more for dusting

2 teaspoons anise seeds

¾ teaspoon baking powder

¼ teaspoon salt

½ cup (96 g) sugar

1 large egg

1 large egg white

3 tablespoons canola or extra-light olive oil

1 tablespoon grated orange zest

1 teaspoon vanilla extract

1. Preheat the oven to 325°F (165°C). Line a baking sheet with parchment paper.

2. Whisk together 1¾ cups (210 g) of the flour, anise seeds, baking powder, and salt in a medium bowl.

3. Use an electric mixer at medium speed to blend the sugar, egg, egg white, oil, orange zest, and vanilla in a large bowl until well mixed, scraping down the sides of the bowl occasionally.

4. Add the flour mixture to the sugar-oil mixture. Beat at low speed until well blended. Add in enough of the remaining ¼ cup (31 g) flour to make a soft dough.

5. Turn the dough out onto a lightly floured surface and divide it in half. Shape it into two 12-inch (30 cm) rolls; transfer them to the lined baking sheet and flatten each to a ½-inch (13 mm) thickness.

6. Bake for 25 minutes. Remove the rolls from the oven, place on a wire rack and let cool for about 5 minutes. Lower the oven temperature to 300°F (150°C). Slice each roll diagonally into twenty ½-inch (13 mm) slices, then place them, cut side down, on the baking sheet.

7. Bake for 6 to 8 minutes, then turn the cookies over and bake for an additional 6 to 8 minutes, until dry.

8. Remove the biscotti to wire racks to cool. Store tightly covered. Freeze for up to 12 months.

Makes 40 biscotti; 20 servings

Per serving (2 biscotti): 81 Calories, 13 g Carbohydrate, 2 g Protein, 2 g Fat,
9 mg Cholesterol, 35 mg Sodium, 0 g Fiber
Exchanges: 1 Starch (1 Carb Choice)

Spicy Nut Clouds

Prep time: 15 minutes • Bake time: 35 minutes

1 cup (130 g) finely chopped walnuts

½ cup (96 g) sugar

1 teaspoon ground cinnamon

½ teaspoon ground nutmeg

¼ teaspoon ground cloves

2 large egg whites, at room temperature

1. Preheat the oven to 350°F (180°C). Place the walnuts on a baking sheet and bake for 3 to 5 minutes, until toasted. Set aside.

2. Lower the oven temperature to 275°F (135°C). Line baking sheets with aluminum foil or parchment paper.

3. Stir together the sugar, cinnamon, nutmeg, and cloves in a small bowl.

4. Use an electric mixer at high speed to beat the egg whites in a large bowl until frothy. Gradually beat in the sugar-spice mixture, beating until the whites form stiff peaks when the beaters are lifted. Use a spatula to gently fold the toasted walnuts into the beaten egg whites.

5. Drop the batter by teaspoonfuls about 1 inch (2.5 cm) apart onto the lined baking sheets. Bake for 20 to 25 minutes or until the cookies are golden brown and crisp.

6. Immediately transfer the aluminum foil or parchment paper with the cookies to wire racks. Cool for 5 minutes, then remove the cookies from the foil and cool completely. Store in a tightly covered container.

Note: *Don't make these on a humid or rainy day because they won't be light in texture.*

Makes 3 dozen cookies; 12 servings

Per serving (3 clouds): 88 Calories, 8 g Carbohydrate, 2 g Protein, 6 g Fat,
0 mg Cholesterol, 9 mg Sodium, 1.5 g Fiber
Exchanges: ½ Starch, 1 Fat (½ Carb Choice)

Chocolate Clouds

Prep time: 15 minutes ◆ Bake time: 30 minutes

2 large egg whites, at room temperature

¼ teaspoon cream of tartar

¼ teaspoon salt

½ cup (96 g) sugar

1 teaspoon vanilla extract

1 tablespoon unsweetened cocoa powder, sifted if lumpy

1. Preheat the oven to 275°F (135°C). Line two baking sheets with aluminum foil or parchment paper.

2. Use an electric mixer at high speed to beat the egg whites in a medium bowl until frothy. Beat in the cream of tartar and salt until soft peaks form.

3. Gradually beat in the sugar and beat until the whites form stiff peaks when the beaters are lifted. Scrape down the sides of the bowl and beat in the vanilla. Use a rubber spatula to gently fold in the cocoa powder until well blended.

4. Drop the batter by teaspoonfuls about 1 inch (2.5 cm) apart onto the lined baking sheets. Bake for 30 to 35 minutes or until the cookies look dry and slightly brown around the edges.

5. Immediately transfer the aluminum foil or parchment paper with the cookies to wire racks. Cool for 1 minute, then remove the cookies from the foil and cool completely. Store in a tightly covered container.

Note: *Don't make these on a humid or rainy day because they won't be light in texture.*

Variation: *If desired, stir ¼ cup (40 g) mini semisweet chocolate morsels into the batter along with the unsweetened cocoa powder.*

Makes 3 dozen cookies; 12 servings

Per serving (3 clouds): 28 Calories, 6 g Carbohydrate, 1 g Protein, 0 g Fat, 0 mg Cholesterol, 58 mg Sodium, 0 g Fiber
Exchanges: ½ Starch (½ Carb Choice)

Easy Apple Bars

Prep time: 20 minutes ◆ Bake time: 45 minutes

Cooking spray

⅓ cup (40 g) chopped pecans

2 cups (250 g) peeled, cored, and chopped tart apples (2 medium)

¼ cup (48 g) sugar

1 teaspoon ground cinnamon

½ cup (60 g) all-purpose flour

½ cup (60 g) whole wheat flour

½ teaspoon baking powder

½ teaspoon baking soda

¼ cup (60 ml) cooled strong coffee

1 large egg, beaten

¼ cup (60 ml) canola or extra-light olive oil

1 teaspoon vanilla extract

1. Preheat the oven to 350°F (180°C). Spray a 9-inch (23 cm) square baking pan with cooking spray.

2. Place the pecans in a small baking pan and bake for 3 to 5 minutes, until toasted; set aside.

3. Place the chopped apples in a large bowl and sprinkle with the sugar and cinnamon. Let stand for 10 minutes to draw out the juices.

4. Stir together the flours, baking powder, and baking soda in a medium bowl, then add to the apple-cinnamon mixture and stir until blended and coated.

5. Use a rubber spatula to stir the coffee, egg, oil, and vanilla into the apple mixture. Spoon the batter into the prepared baking pan. Smooth the top with a spatula and sprinkle with the toasted pecans.

6. Bake for 45 to 50 minutes or until a tester inserted into the center comes out clean. Cool in the pan on a wire rack, then cut into 16 bars. Store covered. Refrigerate after 2 days or freeze for up to 12 months.

Makes 16 bars

Per serving (1 bar): 94 Calories, 11 g Carbohydrate, 2 g Protein, 5 g Fat, 11 mg Cholesterol, 43 mg Sodium, 1 g Fiber
Exchanges: 1 Starch, 1 Fat (1 Carb Choice)

Apple-Raisin Bars

Prep time: 10 minutes ◆ *Bake time: 25 minutes*

Cooking spray

1 cup (120 g) all-purpose flour

1 cup (120 g) whole wheat flour

2 teaspoons baking powder

1 teaspoon baking soda

1½ teaspoons ground cinnamon

1 teaspoon ground nutmeg

½ cup (122 g) unsweetened applesauce

½ cup (120 ml) unsweetened apple juice

3 large eggs, at room temperature

¼ cup (60 ml) canola or extra-light olive oil

½ cup (85 g) golden raisins

1. Preheat the oven to 350°F (180°C). Spray an 8-inch (20 cm) square baking pan with cooking spray.

2. Whisk together the flours, baking powder, baking soda, cinnamon, and nutmeg in a medium bowl.

3. Use an electric mixer at medium speed to beat together the applesauce, juice, eggs, and oil in a large bowl until well blended; scrape down the sides of the bowl. Add the flour mixture and beat at low speed until well blended. Scrape down the sides of the bowl and use a rubber spatula to stir in the raisins. Spoon the batter into the prepared pan.

4. Bake for 25 minutes or until a tester inserted into the center comes out clean.

5. Cool in the pan on a wire rack, then cut into 16 bars. Store covered. Refrigerate after 2 days or freeze for up to 3 months.

Makes 16 bars

Per serving (1 bar): 123 Calories, 18 g Carbohydrate, 3 g Protein, 5 g Fat,
33 mg Cholesterol, 92 mg Sodium, 2 g Fiber
Exchanges: 1 Starch, 1 Fat (1 Carb Choice)

Apple–Oat Bran Bars

Prep time: 10 minutes ◆ Bake time: 20 minutes

Cooking spray

½ cup (65 g) chopped nuts

1 cup (120 g) oat bran

½ cup (60 g) all-purpose flour

½ cup (60 g) whole wheat flour

1 teaspoon baking powder

½ teaspoon baking soda

1½ teaspoons ground cinnamon

½ teaspoon ground nutmeg

¼ teaspoon ground cloves

½ cup (1 stick/113 g) butter,
  softened

½ cup (96 g) granulated sugar

2 large eggs, at room temperature

1 large apple, peeled, cored,
  and coarsely grated (1¼ to
  1½ cups/157 to 188 g)

Confectioners' sugar (optional)

1. Preheat the oven to 375°F (190°C). Spray a 13 x 9 x 2-inch (33 x 23 x 5 cm) baking pan with cooking spray.

2. Place the nuts in a small baking pan and bake for 3 to 5 minutes, until toasted; set aside.

3. Stir together the oat bran, flours, baking powder, baking soda, cinnamon, nutmeg, and cloves in a small bowl.

4. Use an electric mixer at high speed to cream the butter and granulated sugar in a medium bowl until light and fluffy; scrape down the sides of bowl. Add the eggs and beat at medium speed until well blended. Scrape down the sides of the bowl.

5. Add the dry ingredients and mix at low speed until well blended. Use a rubber spatula to gently mix in the apple and toasted nuts. Spoon the batter into the prepared baking pan and smooth the top.

6. Bake for 20 to 25 minutes or until lightly brown. Cool in the pan on a wire rack. If desired, sprinkle with confectioners' sugar. Cut into 24 bars. Store covered. Refrigerate after 2 days or freeze for up to 12 months.

Makes 24 bars

Per serving (1 bar): 99 Calories, 11 g Carbohydrate, 2 g Protein, 6 g Fat,
25 mg Cholesterol, 62 mg Sodium, 1 g Fiber
Exchanges: 1 Starch, 1 Fat (1 Carb Choice)

Golden Apple Bars

Prep time: 15 minutes • Bake time: 20 minutes

PASTRY

Cooking spray

1 large egg

1½ cups (180 g) all-purpose flour

½ cup (60 g) whole wheat flour

½ cup (120 ml) canola or extra-light olive oil

¼ cup (48 g) granulated sugar

1 teaspoon vanilla extract

FILLING

5 cups (550 g) peeled, cored, and sliced Golden Delicious apples (4 to 5 apples)

1 tablespoon grated lemon zest

2 tablespoons fresh lemon juice

1 cup (112 g) shredded sharp cheddar cheese

¼ cup (48 g) granulated sugar

3 tablespoons all-purpose flour

2 teaspoons ground cinnamon

½ teaspoon ground nutmeg

TOPPING

¼ cup (30 g) whole wheat flour

¾ cup (90 g) all-purpose flour

5 tablespoons plus 1 teaspoon butter, softened

3 tablespoons brown sugar

1. Preheat the oven to 425°F (220°C). Spray a 15½ x 10 x 1-inch (38 x 26 x 3 cm) jelly roll pan with cooking spray.

2. **To make the pastry,** with a fork, beat the egg in a medium bowl. Stir in the flours, oil, granulated sugar, and vanilla; mix until well blended. Pat into the bottom of the prepared pan.

3. **To make the filling,** place the apples in a large bowl. Sprinkle with the lemon zest and juice, then add the cheese, granulated sugar, flour, cinnamon, and nutmeg, and stir until well mixed. Spread evenly over the pastry.

4. **To make the topping,** with a fork, mix together the flours, butter, and brown sugar in a medium bowl until the mixture is crumbly. Sprinkle it evenly over the apple filling.

5. Bake for 20 to 25 minutes or until the apples are tender and the topping is brown. Cool in the pan on a wire rack. Cut into 50 bars. Store covered. Refrigerate after 2 days.

Makes 50 bars

Per serving (1 bar): 88 Calories, 11 g Carbohydrate, 1 g Protein, 4 g Fat,
9 mg Cholesterol, 26 mg Sodium, 1 g Fiber
Exchanges: 1 Starch, 1 Fat (1 Carb Choice)

Gingerbread Bars

Prep time: 10 minutes ◆ Bake time: 30 minutes

Cooking spray

½ cup (60 g) all-purpose flour

½ cup (60 g) whole wheat flour

1½ teaspoons ground ginger

1 teaspoon ground cinnamon

½ teaspoon baking soda

¼ teaspoon salt

⅛ teaspoon ground cloves

1 large egg, at room temperature

⅓ cup (107 g) molasses

2 tablespoons brown sugar

½ cup (120 ml) buttermilk
(see page 8)

2 tablespoons canola or extra-light
olive oil

1. Preheat the oven to 350°F (180°C). Spray an 8-inch (20 cm) square baking pan with cooking spray.

2. Whisk together the flours, ginger, cinnamon, baking soda, salt, and cloves in a medium bowl.

3. Use an electric mixer at medium speed to beat the egg, molasses, and brown sugar in a medium bowl until light. Scrape down the sides of the bowl. Add the buttermilk, oil, and the flour mixture; beat at low speed until smooth, scraping down the bowl occasionally. Spoon into the prepared baking pan.

4. Bake for 30 minutes or until a tester inserted into the center comes out clean. Cool in the pan on a wire rack, then cut into 16 bars. Store tightly covered. Refrigerate after 2 days or freeze for up to 12 months.

Makes 16 bars

Per serving (1 bar): 75 Calories, 12 g Carbohydrate, 2 g Protein, 2 g Fat,
11 mg Cholesterol, 97 mg Sodium, 1 g Fiber
Exchanges: 1 Starch (1 Carb Choice)

Simple Banana-Nut Bars

Prep Time: 10 minutes • Bake time: 30 minutes

¼ cup (33 g) chopped nuts

¾ cup (90 g) all-purpose flour

¾ cup (90 g) whole wheat flour

¼ cup (48 g) sugar

1 teaspoon baking powder

¼ teaspoon baking soda

½ teaspoon ground cinnamon

¼ teaspoon ground nutmeg

1 cup (224 g) mashed very ripe
   bananas (2 medium)

2 large eggs, beaten

⅓ cup (80 ml) buttermilk
   (see page 8)

⅓ cup (80 ml) canola or extra-light
   olive oil

1. Preheat the oven to 350°F (180°C). Place the nuts in a small baking pan, and bake for 3 to 5 minutes, until brown; set aside.

2. Place the flours, sugar, baking powder, baking soda, cinnamon, and nutmeg in a 9-inch (23 cm) square baking pan and mix well with a fork.

3. Stir in the mashed bananas, eggs, buttermilk, oil, and toasted nuts; mix until blended. Use a rubber spatula to scrape any ingredients clinging to the sides, corners, or bottom of the pan into the batter.

4. Bake for 30 to 35 minutes or until lightly browned and a tester inserted into the center comes out clean. Cool in the pan on a wire rack, then cut into 16 bars. Store tightly covered. Refrigerate after 2 days or freeze for up to 12 months.

Makes 16 bars

Per serving (1 bar): 125 Calories, 15 g Carbohydrate, 3 g Protein, 7 g Fat,
22 mg Cholesterol, 37 mg Sodium, 1 g Fiber
Exchanges: 1 Starch, 1 Fat (1 Carb Choice)

Banana–Poppy Seed Bars

Prep time: 15 minutes • Bake time: 25 minutes

Cooking spray

¾ cup (90 g) whole wheat flour

¾ cup (90 g) all-purpose flour

⅓ cup (64 g) sugar

2 tablespoons poppy seeds

1 teaspoon baking soda

¾ cup (180 ml) nonfat milk

½ cup (112 g) mashed ripe banana (1 banana)

1 large egg, beaten

1 teaspoon grated lemon zest

3 tablespoons fresh lemon juice

3 tablespoons canola or extra-light olive oil

1⅓ cups (120 g) dried banana chips (32 to 48 chips)

1. Preheat the oven to 375°F (190°C). Spray an 8-inch (20 cm) square baking pan with cooking spray.

2. Use a rubber spatula to mix together the flours, sugar, poppy seeds, and baking soda in a large bowl. Make a well in the center and add the milk, mashed banana, egg, lemon zest and juice, and oil. Use the spatula to thoroughly combine the wet and dry ingredients. Spoon the batter into the prepared baking pan.

3. Bake for 25 minutes or until lightly browned and a tester inserted into the center comes out clean.

4. Cool in the pan on a wire rack, then cut into 16 bars. Store tightly covered. Refrigerate after 2 days or freeze for up to 12 months. Just before serving, add 2 to 3 banana chips on top of each bar.

Makes 16 bars

Per serving (1 bar): 149 Calories, 19 g Carbohydrate, 7 g Protein, 6 g Fat,
11 mg Cholesterol, 88 mg Sodium, 2 g Fiber
Exchanges: 1 Starch, 1 Fat (1 Carb Choice)

Quick Carrot Bars

Prep time: 10 minutes • Bake time: 35 minutes

Cooking spray

½ cup (65 g) chopped walnuts

1 cup (120 g) whole wheat flour

1 cup (120 g) all-purpose flour

1 teaspoon baking powder

1 teaspoon ground cinnamon

½ cup (36 g) unsweetened
   shredded coconut (optional)

½ cup (96 g) packed brown sugar

2 large eggs

½ cup (120 ml) canola or extra-light
   olive oil

¼ cup (61 g) unsweetened
   applesauce

2 cups (240 g) sliced carrots

Confectioners' sugar (optional)

Light Cream Cheese Frosting (page
   90; optional)

1. Preheat the oven to 350°F (180°C). Spray a 13 x 9 x 2-inch (33 x 23 x 5 cm) baking pan with cooking spray.

2. Place the walnuts in a small baking pan and bake for about 5 minutes or until brown; set aside.

3. Mix together the flours, baking powder, cinnamon, and coconut, if using, in a medium bowl.

4. Process the brown sugar, eggs, oil, and applesauce in a food processor until blended; scrape down the sides. With the motor running, gradually add the carrot slices and process until they are coarsely chopped.

5. Use a rubber spatula to stir the carrot mixture and toasted walnuts into the flour mixture until well mixed. Spread into the prepared baking pan.

6. Bake for 35 minutes or until the edges pull away from the sides of the pan and the top is slightly browned. Cool in the pan on a wire rack, then cut into 24 bars.

7. If desired, sprinkle with confectioners' sugar or frost with Light Cream Cheese Frosting. Store tightly covered and refrigerate if frosted.

Makes 24 bars

Per serving (1 bar): 131 Calories, 14 g Carbohydrate, 2 g Protein, 8 g Fat,
15 mg Cholesterol, 13 mg Sodium, 1 g Fiber
Exchanges: 1 Starch, 1½ Fat (1 Carb Choice)

Chocolate Crunch Bars

Prep time: 10 minutes ◆ Chilling time: 1 hour

Cooking spray

¾ cup (192 g) natural peanut butter

3½ cups (140 g) toasted natural brown rice cereal (puffed brown rice)

2 medium bananas, thinly sliced

2 cups (554 g) Chocolate Pudding (page 230)*

*A commercial sugar-free instant chocolate pudding made with ½ cup (120 ml) less nonfat milk works well in place of the homemade version.

1. Spray a 9-inch (23 cm) square baking pan with cooking spray.

2. Spray a large microwave-safe bowl with cooking spray and add the peanut butter. Microwave on high for 1 minute. Spray a heat-proof rubber spatula with cooking spray and use it to stir in the rice cereal until well coated with peanut butter. Use the spatula to press half of the mixture into the prepared baking pan.

3. Layer the bananas over the cereal mixture. Pour the pudding over the bananas. Gently press the remaining cereal mixture onto the pudding. Chill for at least 1 hour or until firm enough to cut into 16 squares. Store, covered, in the refrigerator.

Makes 16 bars

Per serving (1 bar): 58 Calories, 11 g Carbohydrate, 2 g Protein, 1 g Fat,
0 mg Cholesterol, 28 mg Sodium, 1 g Fiber
Exchanges: 1 Starch (1 Carb Choice)

Devilish Chocolate Bars

Prep time: 10 minutes ◆ Bake time: 30 minutes

Cooking spray

1 cup (120 g) all-purpose flour

1 cup (120 g) whole wheat flour

½ cup (40 g) unsweetened cocoa powder, sifted if lumpy

¼ teaspoon salt

½ cup (122 g) unsweetened applesauce

½ cup (96 g) sugar

2 tablespoons canola or extra-light olive oil

1 teaspoon vanilla extract

2 large eggs

1 cup (240 ml) buttermilk (see page 8)

1 tablespoon white vinegar

1½ teaspoons baking soda

1. Preheat the oven to 350°F (180°C). Spray a 13 x 9 x 2-inch (33 x 23 x 5 cm) baking pan with cooking spray.

2. Stir together the flours, cocoa powder, and salt in a medium bowl.

3. Use an electric mixer at medium speed to beat the applesauce, sugar, oil, and vanilla in a large bowl until well blended; scrape down the sides of the bowl. Add the eggs and beat at medium speed until blended; scrape down the sides of the bowl.

4. With the mixer at medium speed, alternately add the flour mixture and the buttermilk to the applesauce mixture, beginning and ending with the flour mixture, until well mixed. Scrape down the sides of the bowl after each addition.

5. Combine the vinegar and baking soda in a small bowl until blended. Using a rubber spatula, carefully fold the vinegar mixture into the batter until blended. Spoon the batter into the prepared baking pan.

6. Bake for 30 to 35 minutes or until a tester inserted into the center comes out clean. Cool in the pan on a wire rack for 15 minutes, then cut into 24 bars. Store tightly covered. Refrigerate after 2 days or freeze for up to 12 months.

> **Variations:** *For cherry or berry chocolate bars, reduce the vanilla extract to ½ teaspoon and add 2 teaspoons cherry, strawberry, or raspberry extract to the applesauce mixture.*

Makes 24 bars

Per serving (1 bar): 73 Calories, 13 g Carbohydrate, 2 g Protein, 2 g Fat, 15 mg Cholesterol, 128 mg Sodium, 1 g Fiber
Exchanges: 1 Starch (1 Carb Choice)

Chocolate Jam Squares

Prep time: 10 minutes ◆ *Bake time: 10 minutes*

Cooking spray

¾ cup (90 g) all-purpose flour

¼ cup (30 g) whole wheat flour

⅓ cup (64 g) sugar

¼ cup (20 g) unsweetened cocoa powder, sifted if lumpy

½ teaspoon baking soda

3 tablespoons canola or extra-light olive oil

3 tablespoons white vinegar

1 tablespoon vanilla extract

½ cup (160 g) no-sugar-added raspberry or strawberry jam

1. Preheat the oven to 375°F (190°C). Spray an 8-inch (20 cm) square baking pan with cooking spray.

2. Use a wooden spoon or rubber spatula to combine the flours, sugar, cocoa powder, and baking soda in a medium bowl.

3. Measure ½ cup (120 ml) water in a 1-cup (240 ml) glass measuring cup and microwave on high for about 1 minute or until boiling. Stir in the oil, vinegar, and vanilla. Stir the oil-vinegar mixture into the dry ingredients until well mixed. Spoon the batter into the prepared baking pan.

4. Bake for 10 minutes. After 7 minutes, place the jam in the same glass measuring cup and microwave on high for 30 seconds. Stir.

5. Remove the pan from then oven and immediately spread the warmed jam over the cookie. Cool on a wire rack, then cut into 16 squares. Store covered. Refrigerate after 2 days or freeze for up to 12 months.

Makes 16 squares

Per serving (1 square): 79 Calories, 13 g Carbohydrate, 1 g Protein, 3 g Fat, 0 mg Cholesterol, 40 mg Sodium, 1 g Fiber
Exchanges: 1 Starch, ½ Fat (1 Carb Choice)

Chewy Coconut Squares

Prep time: 10 minutes ◆ Bake time: 35 minutes

Cooking spray

⅓ cup (43 g) chopped nuts

6 tablespoons (90 g) butter, softened

⅓ cup (60 g) sugar

¾ cup (90 g) whole wheat flour

¼ cup (30 g) all-purpose flour

¾ cup (53 g) unsweetened shredded coconut

2 large eggs

1 teaspoon vanilla extract

1. Preheat the oven to 350°F (180°C). Spray an 8-inch (20 cm) square baking pan with cooking spray.

2. Place the nuts in a small baking pan and bake for 3 to 5 minutes, until toasted; set aside.

3. Use an electric mixer at medium speed to cream the butter and 3 tablespoons of the sugar in a medium bowl until light and fluffy.

4. Blend in the whole wheat flour and 2 tablespoons of the all-purpose flour with the mixer at low speed. Scrape down the sides of the bowl and spoon the batter into the prepared baking pan, spreading evenly. Bake for 10 minutes.

5. Stir together the toasted nuts, the remaining 2 tablespoons sugar, remaining 2 tablespoons all-purpose flour, coconut, eggs, and vanilla in the same bowl until well blended. Spread the mixture evenly over the baked dough.

6. Bake for 25 minutes more or until golden. While warm, cut into 16 squares. Cool in the pan on a wire rack. Store tightly covered. Refrigerate after 2 days or freeze for up to 12 months.

Makes 16 squares

Per serving (1 square): 124 Calories, 10 g Carbohydrate, 2 g Protein, 9 g Fat,
33 mg Cholesterol, 43 mg Sodium, 1 g Fiber
Exchanges: ½ Starch, 2 Fat (½ Carb Choice)

Mix-in-the-Pan Date Bars

Prep time: 5 minutes ◆ Bake time: 30 minutes

¼ cup (33 g) chopped nuts

½ cup (60 g) all-purpose flour

½ cup (60 g) whole wheat flour

2 tablespoons sugar

½ teaspoon baking powder

½ teaspoon ground nutmeg

2 large eggs, beaten

¼ cup (60 ml) canola oil or extra-light olive oil

1 tablespoon fresh lemon juice

1 cup (165 g) chopped pitted dates

1. Preheat the oven to 350°F (180°C). Place the nuts in a small baking pan, and bake for 3 to 5 minutes until brown; set aside.

2. Mix together the flours, sugar, baking powder, and nutmeg in a 9-inch (23 cm) square baking pan. Add the eggs, oil, and lemon juice and mix with a rubber spatula until well blended. Stir in the dates and toasted nuts.

3. Bake for about 30 minutes or until lightly browned and a tester inserted into the center comes out clean. Cool in the pan on a wire rack, then cut into 16 bars. Store covered. Refrigerate after 2 days or freeze for up to 12 months.

Makes 16 bars

Per serving (1 bar): 113 Calories, 15 g Carbohydrate, 2 g Protein, 5 g Fat,
22 mg Cholesterol, 8 mg Sodium, 1 g Fiber
Exchanges: 1 Starch, 1 Fat (1 Carb Choice)

Date Chews

Prep time: 5 minutes • Bake time: 20 minutes

Cooking spray

1 cup (165 g) chopped pitted dates

¼ cup (30 g) all-purpose flour

¼ cup (30 g) whole wheat flour

2 tablespoons granulated sugar

½ teaspoon baking powder

1 large egg, beaten

2 tablespoons canola or extra-light olive oil

Confectioners' sugar (optional)

1. Preheat the oven to 350°F (180°C). Spray a 9-inch (23 cm) square baking pan with cooking spray.

2. Stir together the dates, flours, granulated sugar, and baking powder in a medium bowl. Use a rubber spatula to stir in the egg and oil until well mixed. The dough will be very thick. Spread the dough evenly with the spatula in the prepared baking pan.

3. Bake for 20 minutes or until lightly browned and a tester inserted into the center comes out clean.

4. While still warm, cut into 16 squares. Cool in the pan on a wire rack. If desired, sprinkle with confectioners' sugar before serving. Store covered. Refrigerate after 2 days or freeze for up to 12 months.

Makes 16 chews

Per serving (1 chew): 67 Calories, 12 g Carbohydrate, 1 g Protein, 2 g Fat,
11 mg Cholesterol, 4 mg Sodium, 1 g Fiber
Exchanges: 1 Starch (1 Carb Choice)

Pumpkin Pie Squares

Prep time: 20 minutes ◆ Bake time: 50 minutes ◆ Chilling time: 1 hour

Cooking spray

½ cup (60 g) all-purpose flour

½ cup (60 g) whole wheat flour

½ cup (45 g) old-fashioned rolled oats

⅓ cup (55 g) brown sugar

⅓ cup (80 ml) canola or extra-light olive oil

2 large eggs

One 12-ounce (354 ml) can fat-free evaporated milk

2 cups (460 g) puréed cooked fresh pumpkin or one 16-ounce (454 g) can pumpkin

1 tablespoon pumpkin pie spice

¼ teaspoon salt

¼ cup (33 g) chopped walnuts

1. Preheat the oven to 350°F (180°C). Spray a 9-inch (23 cm) square baking pan with cooking spray.

2. Use a rubber spatula to combine the flours, oats and 2 tablespoons of the brown sugar in a medium bowl. Add the oil and mix until blended.

3. Press 1 cup (120 g) of the mixture onto the bottom of the prepared pan; reserve the remainder. Bake for about 10 minutes or until brown.

4. Meanwhile, whisk the eggs in a large bowl. Shake the can of evaporated milk and add it to the eggs with the pumpkin, the remaining 3 tablespoons brown sugar, pumpkin pie spice, and salt. Whisk until well blended, then pour the mixture over the baked crust. Bake for 30 minutes.

5. Add the walnuts to the reserved flour mixture, mix well, and evenly sprinkle the mixture over the pumpkin filling. Bake for 10 minutes longer or until the filling is set and the top is lightly browned.

6. Cool in the pan on a wire rack. When cool, refrigerate for at least 1 hour before cutting into 16 squares. Store, covered, in the refrigerator.

Makes 16 squares

Per serving (1 square): 140 Calories, 16 g Carbohydrate, 4 g Protein, 7 g Fat,
23 mg Cholesterol, 118 mg Sodium, 2 g Fiber
Exchanges: 1 Starch, 1 Fat (1 Carb Choice)

Raisin Spice Squares

Prep time: 15 minutes ◆ Bake time: 25 minutes

Cooking spray

½ cup (65 g) chopped walnuts

1 cup (120 g) all-purpose flour

1 cup (120 g) whole wheat flour

1 teaspoon baking soda

1 teaspoon ground cinnamon

1 teaspoon ground nutmeg

¼ teaspoon salt

1 cup (170 g) raisins

1 large egg, beaten

¼ cup (61 g) unsweetened applesauce

¼ cup (60 ml) canola or extra-light olive oil

3 tablespoons granulated sugar

Confectioners' sugar (optional)

1. Preheat the oven to 350°F (180°C). Spray a 13 x 9 x 2-inch (33 x 23 x 5 cm) baking pan with cooking spray.

2. Place the walnuts in a small baking pan, and bake for 3 to 5 minutes, until toasted; set aside.

3. Whisk together the flours, baking soda, cinnamon, nutmeg, and salt in a large bowl. Stir in the toasted nuts.

4. In a 4-cup (960 ml) glass measuring cup, combine the raisins and 2 cups (480 ml) water. Microwave on high for 4 to 5 minutes, until the raisins are softened, stirring after 3 minutes. Remove from the microwave; stir. Cool to lukewarm.

5. Use a rubber spatula to stir the egg into the plumped raisins until well mixed. Stir in the applesauce, oil, and granulated sugar until blended.

6. Pour the raisin mixture into the flour mixture and stir until thoroughly blended. Scrape down the sides of the bowl and spoon the batter into the prepared baking pan.

7. Bake for 25 minutes or until a tester inserted into the center comes out clean. Cool in the pan on a wire rack, then cut into 24 squares. If desired, sprinkle with confectioners' sugar. Store tightly covered. Refrigerate after 2 days or freeze for up to 12 months.

Makes 24 squares

Per serving (1 square): 101 Calories, 15 g Carbohydrate, 2 g Protein, 4 g Fat,
7 mg Cholesterol, 80 mg Sodium, 1 g Fiber
Exchanges: 1 Fruit, 1 Fat (1 Carb Choice)

Raspberry Bars

Prep time: 10 minutes • Bake time: 35 minutes

1 cup (90 g) old-fashioned rolled oats

½ cup (60 g) all-purpose flour

½ cup (60 g) whole wheat flour

⅓ cup (80 ml) canola or extra-light olive oil

3 tablespoons light brown sugar

¼ teaspoon baking soda

⅔ cup (212 g) no-sugar-added raspberry jam

1. Preheat the oven to 350°F (180°C). Spray an 8-inch (20 cm) square baking pan with cooking spray. Line the pan with aluminum foil, allowing extra to hang over the sides of the pan for ease in lifting out the baked bars.

2. Stir together the oats, flours, oil, brown sugar, and baking soda in a medium bowl. Press 1 cup (75 g) of the mixture onto the bottom of the lined baking pan.

3. Spread the jam to within ¼ inch (6 mm) of the edge. Sprinkle the remaining crumb mixture over the top and lightly press it into the jam.

4. Bake for 35 to 40 minutes or until lightly browned. Cool in the pan on a wire rack. Lift the bars in the foil from the pan and place on a cutting board. Use a sharp knife to cut the cookie into 16 bars. Remove the bars from the foil with a metal spatula. Store tightly covered. Refrigerate after 2 days or freeze for up to 12 months.

Makes 16 bars

Per serving (1 bar): 111 Calories, 15 g Carbohydrate, 2 g Protein, 5 g Fat,
0 mg Cholesterol, 20 mg Sodium, 1 g Fiber
Exchanges: 1 Starch, 1 Fat (1 Carb Choice)

Tangy Citrus Bars

Prep time: 10 minutes ◆ Bake time: 35 minutes

BARS

Cooking spray

½ cup (65 g) chopped nuts

1 tablespoon grated orange zest

1½ cups (360 ml) fresh orange juice

2 large eggs, at room temperature

¼ cup (60 ml) canola or extra-light olive oil

1½ cups (180 g) whole wheat flour

1 teaspoon ground cinnamon

½ teaspoon ground nutmeg

1½ cups (150 g) whole or chopped cranberries, fresh or frozen

TOPPING

½ cup (60 g) all-purpose flour

½ cup (36 g) unsweetened shredded coconut

2 teaspoons baking powder

1 teaspoon baking soda

One 8-ounce (227 g) can juice-packed crushed pineapple, drained

1. Preheat the oven to 350°F (180°C). Spray a 13 x 9 x 2-inch (33 x 23 x 5 cm) baking pan with cooking spray.

2. **To make the bars,** place the chopped nuts in a small baking pan and bake for 3 to 5 minutes, until toasted; set aside.

3. Use an electric mixer at medium speed to beat the orange zest and juice, eggs, and oil in a medium bowl until well mixed; scrape down the sides of the bowl.

4. Add the flour, cinnamon, and nutmeg and beat at low speed, scraping down the sides of the bowl, until incorporated. Use a rubber spatula to stir in the cranberries and toasted nuts. Spoon the mixture into the prepared baking pan.

5. **To make the topping,** stir together the flour, coconut, baking powder, baking soda, and pineapple in a medium bowl until well mixed. Evenly spoon the topping over the batter.

6. Bake for 35 to 40 minutes or until browned and a tester inserted into the center comes out clean. Cool in the pan on a wire rack, then cut into 24 bars. Store tightly covered. Refrigerate after 2 days or freeze for up to 12 months.

Makes 24 bars

Per serving (1 bar): 136 Calories, 20 g Carbohydrate, 2 g Protein, 5 g Fat, 15 mg Cholesterol, 58 mg Sodium, 2 g Fiber
Exchanges: 1 Starch, 1 Fat (1 Carb Choice)

Fudgy Brownies

Prep time: 10 minutes ◆ Bake time: 20 minutes

½ cup (1 stick/113 g) butter, cut into 4 pieces

1 cup (160 g) semisweet or dark chocolate morsels

½ cup (96 g) sugar

3 large eggs, at room temperature

¼ cup (20 g) cocoa powder, sifted if lumpy

1. Preheat the oven to 325°F (165°C). Line an 11 x 7-inch (28 x 18 cm) baking pan with aluminum foil, allowing extra to hang over two opposite longer sides of the pan for ease in lifting out the baked brownies.

2. Place the butter and chocolate morsels in a medium microwave-safe bowl. Microwave at 50 percent power for 1½ to 2 minutes, until the morsels are mostly melted. Remove from the oven and stir until the chocolate morsels are melted and smooth. Stir in the sugar, then the eggs, one at a time, until well blended and the batter is smooth.

3. Add the cocoa powder and mix with a wooden spoon until well incorporated. Spoon the batter evenly into the prepared pan.

4. Bake for 20 to 25 minutes or until a tester inserted into the center comes out clean. Cool in the pan on a wire rack for 15 minutes. Then lift the brownies out of the pan using the foil as a sling and place on the rack to finish cooling.

5. Cut into 24 squares. Store in a covered container for up to 2 days, or freeze for up to 3 months.

Makes 24 squares

Per serving (1 square): 83 Calories, 8 g Carbohydrate, 1 g Protein, 7 g Fat, 32 mg Cholesterol, 39 mg Sodium, 0 g Fiber
Exchanges: ½ Starch, 1 Fat (½ Carb Choice)

Cakes

Tips & Tricks

» Chiffon, angel food, and sponge cakes are light, delicate, and easy to modify for people with diabetes. Chiffon cake combines beaten egg whites, egg yolks, leavening, and a small amount of oil. Angel food cake has no leavening, no added fat or oil, and no egg yolks; therefore, it has no cholesterol and no fat. Sponge cake uses both egg whites and egg yolks, with no other fats added. Sponge cake may also be used as a roll cake.

» These cakes can be baked in a tube pan or a loaf pan. For angel food and chiffon cakes, the pan is not greased.

» When baking these cakes, place the tube pan on the bottom rack of the oven.

» Don't open the oven door until the minimum baking time has elapsed.

» Cakes baked in a tube pan are done when cracks in the top feel dry and no imprint remains when the top is lightly touched. Foam-type cakes baked in oblong or jelly roll pans are done when a tester inserted into the center comes out clean.

» To remove a cooled cake from a tube pan, loosen it first by moving a thin knife up and down against the sides and center tube of the pan. Turn the cake upside down on a wire rack or serving plate and remove the pan.

» An unopened carbonated beverage glass bottle, a wine bottle, or funnel makes a convenient stand for a tube or Bundt pan that must be inverted to cool.

» Whole wheat flour and all-purpose should be stirred with a fork or whisked before measuring to ensure a light-textured baked good. Whole wheat pastry flour can be substituted for whole wheat flour; the texture of the cake, cookies, or pie crusts will be lighter. Whole wheat pastry flour is preferred, if available.

» Use white whole wheat flour, if available, in place of darker whole wheat flour. Its texture and color are lighter, but it has all the nutrients and fiber of regular whole wheat flour. If you prefer to use only white all-purpose flour, do so. I prefer combining all-purpose flour and whole wheat flour, because whole wheat flour has natural nutrients and fiber. By combining both flours, we get a more healthful, yet tasty baked good.

Raspberry Angel Food Cake

Prep time: 10 minutes • Bake time: 40 minutes • Cooling time: 1 hour

10 large egg whites, at room temperature

1¼ teaspoons cream of tartar

1 teaspoon vanilla extract

½ teaspoon almond extract

½ cup (96 g) sugar

1 cup (90 g) cake flour

2 cups (300 g) fresh raspberries

1. Preheat the oven to 325°F (165°C). Set out a 10-inch (25 cm) tube pan.

2. Use an electric mixer at high speed to beat the egg whites in a large bowl until frothy; beat in the cream of tartar until soft peaks form. Add the extracts, then gradually beat in the sugar, beating until the whites form stiff peaks when the beaters are lifted.

3. Sift the cake flour over the beaten egg whites and sprinkle in the raspberries. Use a rubber spatula to gently fold the flour and raspberries into the batter, mixing thoroughly but lightly to incorporate all of the flour. Spoon the batter into the tube pan, then gently cut through the batter with a clean table knife.

4. Bake for 40 to 45 minutes or until the cake is lightly browned and a tester inserted into the center comes out clean. Immediately invert the cake pan over a sturdy glass bottle or funnel and let it cool completely, about 1 hour.

5. Use a knife to loosen the cake from the sides, center tube, and bottom of the pan. Remove it from the pan and place the cake on a plate. Store, covered, at room temperature for up to 2 days. This cake can be frozen for up to 3 months. Use a serrated knife for easy slicing.

Makes one 10-inch (25 cm) cake; 16 servings

Per serving (1 slice): 64 Calories, 13 g Carbohydrate, 3 g Protein, 0 g Fat,
0 g Cholesterol, 34 mg Sodium, 0 g Fiber
Exchanges: 1 Starch (1 Carb Choice)

Orange Chiffon Cake

Prep time: 10 minutes ◆ Bake time: 55 minutes ◆ Cooling time: 1 hour

7 large eggs, separated, at room temperature

½ teaspoon cream of tartar

½ cup (96 g) sugar

2¼ cups (203 g) sifted cake flour

1 tablespoon baking powder

½ teaspoon salt

½ cup (120 ml) canola or extra-light olive oil

1 tablespoon grated orange zest

¾ cup (180 ml) fresh orange juice

1 teaspoon vanilla extract

1. Preheat the oven to 325°F (165°C). Set out a 10-inch (25 cm) tube pan.

2. Use an electric mixer at high speed to beat the egg whites in a large bowl until frothy; beat in the cream of tartar until soft peaks form. Gradually beat in ¼ cup (48 g) of the sugar, beating until the whites form stiff peaks when the beaters are lifted. Set aside.

3. Whisk together the cake flour, remaining ¼ cup sugar, baking powder, and salt in another large bowl. Make a well in the center and add the oil, egg yolks, orange zest and juice, and vanilla. Use the same beaters at medium speed to beat the egg yolks and juice into the flour mixture until smooth, scraping down the sides of the bowl occasionally.

4. Add the flour mixture to the beaten whites. Use a rubber spatula to gently fold the flour mixture into the egg whites until no white streaks remain. Spoon the batter into the tube pan.

5. Bake for 55 minutes or until a tester inserted into the center comes out clean and the cake springs back when lightly touched.

6. Immediately invert the cake over a sturdy glass bottle or funnel and let cool completely, about 1 hour. Use a knife to loosen the cake from the sides, center tube, and bottom of the pan. Remove it from the pan and place the cake on plate. Store, covered, at room temperature for up to 2 days. This cake can be frozen for up to 3 months. Use a serrated knife for easy slicing.

Makes one 10-inch (25 cm) cake; 16 servings

Per serving (1 slice): 184 Calories, 21 g Carbohydrate, 5 g Protein, 9 g Fat, 81 mg Cholesterol, 101 mg Sodium, 0 g Fiber
Exchanges: 1½ Starch, 2 Fat (1½ Carb Choices)

Nutty Maple Chiffon Cake

Prep time: 10 minutes • Bake time: 55 minutes • Cooling time: 1 hour

1 cup (121 g) finely chopped pecans or walnuts

7 large eggs, separated, at room temperature

½ teaspoon cream of tartar

⅓ cup (64 g) granulated sugar

1 cup (120 g) all-purpose flour

1 cup (120 g) whole wheat flour

⅓ cup (64 g) packed brown sugar

1 tablespoon baking powder

½ teaspoon salt

½ cup (120 ml) canola or extra-light olive oil

2 teaspoons maple extract

1. Preheat the oven to 325°F (165°C). Set out a 10-inch (25 cm) tube pan.

2. Place the nuts in a small baking pan, and bake for 3 to 5 minutes, until toasted; set aside.

3. Use an electric mixer at high speed to beat the egg whites in a large bowl until frothy; beat in the cream of tartar until soft peaks form. Gradually beat in the granulated sugar, beating until the whites form stiff peaks when the beaters are lifted. Set aside.

4. Whisk together the flours, brown sugar, baking powder, and salt in a large bowl. Make a well in the center and add the oil, egg yolks, ¾ cup (180 ml) cold water, and maple extract. Use the same beaters at medium speed to beat the egg yolk mixture into the flour mixture, beating until smooth.

5. Add the flour mixture to the beaten whites. Use a rubber spatula to gently fold the egg whites into the batter until no white streaks remain. Fold in the toasted nuts. Spoon the batter into the tube pan.

6. Bake for 55 to 65 minutes or, until a tester inserted into the center of the cake comes out clean. Immediately invert the pan over a glass bottle or funnel and let cool completely, about 1 hour.

7. Use a knife to loosen the cake from the sides, center tube, and bottom of the pan. Remove it from the pan and place the cake on a plate. Store, covered, at room temperature for up to 2 days This cake can be frozen for up to 3 months. Use a serrated knife for easy slicing.

Makes one 10-inch (25 cm) cake; 16 servings

Per serving (1 slice): 225 Calories, 21 g Carbohydrate, 5 g Protein, 14 g Fat, 81 mg Cholesterol, 100 mg Sodium, 2 g Fiber
Exchanges: 1½ Starch, 3 Fat (1½ Carb Choices)

Tropical Chiffon Cake

Prep time: 10 minutes ◆ Bake time: 55 minutes ◆ Cooling time: 1 hour

7 large eggs, separated, at room temperature

½ teaspoon cream of tartar

½ cup (96 g) granulated sugar

1 cup (120 g) whole wheat flour

1 cup (120 g) all-purpose flour

1 tablespoon baking powder

1 tablespoon grated lemon zest

1 teaspoon ground cinnamon

½ teaspoon salt

½ teaspoon ground nutmeg

½ cup (120 ml) canola or extra-light olive oil

1 cup (224 g) mashed ripe bananas (2 medium)

One 6-ounce (177 ml) can unsweetened pineapple juice (about ¾ cup)

Confectioners' sugar (optional)

1. Preheat the oven to 325°F (165°C). Set out a 10-inch (25 cm) tube pan.

2. Use an electric mixer at high speed to beat the egg whites in a large bowl until frothy; beat in the cream of tartar until soft peaks form. Gradually beat in ¼ cup (48 g) of the granulated sugar, beating until the whites form stiff peaks when the beaters are lifted. Set aside.

3. Whisk together the remaining ¼ cup granulated sugar, the flours, baking powder, lemon zest, cinnamon, salt, and nutmeg in another large bowl. Make a well in the center and add the oil, bananas, egg yolks, and pineapple juice. Use the same beaters at medium speed to beat the egg mixture into the flour mixture until smooth, scraping the bowl occasionally.

4. Add the flour mixture to the beaten whites. Use a rubber spatula to gently fold the egg whites into the batter until no white streaks remain. Spoon the batter into the tube pan.

5. Bake for 55 minutes or until the cake is browned and springs back when lightly touched. Immediately invert the pan over a sturdy glass bottle or funnel and let cool, about 1 hour.

6. Use a knife to loosen the cake from the sides, center tube, and bottom of the pan. Remove it from the pan and place the cake on a plate. If desired, sprinkle with confectioners' sugar. Store, covered, at room temperature for up to 2 days. The cake can be frozen for up to 3 months. Use a serrated knife for easy slicing.

Makes one 10-inch (25 cm) cake; 16 servings

Per serving (1 slice): 178 Calories, 21 g Carbohydrates, 4 g Protein, 9 g Fat, 68 mg Cholesterol, 97 mg Sodium, 2 g Fiber
Exchanges: 1 Starch, ½ Fruit, 2 Fat (1½ Carb Choices)

Featherweight Sponge Cake

Prep time: 15 minutes ◆ Bake time: 25 minutes ◆ Cooling time: 40 minutes

Cooking spray

3 large eggs, separated, at room temperature

½ teaspoon cream of tartar

½ cup (60 g) confectioners' sugar

¼ cup (60 ml) warm water

1 tablespoon grated orange zest

1 teaspoon vanilla extract

1 cup (90 g) cake flour

1 teaspoon baking powder

Blueberry Topping (page 93; optional)

1. Preheat the oven to 350°F (180°C). Spray two 8-inch (20 cm) cake pans with cooking spray, line with rounds of parchment paper, cut to fit, and spray the paper with cooking spray.

2. Use an electric mixer at high speed to beat the egg whites in a large bowl; beat in the cream of tartar until soft peaks form. Gradually beat in ¼ cup (30 g) of the confectioners' sugar, beating until the whites form stiff peaks when the beaters are lifted. Set aside.

3. Use the same beaters at medium speed (or a whisk) to beat the egg yolks in another large bowl, until thick and lemon colored; add the remaining ¼ cup confectioners' sugar and beat until thick and smooth, scraping down the sides of the bowl occasionally. Beat in the warm water, orange zest, and vanilla until blended.

4. Whisk the flour and baking powder in a small bowl. Gradually beat the flour mixture into the egg yolk mixture at medium speed, scraping down the sides of the bowl after each addition, until smooth. Use a rubber spatula to gently fold the egg yolk mixture into the beaten whites until no white streaks remain. Spoon the batter evenly into the lined cake pans.

5. Bake for 25 minutes or until the cakes are lightly browned and a tester inserted into the center comes out clean.

6. Cool in the pans on wire racks for 10 minutes. Use a knife to loosen the cakes; remove them from the pans and let cool completely on the racks, about 30 minutes. Peel off the parchment paper. Fill and frost with Blueberry Topping as desired. Store, covered, in the refrigerator. This cake can be frozen without filling and frosting for up to 3 months. Use a serrated knife for easy slicing.

Makes two 8-inch (20 cm) round cakes; 12 servings

Per serving (1 slice): 72 Calories, 12 g Carbohydrate, 3 g Protein, 1 g Fat,
44 mg Cholesterol, 15 mg Sodium, 0 g Fiber
Exchanges: 1 Starch (1 Carb Choice)

Simple Apple Cake

Prep time: 5 minutes ◆ *Bake time: 30 minutes*

Cooking spray

¼ cup (33 g) chopped nuts

½ cup (60 g) all-purpose flour

½ cup (60 g) whole wheat flour

¼ cup (48 g) packed brown sugar

¾ teaspoon ground cinnamon

½ teaspoon baking soda

2 large eggs

⅓ cup (80 ml) canola or extra-light olive oil

1 teaspoon vanilla extract

2 cups (250 g) peeled, cored, and chopped apples (2 medium)

Confectioners' sugar (optional)

1. Preheat the oven to 350°F (180°C). Spray a 9-inch (23 cm) square baking pan with cooking spray.

2. Place the nuts in a small baking pan; bake for 3 to 5 minutes, until toasted; set aside.

3. Use an electric mixer at low speed to beat the flours, brown sugar, cinnamon, baking soda, eggs, oil, and vanilla in a large bowl for 1 minute, scraping down the sides of the bowl occasionally. Use a rubber spatula to mix in the apples and toasted nuts until well blended. Spoon the batter into the prepared baking pan.

4. Bake for 30 minutes or until a tester inserted into the center of the cake comes out clean.

5. Cool in the pan on a wire rack for 20 minutes. Use a knife to loosen the cake and invert it onto a plate. Turn the cake right side up on a wire rack to cool completely, about 30 minutes. Place the cake on a serving plate and, if desired, sprinkle with confectioners' sugar. Store covered. Refrigerate after 2 days. This cake can be frozen for up to 3 months.

Makes one 9-inch (23 cm) square cake; 9 servings

Per serving (1 piece): 196 Calories, 21 g Carbohydrate, 3 g Protein, 11 g Fat, 39 mg Cholesterol, 84 mg Sodium, 2 g Fiber
Exchanges: 1 Starch, ½ Fruit, 2 Fat (1½ Carb Choices)

Spicy Apple Upside-Down Cake

Prep time: 15 minutes ◆ *Bake time: 30 minutes*

2 tablespoons brown sugar

2 tablespoons butter, melted

1 tablespoon fresh lemon juice

1 large unpeeled baking apple, cored and thinly sliced

½ cup (60 g) all-purpose flour

½ cup (60 g) whole wheat flour

½ teaspoon ground cinnamon

¼ teaspoon ground nutmeg

⅛ teaspoon ground cloves

¼ teaspoon salt

2 large eggs

⅓ cup (80 ml) canola or extra-light olive oil

⅓ cup (80 ml) nonfat milk

¼ cup (48 g) granulated sugar

1 teaspoon butter extract

½ teaspoon vanilla extract

1. Preheat the oven to 350°F (180°C).

2. Add the brown sugar, melted butter, and lemon juice to an 8-inch (20 cm) square baking pan. Use a rubber spatula to mix the ingredients well, then spread the mixture evenly over the bottom of the pan.

3. Bake for 1 minute. Stir again and arrange the apple slices over the brown sugar mixture in the pan. Press any additional apple slices onto the sides of the pan. Set aside.

4. Stir together the flours, cinnamon, nutmeg, cloves, and salt in a medium bowl. Add the eggs, oil, milk, granulated sugar, and extracts. Use an electric mixer at medium speed to beat the mixture for 2 minutes, scraping down the bowl occasionally.

5. Spread the batter over the apple slices. Bake for 30 to 35 minutes or until a tester inserted into the center of the cake comes out clean.

6. Cool in the pan on a wire rack for 10 minutes. Use a knife to loosen the cake and invert it onto the rack. Cool completely, at least 30 minutes, before serving. Store covered. Refrigerate after 2 days. This cake can be frozen for up to 3 months.

Makes one 8-inch (20 cm) square cake; 8 servings

Per serving (1 piece): 235 Calories, 26 g Carbohydrate, 4 g Protein, 13 g Fat,
52 mg Cholesterol, 116 mg Sodium, 2 g Fiber
Exchanges: 2 Starch, 2½ Fat (2 Carb Choices)

Date Nut Apple Cake

Prep time: 15 minutes • Bake time: 55 minutes

Cooking spray

½ cup (65 g) chopped walnuts

1 cup (120 g) all-purpose flour

¾ cup (90 g) whole wheat flour

2 teaspoons unsweetened cocoa
powder

1 teaspoon baking powder

1 teaspoon baking soda

1 teaspoon ground cinnamon

½ teaspoon ground cloves

4 cups (500 g) peeled, cored,
and chopped tart apples
(3 or 4 medium)

½ cup (83 g) chopped pitted dates

2 large eggs, at room temperature

½ cup (120 ml) canola or extra-light
olive oil

¼ cup (48 g) sugar

½ cup (120 ml) cold coffee (or
dissolve 1 teaspoon instant coffee
in ½ cup/120 ml boiling water,
then cool)

1. Preheat the oven to 350°F (180°C). Spray a 10-inch (25 cm) tube or Bundt pan with cooking spray.

2. Put the walnuts in a small baking pan and bake for 3 to 5 minutes, until toasted; set aside.

3. Whisk together the flours, cocoa powder, baking powder, baking soda, cinnamon, and cloves in a medium bowl. Reserve ½ cup (105 g) of the flour mixture.

4. Mix the apples, toasted walnuts, dates, and the reserved flour mixture in another medium bowl; toss together until the fruit is well coated.

5. Use an electric mixer at medium speed to beat the eggs, oil, and sugar in a large bowl until well blended; scrape down the sides of the bowl.

6. With the mixer at low speed, beat in the remaining flour mixture alternately with the coffee, beginning and ending with the flour mixture, until the batter is smooth. Scrape down the bowl after each addition.

7. Stir in the fruit mixture and mix well. Spoon the batter into the prepared cake pan, and smooth the top.

8. Bake for 55 to 60 minutes or until the cake is browned and a tester inserted into the center comes out clean.

9. Cool in the pan on a wire rack for 20 minutes. Use a knife to loosen the cake from the sides, center tube, and bottom of the pan. Remove the cake from the pan and let cool completely on the rack, for about 1 hour. Store covered. Refrigerate after 2 days. This cake can be frozen for up to 3 months.

Makes one 10-inch (25 cm) tube or Bundt cake; 16 servings

Per serving: 181 Calories, 21 g Carbohydrate, 3 g Protein, 10 g Fat,
22 mg Cholesterol, 87 mg Sodium, 2 g Fiber
Exchanges: 1 Starch, ½ Fruit, 2 Fat (1½ Carb Choices)

Blueberry Bundt Cake

Prep time: 15 minutes ◆ *Bake time: 1 hour*

Cooking spray

1¼ cups (150 g) all-purpose flour

1 cup (120 g) whole wheat flour

2½ teaspoons baking powder

1 teaspoon baking soda

½ teaspoon ground nutmeg

¼ teaspoon salt

4 large eggs, separated, at room
temperature

½ teaspoon cream of tartar

½ cup (96 g) sugar

½ cup (120 ml) buttermilk
(see page 8)

½ cup (120 ml) canola or extra-light
olive oil

½ cup (120 ml) fresh orange juice

1 tablespoon grated lemon zest

2 cups (290 g) fresh or frozen
blueberries

1. Preheat the oven to 350°F (180°C). Spray a 10-inch (25 cm) Bundt or tube pan with cooking spray.

2. Whisk together the flours, baking powder, baking soda, nutmeg, and salt in a medium bowl. Reserve ½ cup (60 g) of the flour mixture.

3. Use an electric mixer at high speed to beat the egg whites in a medium bowl until frothy; beat in the cream of tartar until soft peaks form. Gradually beat in ¼ cup (48 g) of the sugar, beating until the whites form stiff peaks when the beaters are lifted. Set aside.

4. Use the same beaters at medium speed to beat the egg yolks and remaining ¼ cup (48 g) sugar in a large bowl until thick and lemon colored, 1 to 2 minutes. Scrape down the bowl and beat in the buttermilk, oil, orange juice, and lemon zest.

5. With the mixer at low speed, gradually beat in all but the reserved flour mixture; scrape down the sides of the bowl. Combine the blueberries with the reserved flour mixture until the berries are coated. Stir the coated blueberries into the batter. Use a rubber spatula to gently fold the egg whites into the batter until no white streaks remain.

6. Spoon the batter into the prepared Bundt pan. Bake for 60 to 65 minutes or until the cake is lightly browned and a tester inserted into the center comes out clean.

7. Cool in the pan on a wire rack for 20 minutes. Use a knife to loosen the cake. Remove the cake from the pan and let cool completely on the rack, about 1 hour. Store covered. Refrigerate after 2 days. This cake can be frozen for up to 3 months.

Makes one 10-inch (25 cm) Bundt or tube cake; 16 servings

Per serving (1 slice): 174 Calories, 22 g Carbohydrate, 4 g Protein, 8 g Fat,
46 mg Cholesterol, 146 mg Sodium, 2 g Fiber
Exchanges: 1½ Starch, 1½ Fat (1½ Carb Choices)

Apple-Raisin Cake

Prep time: 20 minutes ◆ Bake time: 75 minutes

4 cups (500 g) unpeeled cored, diced apples (3 or 4 medium)

½ cup (96 g) sugar

Cooking spray

½ cup (65 g) chopped walnuts

1½ cups (180 g) all-purpose flour

1½ cups (180 g) whole wheat flour

2 teaspoons baking soda

2 teaspoons ground cinnamon

1 teaspoon ground allspice

½ teaspoon ground cloves

½ teaspoon ground nutmeg

½ cup (122 g) unsweetened applesauce

2 large eggs, beaten

½ cup (120 ml) canola or extra-light olive oil

1 tablespoon Worcestershire sauce

½ cup (85 g) raisins

1. Combine the apples and sugar in a medium bowl; set aside for 15 minutes.

2. Preheat the oven to 325°F (165°C). Spray a 10-inch (25 cm) tube pan with cooking spray.

3. Place the walnuts in a small baking pan and bake for 3 to 5 minutes, until toasted; set aside.

4. Whisk together the flours, baking soda, cinnamon, allspice, cloves, and nutmeg in a large bowl.

5. Use a rubber spatula to stir in the applesauce, eggs, oil, and Worcestershire sauce; blend thoroughly. Stir in the apple mixture, raisins, and toasted walnuts; mix well, scraping down the sides of the bowl. Spoon the batter into the prepared cake pan.

6. Bake for 75 minutes or until the cake is brown and a tester inserted into the center comes out clean.

7. Cool in the pan on a wire rack for 20 minutes. Use a knife to loosen the cake from the sides, center tube, and bottom of the pan. Remove the cake from the pan and let cool completely on the rack, about 1 hour. Store covered. Refrigerate after 2 days. This cake can be frozen for up to 3 months.

Makes one 10-inch (25 cm) tube cake; 16 servings

Per serving (1 slice): 225 Calories, 31 g Carbohydrate, 4 g Protein, 10 g Fat, 22 mg Cholesterol, 178 mg Sodium, 3 g Fiber
Exchanges: 1½ Starch, ½ Fruit, 2 Fat (2 Carb Choices)

Carrot-Applesauce Cake

Prep time: 10 minutes • Bake time: 1 hour

Cooking spray

1 cup (120 g) all-purpose flour

1 cup (120 g) whole wheat flour

½ cup (29 g) wheat bran

1 tablespoon baking soda

2 teaspoons ground cinnamon

1 teaspoon ground cloves

1 teaspoon ground nutmeg

3 large eggs, at room temperature

½ cup (96 g) granulated sugar

⅓ cup (80 ml) canola or extra-light olive oil

1½ teaspoons vanilla extract

1⅔ cups (203 g) unsweetened applesauce

3½ cups (1 pound/454 g) shredded carrots

Confectioners' sugar (optional)

1. Preheat the oven to 350°F (180°C). Spray a 10-inch (25 cm) tube or Bundt pan with cooking spray.

2. Whisk together the flours, wheat bran, baking soda, cinnamon, cloves, and nutmeg in a large bowl.

3. Use an electric mixer at medium speed to beat the eggs, granulated sugar, oil, and vanilla in a medium bowl until well blended. Use a rubber spatula to stir in the applesauce and carrots until blended. Pour the applesauce-carrot mixture into the flour mixture and stir just to moisten; do not overmix. Spoon the batter into the prepared cake pan.

4. Bake for 60 to 65 minutes or until a tester inserted into the center comes out clean.

5. Cool in the pan on a wire rack for 15 minutes. Use a knife to loosen the cake from the sides, center tube, and bottom of the pan. Remove the cake from the pan and let cool completely on the rack, about 1 hour. If desired, sprinkle with confectioners' sugar. Store covered. Refrigerate after 2 days.

Makes one 10-inch (25 cm) tube or Bundt cake; 16 servings

Per serving (1 slice): 150 Calories, 22 g Carbohydrate, 3 g Protein, 6 g Fat,
33 mg Cholesterol, 255 mg Sodium, 3 g Fiber
Exchanges: 1½ Starch, 1 Fat (1½ Carb Choices)

Pineapple-Carrot Cake

Prep time: 10 minutes • Bake time: 30 minutes

Cooking spray

½ cup (65 g) chopped nuts (optional)

1 cup (120 g) all-purpose flour

1 cup (120 g) whole wheat flour

2 teaspoons baking soda

1 teaspoon baking powder

1 teaspoon ground cinnamon

½ teaspoon ground nutmeg

3 large eggs, at room temperature

½ cup (120 ml) canola or extra-light olive oil

½ cup (96 g) granulated sugar

One 8-ounce (227 g) can juice-packed crushed pineapple

1 teaspoon vanilla extract

3½ cups (1 pound/454 g) shredded carrots

½ cup (85 g) raisins (optional)

Confectioners' sugar (optional)

Light Cream Cheese Frosting (page 90; optional)

1. Preheat the oven to 350°F (180°C). Spray a 13 x 9 x 2-inch (33 x 23 x 5 cm) baking pan with cooking spray.

2. If using nuts, place them in a small baking pan and bake for 3 to 5 minutes, until toasted; set aside.

3. Whisk together the flours, baking soda, baking powder, cinnamon, and nutmeg in a medium bowl.

4. Use an electric mixer at medium speed to beat the eggs in a large bowl until frothy. Beat in the oil and granulated sugar until well blended; scrape down the sides of the bowl.

5. With the mixer at low speed, beat in the pineapple with its juice, the flour mixture, and vanilla and beat until well blended. Use a rubber spatula to stir in the carrots, toasted nuts, and raisins, if desired. Spoon the batter into the prepared baking pan.

6. Bake for 30 to 35 minutes or until a tester inserted into the center of the cake comes out clean.

7. Cool completely in the pan on a wire rack, about 1 hour. Use a knife to loosen the cake and invert it onto the rack. Place the cake right side up on a serving plate. Sprinkle with confectioners' sugar or frost with Light Cream Cheese Frosting, if desired. Store covered. Refrigerate after 2 days or if the cake is frosted.

Makes one 13 x 9-inch (33 x 23 cm) cake; 20 servings

Per serving (1 piece): 156 Calories, 19 g Carbohydrate, 3 g Protein, 8 g Fat, 26 mg Cholesterol, 142 mg Sodium, 2 g Fiber
Exchanges: 1 Starch, 1½ Fat (1 Carb Choice)

Spicy Pumpkin Cake

Prep time: 10 minutes • Bake time: 60 minutes

Cooking spray

1½ cups (180 g) all-purpose flour

1½ cups (180 g) whole wheat flour

1 tablespoon baking powder

2 teaspoons pumpkin pie spice

1 teaspoon ground cinnamon

½ teaspoon baking soda

3 large eggs, at room temperature

½ cup (96 g) granulated sugar

½ cup (96 g) packed brown sugar

One 16-ounce (454 g) can pumpkin or 2 cups puréed cooked fresh pumpkin

¾ cup (180 ml) nonfat milk

½ cup (120 ml) canola or extra-light olive oil

1½ cups (135 g) old-fashioned rolled oats

Confectioners' sugar (optional)

1. Preheat the oven to 350°F (180°C). Spray a 10-inch (25 cm) tube pan or Bundt pan with cooking spray.

2. Whisk together the flours, baking powder, pumpkin pie spice, cinnamon, and baking soda in a medium bowl.

3. Use an electric mixer at medium speed to beat the eggs in large bowl until frothy; add the granulated sugar and brown sugar and beat at medium speed until thick.

4. Scrape down the sides of the bowl and add the pumpkin, milk, and oil; beat at medium speed until well blended, scraping down the bowl occasionally.

5. With the mixer at low speed, beat in the flour mixture until well blended. Use a rubber spatula to stir in the oats until all ingredients are well mixed.

6. Pour the batter into the prepared cake pan. Bake for 60 to 65 minutes or until a tester inserted into the center comes out clean.

7. Cool in the pan on a wire rack for about 20 minutes. Use a knife to loosen the cake from the sides, center tube, and bottom of the pan. Remove it from the pan and let cool completely on the rack, about 1 hour. If desired, sprinkle with confectioners' sugar before serving. Store covered. Refrigerate after 2 days.

Makes one 10-inch (25 cm) tube or Bundt cake; 16 servings

Per serving (1 slice): 242 Calories, 37 g Carbohydrate, 5 g Protein, 9 g Fat,
33 mg Cholesterol, 57 mg Sodium, 3 g Fiber
Exchanges: 2½ Starch, 2 Fat (2½ Carb Choices)

Orange-Zucchini Cake

Prep time: 15 minutes ◆ Bake time: 35 to 40 minutes

Cooking spray

½ cup (65 g) chopped nuts (optional)

1 cup (120 g) all-purpose flour

1 cup (120 g) whole wheat flour

½ cup (45 g) old-fashioned rolled oats

2 teaspoons baking powder

2 teaspoons ground cinnamon

1 teaspoon baking soda

½ teaspoon ground cloves

3 large eggs, at room temperature

½ cup canola (120 ml) or extra-light olive oil

1 tablespoon grated orange zest

½ cup (120 ml) fresh orange juice

¼ cup (48 g) packed brown sugar

¼ cup (48 g) granulated sugar

1 teaspoon almond extract

2 cups (254 g) shredded zucchini (about 1 medium)

1. Preheat the oven to 350°F (180°C). Spray a 13 x 9 x 2-inch (33 x 23 x 5 cm) baking pan or two 8½ x 4½ x 2-inch (22 x 11 x 5 cm) loaf pans with cooking spray.

2. If using nuts, place them in a small baking pan and bake for 3 to 5 minutes, until toasted; set aside.

3. Stir together the flours, oats, baking powder, cinnamon, baking soda, and cloves in a large bowl.

4. Whisk the eggs in another large bowl. Whisk in the oil, orange zest and juice, sugars, and almond extract. Stir in the zucchini.

5. Add the egg mixture and toasted nuts, if using, to the flour mixture, stirring just to moisten. Spoon the batter into the chosen prepared baking pan(s).

6. Bake for 35 to 40 minutes for a 13 x 9-inch (33 x 23) pan or 40 to 45 minutes for the loaf pans or until a tester inserted into the center of the cake comes out clean.

7. Cool in the pan(s) on a wire rack for 10 minutes. Use a knife to loosen the cake and invert it onto a rack to cool completely. Store covered. Refrigerate after 2 days. This cake can be frozen for up to 3 months.

Makes 16 servings

Per serving (1 slice): 192 Calories, 21 g Carbohydrate, 4 g Protein, 11 g Fat,
33 mg Cholesterol, 92 mg Sodium, 2 g Fiber
Exchanges: 1½ Starch, 2 Fat (1½ Carb Choices)

Strawberry Shortcake

Prep time: 10 minutes ◆ *Chilling time: 1 hour*

1 cup (245 g) plain Greek yogurt

1 tablespoon sugar-free vanilla syrup (such as Torani, Amoretti, or Jordan's)

1 teaspoon grated orange zest

¾ cup (120 ml) fresh orange juice

½ cup (60 ml) dry red wine

2 tablespoons (24 g) sugar

1 tablespoon plus 1 teaspoon cornstarch

1 recipe Featherweight Sponge Cake (page 62)

1 cup (165 g) sliced fresh strawberries

1 cup (151 g) halved fresh strawberries

1 whole strawberry, for garnish (optional)

1. **To make the topping,** combine the yogurt and vanilla syrup in a small bowl. Refrigerate, covered, until ready to use.

2. Stir together the orange zest and juice, wine, sugar, and cornstarch in a 4-cup (960 ml) glass measuring cup. Microwave on high for 3 minutes or until the mixture boils; stir, then cover and chill for 1 hour.

3. Up to an hour before serving, place a sponge cake layer on a serving plate. Stir the orange juice mixture, then spread half of the mixture over the cake layer. Arrange the sliced strawberries on top.

4. Top with the remaining cake layer, then spoon the remaining orange mixture evenly over the cake.

5. Arrange the strawberry halves on top of the cake; top with the yogurt mixture. If desired, garnish with a whole strawberry in the center. Serve immediately. Cover and refrigerate leftovers.

Makes one 8-inch (20 cm) round cake; 12 servings

Per serving (1 piece): 159 Calories, 27 g Carbohydrate, 5 g Protein, 3 g Fat,
50 mg Cholesterol, 25 mg Sodium, 1 g Fiber
Exchanges: 1 Starch, 1 Fruit, ½ Fat (2 Carb Choices)

Cocoa-Zucchini Cake

Prep time: 15 minutes • Bake time: 45 to 60 minutes

Cooking spray

1½ cups (180 g) all-purpose flour

⅔ cup (80 g) whole wheat flour

½ cup (120 g) unsweetened cocoa
   powder, sifted if lumpy

1 teaspoon baking soda

½ teaspoon ground cinnamon

½ teaspoon salt

½ cup (96 g) sugar

¼ cup (60 ml) canola or extra-light
   olive oil

¼ cup (61 g) unsweetened
   applesauce

½ cup (120 ml) nonfat milk

2 large eggs

1 teaspoon vanilla extract

2 cups (254 g) shredded zucchini
   (1 medium)

1. Preheat the oven to 350°F (180°C). Spray a 10-inch
   (25 cm) Bundt pan or a 13 x 9 x 2-inch (33 x 23 x 5
   cm) baking pan with cooking spray.

2. Stir together the flours, cocoa powder, baking
   soda, cinnamon, and salt in a medium bowl.

3. Use an electric mixer at medium speed to beat
   the sugar, oil, applesauce, milk, eggs, and vanilla
   in a large bowl until well blended; scrape down
   the sides of the bowl.

4. With the mixer at low speed, beat in the flour
   mixture in two additions, until well blended,
   scraping down the bowl occasionally. Use a
   rubber spatula to fold in the zucchini. Spoon the
   batter into the chosen prepared cake pan.

5. Bake for 60 minutes for a Bundt pan or 45
   minutes for a 13 x 9-inch (33 x 23) pan or until a
   tester inserted into the center of the cake comes
   out clean.

6. Cool in the pan on a wire rack for 10 or 15
   minutes. Use a knife to loosen the cake and invert
   it onto the rack to cool completely, about 1 hour.
   Store covered. Refrigerate after 2 days. This cake
   can be frozen for up to 3 months.

Makes 16 servings

Per serving (1 slice): 127 Calories, 20 g Carbohydrate, 4 g Protein, 5 g Fat,
22 mg Cholesterol, 164 mg Sodium, 2 g Fiber
Exchanges: 1 Starch, 1 Fat (1 Carb Choice)

Speedy Chocolate Cake

Prep time: 5 minutes • Bake time: 20 minutes

Cooking spray

2 squares (1 ounce/29 g each)
unsweetened baking chocolate

¾ cup (90 g) all-purpose flour

¼ cup (30 g) whole wheat flour

⅓ cup (64 g) granulated sugar

2 teaspoons baking powder

1 teaspoon baking soda

¾ teaspoon ground cinnamon

½ cup (122 g) unsweetened
applesauce

½ cup (120 ml) nonfat milk

2 large eggs, at room temperature

1 teaspoon vanilla extract

Confectioners' sugar (optional)

Fresh fruit (optional)

Whipped Topping (page 91;
optional)

1. Preheat the oven to 375°F (190°C). Spray a 9-inch (23 cm) square baking pan with cooking spray.

2. Place the chocolate squares in a small microwave-safe bowl. Microwave on high for 1 minute. Stir, then microwave on high for another 10 seconds or until melted; set aside.

3. Mix together the flours, granulated sugar, baking powder, baking soda, and cinnamon in a large bowl, until well blended. Add the applesauce, milk, eggs, vanilla, and melted chocolate; beat with a wooden spoon or an electric mixer at medium speed for 1 minute, until smooth. Scrape down the bowl, and pour the batter into the prepared baking pan.

4. Bake for 20 to 25 minutes or until a tester inserted into the center of the cake comes out clean and the sides pull away from the pan.

5. Cool for 10 minutes on a wire rack. Cut into 9 squares to serve warm or at room temperature. If desired, sprinkle with confectioners' sugar or serve with fresh fruit and Whipped Topping, if you wish. Store covered. Refrigerate after 2 days.

Makes one 9-inch (23 cm) square cake; 9 servings

Per serving (1 square): 137 Calories, 20 g Carbohydrate, 4 g Protein, 5 g Fat,
39 mg Cholesterol, 166 mg Sodium, 1 g Fiber
Exchanges: 1 Starch, 1 Fat (1 Carb Choice)

Chocolate Cloud Cake

Prep time: 15 minutes ◆ Bake time: 20 minutes ◆ Cooling time: 50 minutes

⅓ cup (27 g) unsweetened cocoa powder, sifted if lumpy

½ teaspoon vanilla extract

¼ cup (30 g) all-purpose flour

2 teaspoons baking powder

4 large egg whites, at room temperature

¼ teaspoon salt

⅓ cup (48 g) granulated sugar

Cooking spray

Confectioners' sugar

1. Preheat the oven to 350°F (180°C). Place an 8-inch (20 cm) round cake pan on a piece of parchment paper or wax paper. Trace the pan and cut out two rounds of paper to fit on the bottom of the pan. Line the pan with one of the rounds; reserve the other for later.

2. Use a small whisk, mix the cocoa powder and ⅓ cup (80 ml) water in a 1-cup (240 ml) glass measuring cup. Microwave on high for 1 minute, stir, and microwave 1 more minute or until the mixture becomes thick and smooth. Stir in the vanilla; let cool.

3. Mix together the flour and baking powder in a small bowl. Set aside.

4. Use an electric mixer at high speed to beat the egg whites and salt in a large bowl until foamy. Gradually beat in the granulated sugar, beating until soft peaks form when the beaters are lifted.

5. Immediately add the cocoa powder mixture to the whites and beat just until blended; scrape down the sides of the bowl. Use a rubber spatula to fold in the flour mixture just until blended. Do not overmix. Pour the batter into the lined cake pan and smooth the top with a rubber spatula.

6. Bake for 20 to 25 minutes or until the top of the cake cracks and looks dry and a tester inserted into the center comes out clean.

7. Spray the reserved parchment or wax paper round with cooking spray and place sprayed side up on a wire rack. Invert the cake pan on top of the sprayed piece of paper. Cool for 20 minutes.

8. Turn the pan right side up; discard the paper from the top, and use a knife to loosen the cake. Carefully invert the cake onto the rack; remove the other piece of paper and turn the cake right side up. Cool completely, about 30 minutes. To serve, sprinkle with confectioners' sugar. Store, covered, in the refrigerator.

Makes one 8-inch (20 cm) round cake; 8 servings

Per serving (1 slice): 52 Calories, 11 g Carbohydrate, 3 g Protein, 1 g Fat,
0 mg Cholesterol, 101 mg Sodium, 1 g Fiber
Exchanges: 1 Starch (1 Carb Choice)

Chocolate Upside-Down Cake

Prep time: 15 minutes ◆ Bake time: 40 minutes

Cooking spray

2 tablespoons canola or extra-light olive oil

1 tablespoon brown sugar

⅓ cup (43 g) chopped walnuts

2 squares (1 ounce/29 g each) unsweetened baking chocolate

1 cup (90 g) cake flour

2 teaspoons baking powder

¼ teaspoon salt

½ cup (112 g) mashed ripe banana (1 medium)

¼ cup (61 g) unsweetened applesauce

1 large egg

2 tablespoons granulated sugar

¾ cup (180 g) buttermilk (see page 8)

1. Preheat the oven to 350°F (180°C). Spray a 9-inch (23 cm) square baking pan with cooking spray, then add the oil and brown sugar. Use a rubber spatula to mix and spread the mixture evenly on the bottom of the pan.

2. Place the pan in the oven for 2 minutes to melt the brown sugar mixture. Add the walnuts and stir until they are coated in the mixture; spread them in an even layer, then set aside.

3. Place the chocolate in a small microwave-safe bowl. Microwave on high for 1 minute, then stir. Microwave for another 10 seconds or until melted; stir, then set aside.

4. Whisk together the cake flour, baking powder, and salt in a small bowl.

5. Use an electric mixer at medium speed to beat the banana, applesauce, egg, granulated sugar, and melted chocolate in a medium bowl, scraping down the bowl occasionally, until well blended, about 2 minutes.

6. With the mixer at medium speed, beat in the flour mixture alternately with the buttermilk, beginning and ending with the flour mixture, until well blended. Spoon the batter into the prepared baking pan.

7. Bake for 40 minutes or until a tester inserted into the center of the cake comes out clean.

8. Cool in the pan on a wire rack for 5 minutes. Use a knife to loosen the cake and invert the cake onto a plate, then remove the pan. Cool the cake on the plate on top of the rack for about 30 minutes. Store covered. Refrigerate after 2 days.

Makes one 9-inch (23 cm) square cake; 9 servings

Per serving (1 piece): 194 Calories, 22 g Carbohydrate, 5 g Protein, 10 g Fat, 20 mg Cholesterol, 117 mg Sodium, 2 g Fiber
Exchanges: 1½ Starch, 2 Fat (1½ Carb Choices)

Chocolate Roll

Prep time: 20 minutes • Bake time: 15 minutes • Cooling time: 15 minutes • Chilling time: 1 hour

CAKE

Cooking spray

¼ cup (20 g) unsweetened cocoa powder

2 tablespoons all-purpose flour

⅛ teaspoon salt

4 large eggs, separated, at room temperature

½ teaspoon cream of tartar

⅓ cup (40 g) confectioners' sugar, sifted, plus more for dusting

1 teaspoon vanilla extract

FILLING

2 cups (454 g) reduced-fat ricotta

3 tablespoons granulated sugar

2 tablespoons dark rum

1 tablespoon finely chopped blanched almonds, toasted

1 tablespoon mini semisweet or dark chocolate morsels

2 tablespoons grated orange zest

½ teaspoon vanilla extract

1. Preheat the oven to 325°F (165°C). Line a 15 x 10 x 1-inch (39 x 27 x 2.5 cm) jelly roll pan with parchment paper and spray with cooking spray.

2. **To make the cake,** sift the together the cocoa powder, flour, and salt into a small bowl.

3. Use an electric mixer at high speed to beat the egg whites in a medium bowl until frothy; beat in the cream of tartar. Continue beating until the whites form stiff peaks when the beaters are lifted.

4. Use the same beaters at medium speed to beat the egg yolks in a large bowl until thick and lemon colored, 2 to 3 minutes. Gradually beat in the confectioners' sugar and vanilla; scrape down the bowl.

5. Use a rubber spatula to stir the cocoa powder mixture into the yolks. Gently fold the egg whites into the batter until no white streaks remain.

6. Spoon the batter into the pan and smooth the top with a rubber spatula. Bake for 12 to 15 minutes or until the center of the cake springs back when lightly pressed.

7. Meanwhile, **prepare the filling.** Use an electric mixer at low speed to beat the ricotta in a medium bowl until smooth. Use a rubber spatula to stir in the granulated sugar, rum, almonds, chocolate morsels, orange zest, and vanilla until well blended.

8. Lay a clean kitchen towel on the counter and sprinkle it with sifted confectioners' sugar.

9. Remove the cake from oven and loosen the edges with knife. Place the cake upside down on the towel; lift off the pan and gently peel off the parchment paper.

(continued)

10. Starting at a short end, roll up the cake and towel together. Place the cake, seam side down, on a wire rack to cool for about 15 minutes.

11. Unroll the cake and spread the filling to within ½ inch (2.5 cm) of the edges. Reroll the cake with the filling; place with the seam side down on a serving plate and cover.

12. Refrigerate for at least 1 hour or up to 4 hours. Sprinkle the cake with sifted confectioners' sugar before serving. Cover and refrigerate leftovers.

Makes one 10-inch (25 cm) roll; 10 servings

Per serving (1 slice): 139 Calories, 12 g Carbohydrate, 9 g Protein, 6 g Fat,
82 mg Cholesterol, 110 mg Sodium, 1 g Fiber
Exchanges: 1 Starch, 1 Fat (1 Carb Choice)

Strawberry-Pineapple Roll

Prep time: 20 minutes • Bake time: 30 minutes • Cooling time: 15 minutes • Chilling time: 1 hour

CAKE

Cooking spray

¾ cup (90 g) all-purpose flour

¼ cup (30 g) whole wheat flour

2 teaspoons baking powder

¼ teaspoon salt

4 large eggs, at room temperature

½ cup (96 g) granulated sugar

1 teaspoon vanilla extract

Sifted confectioners' sugar

FILLING

2 cups (454 g) reduced-fat ricotta

2 tablespoons granulated sugar

2 tablespoons plain Greek yogurt

1 teaspoon rum extract

One 8-ounce (227 g) can juice-packed crushed pineapple, drained, juice reserved

3 cups (1 pound/454 g) fresh strawberries

1. Preheat the oven to 350°F (180°C). Line a 15 x 10 x 1-inch (39 x 27 x 2.5 cm) jelly roll pan with parchment paper and spray with cooking spray.

2. **To make the cake,** whisk together the flours, baking powder, and salt in a small bowl.

3. Use an electric mixer at medium speed to beat the eggs in a large bowl until frothy; gradually beat in the granulated sugar until the mixture is thick and lemon colored, 2 to 3 minutes. Scrape down the bowl. With the mixer at low speed, beat in 2 tablespoons water and the vanilla. Use a rubber spatula to stir in the flour mixture until well blended.

4. Spoon the batter into the lined pan and smooth the top with a rubber spatula. Bake for 15 to 20 minutes or until the cake pulls away from the sides of the pan and the center springs back when lightly touched.

5. Meanwhile, lay a clean kitchen towel on the counter and sprinkle it with sifted confectioners' sugar.

6. **Prepare the filling.** Use an electric mixer at low speed to beat the ricotta in a medium bowl until smooth. Beat in 3 tablespoons of the reserved pineapple juice, the sugar, yogurt, and rum extract until well blended; scrape down the sides of the bowl. Use a rubber spatula to stir in the crushed pineapple.

7. Remove the cake from the oven and loosen the edges with a knife. Place the cake upside down on the towel; lift off the pan and gently peel off the parchment paper.

(continued)

8. Starting from one long side, roll up the cake and towel together. Place the cake, seam side down, on a wire rack to cool for about 15 minutes. Unroll the cake and spread the filling to within ½-inch (13 mm) of the edges.

9. Hull and slice 4 strawberries, then hull and dice the rest. Arrange the diced berries evenly over the filling.

10. Reroll the cake with the filling and diced berries. Place the cake, seam side down, on a large serving plate and cover. Refrigerate for at least 1 hour or up to 4 hours before serving. Sprinkle with sifted confectioners' sugar; garnish with the sliced berries. Cover and refrigerate leftovers.

Makes one 15-inch (39 cm) roll; 12 servings

Per serving (1 slice): 167 Calories, 30 g Carbohydrate, 7 g Protein, 3 g Fat,
25 mg Cholesterol, 102 mg Sodium, 2 g Fiber
Exchanges: 1 Starch, 1 Fruit, ½ Fat (2 Carb Choices)

Pumpkin Cheese Roll

Prep time: 20 minutes • Bake time: 20 minutes • Cooling time: 15 minutes • Chilling time: 1 hour

CAKE

Cooking spray

½ cup (60 g) all-purpose flour

¼ cup (30 g) whole wheat flour

2 teaspoons ground cinnamon

1 teaspoon baking powder

1 teaspoon ground ginger

½ teaspoon ground nutmeg

¼ teaspoon salt

3 large eggs, at room temperature

½ cup (96 g) granulated sugar

⅔ cup (152 g) canned pumpkin or puréed cooked fresh pumpkin

1 teaspoon fresh lemon juice

1 cup (130 g) finely chopped nuts (walnuts or pecans)

Sifted confectioners' sugar

FILLING

One 8-ounce (226 g) package reduced-fat cream cheese, softened

¼ cup (30 g) confectioners' sugar

⅓ cup (75 g) reduced-fat ricotta

2 teaspoons butter extract

1 teaspoon vanilla extract

1. Preheat the oven to 375°F (190°C). Line a 15 x 10 x 1-inch (39 x 27 x 2.5 cm) jelly roll pan with with parchment paper and spray with cooking spray.

2. **To make the cake,** whisk together the flours, cinnamon, baking powder, ginger, nutmeg, and salt in a small bowl.

3. Use an electric mixer at medium speed to beat the eggs and granulated sugar in a large bowl until thick and lemon colored, 2 to 3 minutes. Beat in the pumpkin and lemon juice; scrape down the sides of the bowl. Use a rubber spatula to stir in the dry ingredients all at once until well blended.

4. Pour the batter into the lined pan and smooth the top with a rubber spatula. Sprinkle the nuts over the top. Bake for 12 to 15 minutes or until the center of the cake springs back when lightly touched.

5. Meanwhile, sprinkle a clean kitchen towel with sifted confectioners' sugar. **Prepare the filling.** Use an electric mixer at medium speed to beat the cream cheese in a small bowl until smooth. Scrape down the bowl and beat in the confectioners' sugar, ricotta, and extracts until light and fluffy, about 30 seconds, scraping down the bowl occasionally.

6. Remove the cake from the oven and loosen the edges with a knife. Place the cake upside down on the towel; lift off the pan, and gently peel off the parchment paper.

7. Starting at a short end, roll up the cake and towel together. Place the cake, seam side down, on a wire rack to cool, about 15 minutes. Unroll the cake and spread the filling to within ½-inch (2.5 cm) of the edges.

8. Reroll the cake; place with seam side down on a serving plate and cover. Refrigerate for at least 1 hour or up to 4 hours before serving. Cover and refrigerate leftovers.

Makes one 10-inch (25 cm) roll; 10 servings

Per serving (1 slice): 246 Calories, 23 g Carbohydrate, 7 g Protein, 15 g Fat, 73 mg Cholesterol, 163 mg Sodium, 2 g Fiber

Exchanges: 1½ Starch, 3 Fat (1½ Carb Choices)

Healthy Holiday Fruitcake

Prep time: 20 minutes ◆ Bake time: 1 hour

Cooking spray

¼ cup (30 g) all-purpose flour

¼ cup (30 g) whole wheat flour

½ teaspoon baking powder

½ teaspoon ground cinnamon

¼ teaspoon salt

¼ teaspoon ground allspice

⅛ teaspoon ground nutmeg

5 tablespoons plus 1 teaspoon unsalted butter, softened

1 tablespoon brown sugar

2 large eggs, at room temperature

1 tablespoon honey

2 tablespoons fat-free evaporated milk

2 cups (227 g) pecan halves

1 cup (160 g) dried apricots, finely chopped

1 cup (165 g) chopped pitted dates

½ cup (85 g) raisins

1. Preheat the oven to 300°F (150°C). Spray two 7¼ x 3⅝ x 2¼-inch (20 x 10 x 6 cm) loaf pans with cooking spray. Line the pans with aluminum foil, allowing the foil to hang over the sides, and spray again.

2. Stir together the flours, baking powder, cinnamon, salt, allspice, and nutmeg in a small bowl.

3. Use an electric mixer at medium speed to cream the butter, sugar, eggs, and honey in a large bowl.

4. Add the flour mixture to the creamed mixture alternately with the evaporated milk, beginning and ending with the flour mixture. Stir in the pecans, apricots, dates, and raisins until the fruit and nuts are well coated with batter.

5. Spoon the batter into the lined pans and spread evenly. Place the pans on the middle rack of the oven. Place a shallow baking pan on the lowest rack underneath the cakes. Fill the pan halfway with hot water. Bake for 60 to 65 minutes or until a tester inserted into the center of the cakes comes out clean.

6. Place the pans on a wire rack to cool, about 10 minutes. Using the foil as a lifter, remove the cakes to the rack and let cool completely. Remove the foil and store the cakes in an airtight container in the refrigerator. Use a serrated knife to slice.

Makes two 7¼ x 3⅝-inch (20 x 10 cm) loaves; 20 servings

Per serving (1 slice): 173 Calories, 19 g Carbohydrate, 2 g Protein, 11 g Fat, 26 mg Cholesterol, 39 mg Sodium, 3 g Fiber
Exchanges: 1 Fruit, 2 Fat (1 Carb Choice)

Cream Puffs

Prep time: 15 minutes • Bake time: 25 minutes

½ cup (60 g) all-purpose flour or bread flour*

¼ teaspoon salt

3 tablespoons canola or extra-light olive oil

2 large eggs, at room temperature

Chocolate Pudding (page 230) or Simple Vanilla Pudding (page 234), for filling

1. Preheat the oven to 450°F (230°C). Line a baking sheet with parchment paper. Whisk together the flour and salt in a small bowl; set aside.

2. Combine ½ cup (120 ml) water and the oil in a heavy medium saucepan over high heat. Bring to a boil.

3. Use a wooden spoon to stir in the flour mixture all at once. Stir vigorously until the mixture pulls away from the sides of the pan and forms a ball, about 1 minute.

4. Remove the pan from the heat and use a wooden spoon, whisk, or portable electric mixer to beat in the eggs, one at a time, until the mixture is smooth and shiny.

5. Spoon the mixture onto the lined baking sheet in 6 mounds, leaving about 2 inches (5 cm) between the puffs, to account for spreading.

6. Bake for 10 minutes, then reduce the oven temperature to 400°F (200°C) and continue baking for 15 to 20 minutes, until the pastry is puffed and golden brown.

7. Cool on a wire rack. Just before serving, cut a slice horizontally from the top of each puff, then remove any soft dough from inside each puff. Spoon the filling into each puff and replace the tops. Serve immediately; store the extras in a covered container.

Variation: *For petite cream puffs, follow steps 1 through 4, then drop the cream puff mixture by 24 rounded teaspoonfuls onto the lined baking sheet. Bake at 450°F (230°C) for 5 minutes, then reduce the oven temperature to 400°F (200°C) and bake 10 to 15 minutes more, until the pastry is puffed and golden brown. Cool on a wire rack and fill as desired just before serving.*

*Puffs made with bread flour will be larger and crispier.

Makes 6 puffs; 6 servings

Per serving (1 puff): 185 Calories, 21 g Carbohydrate, 6 g Protein, 9 g Fat, 60 mg Cholesterol, 152 mg Sodium, 1 g Fiber
Exchanges: 1½ Starch, 2 Fat (1½ Carb Choices)

Chocolate Cupcakes

Prep time: 5 minutes • Bake time: 15 minutes

Cooking spray

¾ cup (90 g) all-purpose flour

¾ cup (90 g) whole wheat flour

½ cup (40 g) unsweetened cocoa
powder, sifted if lumpy

½ cup (96 g) sugar

1 teaspoon baking soda

¼ teaspoon salt

¾ cup (180 ml) fresh orange juice

3 tablespoons canola or extra-light
olive oil

1 tablespoon white vinegar

1 teaspoon vanilla extract

⅓ cup (53 g) mini semisweet or dark
chocolate morsels

Light Cream Cheese Frosting
(page 90; optional)

1. Preheat the oven to 375°F (190°C). Spray a 12-cup muffin pan with cooking spray or line with paper liners.

2. Whisk together the flours, cocoa powder, sugar, baking soda, and salt in a large bowl. Make a well in center and add the orange juice, oil, vinegar, vanilla, and ½ cup (120 ml) water. Stir the ingredients just to moisten the batter. Add the chocolate morsels and mix gently to combine.

3. Evenly spoon the batter into the prepared muffin cups. Bake for about 15 minutes or until a tester inserted into the center of the cupcakes comes out clean. Immediately remove the cupcakes from the pan and cool completely on a wire rack.

4. If frosting the cupcakes, allow the cupcakes to cool completely. Prepare the Light Cream Cheese Frosting. Frost cupcakes using a pastry bag or by hand, allowing up to 2 tablespoons of frosting for each cupcake.

> **Variation:** *This recipe can also be used to make about 42 mini cupcakes. Use mini muffin pans and spray them with cooking spray or line with foil or paper liners. Bake for about minutes, until a tester inserted into the center of the cupcakes comes out clean.*

Makes 12 cupcakes; 12 servings

Per serving (1 cupcake): 144 Calories, 24 g Carbohydrate, 3 g Protein, 6 g Fat,
0 mg Cholesterol, 155 mg Sodium, 2 g Fiber (without frosting)
Exchanges: 1½ Starch, 1 Fat (1½ Carb Choices)

Light Cream Cheese Frosting

Prep time: 15 minutes

¼ cup (48 g) sugar

2 tablespoons fresh orange juice

2 teaspoons dried egg whites

2 tablespoons warm water

One 8-ounce (226 g) package
   nonfat cream cheese, softened

2 teaspoons grated orange zest

½ teaspoon vanilla extract

1. Add the sugar and orange juice to a 1-cup (240 ml) glass measuring cup and microwave for 1 minute; stir.

2. Use an electric mixer at high speed to beat the egg white powder and warm water in a small bowl until soft peaks form; gradually add the sugar mixture in a thin stream. Continue beating at high speed until the mixture is thick and glossy, about 4 minutes; scrape down the sides of the bowl occasionally.

3. Use the same beaters at high speed to beat the cream cheese, orange zest, and vanilla in a medium bowl until light and fluffy, about 5 minutes; scrape down the bowl occasionally.

4. Add one third of the egg white mixture to the cream cheese mixture, beating at low speed, just until blended. Use a rubber spatula to gently fold in the remaining egg white mixture until it is completely blended into the cream cheese mixture.

5. Frost your cake and store it, covered, in the refrigerator.

Makes 1½ cups (303 g); 12 servings

Per serving (2 tablespoons): 42 Calories, 6 g Carbohydrate, 4 g Protein, 0 g Fat,
3 mg Cholesterol, 73 mg Sodium, 0 g Fiber
Exchanges: ½ Starch (½ Carb Choice)

Whipped Topping

Chilling time: 90 minutes ◆ *Prep time: 5 minutes*

One 0.25-ounce (7 g) envelope unflavored gelatin

¼ cup (60 ml) cold water

¼ cup boiling water

1 tablespoon fresh lemon juice

½ cup (34 g) nonfat milk powder

2 tablespoons sugar

½ teaspoon vanilla extract

1. Place a small mixer bowl and beaters in the refrigerator for at least 1 hour.

2. Sprinkle the gelatin over the cold water in a small saucepan and let stand for 1 minute. Stir in the boiling water and stir constantly until the gelatin is dissolved. Refrigerate until cold but not set.

3. Add the cold gelatin mixture and lemon juice to the chilled bowl. Use an electric mixer with the chilled beaters at medium speed to beat the ingredients until well blended. Gradually beat in the milk powder until moistened, scraping down the sides of the bowl occasionally.

4. Turn the mixer to high speed and beat the mixture until light and fluffy, scraping down the sides of the bowl occasionally, until soft peaks form when the beaters are lifted. Gradually beat in the sugar and vanilla at high speed until stiff peaks form.

5. Serve immediately. Store leftovers, covered, in the refrigerator. If the topping loses volume after chilling, rewhip before serving.

Makes 2 cups (80 g); 8 servings

Per serving (¼ cup/10 g): 25 Calories, 5 g Carbohydrate, 2 g Protein, 0 g Fat,
1 mg Cholesterol, 25 mg Sodium, 0 g Fiber
Exchanges: FREE

Easy Fat-Free Topping

Chilling time: 1 hour • Prep time: 5 minutes

One 12-ounce (354 ml) can fat-free evaporated milk

1 tablespoon sugar

1 teaspoon vanilla extract

1. Place the unopened can of evaporated milk in the freezer for 1 hour. Meanwhile, refrigerate a small bowl and beaters for 1 hour.

2. Shake the can and pour the milk into the bowl. Use an electric mixer with the chilled beaters at high speed to beat the milk until slightly stiff.

3. Gradually beat in the sugar and vanilla, scraping down the bowl occasionally, until the mixture is very stiff when lifted with a rubber spatula.

4. Serve immediately.

Tip: If the milk doesn't whip well, it needs to be colder. Put the bowl filled with milk and the beaters back into the freezer for about 15 minutes and then try again.

Makes 3 cups (360 g); 12 servings

Per serving (¼ cup/30 g): 25 Calories, 4 g Carbohydrate, 2 g Protein, 0 g Fat, 1 mg Cholesterol, 32 mg Sodium, 0 g Fiber
Exchanges: FREE

Blueberry Topping

Prep time: 10 minutes

2 tablespoons cornstarch

1¼ cups (180 g) fresh or frozen
blueberries

2 tablespoons honey

2 teaspoons fresh lemon juice

1. Whisk the cornstarch and 2 tablespoons water in a 4-cup (960 ml) glass measuring cup until smooth.

2. Use a wooden spoon to stir in an additional ⅓ cup (80 ml) water, the blueberries and honey until well mixed. Microwave on high for 2 minutes; stir. Microwave for 2 to 4 minutes longer or until thickened and translucent, stirring every 2 minutes. Stir in the lemon juice.

3. Cool completely before spreading on a cake or cheesecake. Cool slightly before topping pancakes or waffles. Store, covered, in the refrigerator.

Tip: An excellent topping for Blueberry Bundt Cake (page 66), Creamy Ricotta Cheesecake (page 100), or Fruity Cheesecake (page 104).

Makes 1½ cups (253 g); 6 servings

Per serving (¼ cup/42 g): 99 Calories, 26 g Carbohydrate, 1 g Protein, 0 g Fat,
0 mg Cholesterol, 2 mg Sodium, 2 g Fiber
Exchanges: 2 Fruit (2 Carb Choices)

Cheesecakes

Tips & Tricks

» Cheesecakes are decadent and luxurious. They're an elegant dessert to serve after any meal and are also a great alternative to ordinary birthday cakes.

» These recipes won't tip the scales by adding too much fat or too many calories. Products such as reduced-fat ricotta and cream cheese add creaminess while keeping the calories and total fat content low.

» Peaches, kiwi, citrus, and pumpkin offer varying flavors and health benefits.

» Several of these cheesecakes call for homemade Yogurt Cheese (page 96), which adds a tangy flavor and enhances the firmness of the cheesecake.

» Many cheesecakes use freshly grated orange, lemon, or lime zest and freshly squeezed orange, lemon, or lime juice. They pack a distinctive punch of flavor, giving that "something extra" to your cheesecake.

» Finely grated fresh lemon, orange, or lime zest can be frozen in airtight, sealable freezer-safe containers for six months. Measure and use what you need for your recipe and reseal; there's no need to thaw the zest before using.

» Sometimes, cracks appear in the top of the cheesecake while it's baking or cooling. There are many reasons for this; most cracks appear because the cake has released its moisture (or steam) too quickly. This can happen when the cake is exposed to extreme temperatures, such as baking in too hot an oven, baking for too long (use an instant-read thermometer and take the cake out when it registers 150°F/65°C), or being placed in a cool spot or draft immediately after baking.

» Shallow cracks often occur despite our best efforts and generally can be ignored. If they show up during baking, remember that the cake will sink down as it cools and these cracks will get smaller. To repair shallow cracks, remove the sides from the springform pan while the cheesecake is warm. Gently wrap a cloth ribbon (about 3 inches/8 cm wide) snugly around the cake until the entire sides are covered. Secure the ribbon with a binder clip and leave it in place until the cake has completely cooled.

» To help prevent cracks, bake at the correct temperature given in the recipe and don't open the oven door during the first half of the baking time to keep the temperature steady. In most cases, we keep the cake in the oven after baking, with the heat turned off, for an additional hour to allow the cake to cool very slowly away from drafts. One last effort to prevent cracking (after it has baked) is to make a cardboard disk or use overlapping paper towels to top the cooling cheesecake; the cardboard or towels help to absorb the moisture as the cake cools and keeps away drafts.

Yogurt Cheese

Prep time: 5 minutes ◆ Draining time: 12 hours to overnight

2½ cups* (612 g) reduced-fat or full-fat plain yogurt

Kosher salt

*Use 2½ cups (612 g) yogurt to yield 1 cup yogurt cheese, 3⅔ cups (898 g) yogurt to yield 1½ cups yogurt cheese, and 5 cups (1,225 g) yogurt to yield 2 cups yogurt cheese.

1. Cut two 14-inch (35.5 cm) square pieces of triple-thickness cheesecloth. Line a colander, set on a rimmed baking pan, with the cheesecloth, or lay the cheesecloth across a mesh strainer suspended over a bowl. (You need somewhere to collect the whey as it drips.) If you don't have cheesecloth, you can use 2 coffee filters.

2. Spoon the amount of yogurt you need into a small bowl, add a pinch of kosher salt, and mix together. Spoon the yogurt onto the cheesecloth or into the coffee filter.

3. Gather together the ends of the cheesecloth squares, give a relaxed twist and either lay the ends on top of the yogurt or tie them with string.

4. Allow the yogurt to drain for 12 hours to overnight in the refrigerator, until the cheese reaches a firm consistency. After draining for 2 hours, you will have made Greek yogurt, which can be eaten or used in baked recipes that call for Greek yogurt.

5. Drain the whey as it collects. Save this liquid to add to other recipes where water is needed or add to a smoothie, soup, or casserole. Whey is an excellent source of protein with magnesium and potassium; don't throw it away.

6. Store the finished yogurt cheese in a covered container in the refrigerator. The whey may continue to drain; pour off any excess whey as necessary.

Tip: This is a mild yet creamy substitute for cream cheese with fewer calories, less fat, and 60 percent less saturated fat. Yogurt cheese is simply yogurt allowed to drain away all its moisture (the whey), leaving you with a firm, creamy, spreadable cheese that can be used to make cheesecake. If you're lucky enough to have any yogurt cheese remaining, add chopped fresh herbs and garlic and serve alongside fresh vegetables or on top of your favorite crackers. Plan on making yogurt cheese a day ahead of making your cheesecake.

Makes 1 cup (245 g)

Per serving (1 cup/245 g): 227 Calories, 16 g Carbohydrate, 12 g Protein, 13 g Fat, 54 mg Cholesterol, 183 mg Sodium, 0 g Fiber
Exchanges: 1 Reduced-Fat Milk, 1 Fat (1 Carb Choice)

No-Bake Peachy Ricotta Cheesecake

Prep time: 20 minutes • Chilling time: 4 hours

Cooking spray

¼ cup (43 g) plus 2 tablespoons instant meringue mix or 2 tablespoons dried egg whites

⅓ cup (80 ml) cold water, or ⅓ cup (80 ml) warm water if using dried egg whites

¼ cup (48 g) sugar

Two 0.25-ounce (7 g) envelopes unflavored gelatin

¼ cup (75 g) sweetened condensed milk, chilled

Two 16-ounce (454 g) cans juice-packed sliced peaches, drained, juice reserved

1 teaspoon vanilla extract

½ teaspoon almond extract

3 cups (681 g) reduced-fat ricotta, at room temperature

½ cup (34 g) nonfat milk powder

1 tablespoon grated orange zest

1 tablespoon grated lemon zest

1 tablespoon fresh lemon juice

1. Spray a 10-inch (25 cm) springform pan with cooking spray.

2. Use an electric mixer at high speed to beat the meringue mix and water in a medium bowl until soft peaks form. Gradually beat in 2 tablespoons of the sugar, beating until stiff peaks form when the beaters are lifted; set aside.

3. Combine the remaining 2 tablespoons sugar and gelatin in a 4-cup (960 ml) glass measuring cup or microwave-safe bowl. Stir in the sweetened condensed milk. Let stand for 1 minute to soften the gelatin, then stir until well blended.

4. Stir in the reserved peach juice and the extracts. Microwave on high for 2 minutes, then stir, and microwave for another minute or until the mixture comes to a boil; set aside to cool.

5. Process the ricotta and milk powder in a food processor or blender until smooth; scrape down the sides. With the machine running, gradually drop in 1 cup (227 g) of the peaches and process just until small pieces of peach are visible; scrape down the sides.

6. Combine the ricotta and peach mixture, the gelatin mixture, orange and lemon zests, and the lemon juice in a large bowl; stir to mix well. Use a rubber spatula to gently fold the meringue mixture into the peach mixture until no white streaks remain. Pour the mixture into the prepared pan, spreading evenly.

7. Cut each remaining peach slice into 2 thin slices each and arrange on top of the cheesecake in a circular manner. Cover the cake loosely with plastic wrap and refrigerate for at least 4 hours or overnight.

8. To serve, use a sharp knife to loosen the sides of the cake. Remove the sides of the pan, leaving the cake on the bottom. Place the cake on a serving plate. Cover and refrigerate leftovers.

Makes one 10-inch (25 cm) cheesecake; 10 servings

Per serving: 187 Calories, 18 g Carbohydrate, 13 g Protein, 7 g Fat, 13 mg Cholesterol, 130 mg Sodium, 1 g Fiber
Exchanges: 1 Starch, 2 Lean Meat (1 Carb Choice)

No-Bake Swirl Cheesecake

Prep time: 15 minutes • Chilling time: 4 hours

Cooking spray

½ cup (51 g) graham cracker crumbs

¼ cup (43 g) plus 2 tablespoons instant meringue mix or 2 tablespoons dried egg whites

⅓ cup/80 ml cold water, or ⅓ cup/80 ml warm water if using dried egg whites

¼ cup (48 g) sugar

Two 0.25-ounce (7 g) envelopes unflavored gelatin

¼ cup (75 g) sweetened condensed milk, chilled

1½ cups (360 ml) nonfat milk

3 cups (681 g) reduced-fat ricotta, at room temperature

¼ cup (17 g) nonfat milk powder

1 tablespoon grated orange zest

1 tablespoon grated lemon zest

3 tablespoons fresh lemon juice

1 teaspoon vanilla extract

½ cup (160 g) no-sugar-added raspberry or strawberry jam

Raspberries or strawberries for serving (optional)

1. Spray an 8-inch (21 cm) springform pan with cooking spray. Sprinkle the inside of the pan with graham cracker crumbs. Refrigerate.

2. Use an electric mixer at high speed to beat the meringue mix and water in a medium bowl until soft peaks form. Gradually beat in 2 tablespoons of the sugar, beating until stiff peaks form when the beaters are lifted; set aside.

3. Mix the remaining 2 tablespoons sugar and gelatin in the top of a double boiler (or a bowl that will fit on top of a medium saucepan). Stir in the sweetened condensed milk. Let stand for 1 minute to soften the gelatin, then stir until well blended; stir or whisk in the milk.

4. Place the gelatin mixture over a saucepan of simmering water over medium heat. Use a spoon or heat-proof spatula to continuously stir the mixture until it forms a custard thick enough to coat the back side of a spoon, 8 to 12 minutes. Remove from the heat; transfer to a large bowl.

5. Process the ricotta in a food processor or blender until smooth. Stir the ricotta into the custard along with the milk powder, orange zest, lemon zest and juice, and vanilla, until well blended.

6. Use a rubber spatula to gently fold the meringue mixture into the ricotta mixture until no white streaks remain. Remove the springform pan from the refrigerator and pour in the ricotta mixture, spreading evenly.

7. Microwave the jam in a small microwave-safe bowl for 20 to 30 seconds, until melted; stir. Drizzle the jam over the top of the cake and swirl with a table knife to marble.

8. Cover the cake loosely with plastic wrap and refrigerate for at least 4 hours or overnight.

9. To serve, use a sharp knife to loosen the sides of the cake. Remove the sides of the pan, leaving the cake on the bottom. Place the cake on a serving plate. Serve with fresh raspberries or strawberries, if desired. Cover and refrigerate leftovers.

Makes one 8-inch (21 cm) cheesecake; 8 servings

Per serving (1 slice): 254 Calories, 28 g Carbohydrate, 16 g Protein, 9 g Fat, 14 mg Cholesterol, 210 mg Sodium, 0 g Fiber
Exchanges: 2 Starch, 2 Lean Meat, ½ Fat (2 Carb Choices)

Creamy Ricotta Cheesecake

Prep time: 10 minutes • Bake time: 2 hours • Cooling time: 1 hour • Chilling time: 4 hours

Cooking spray

½ cup (51 g) graham cracker crumbs

3¾ cups (852 g) reduced-fat ricotta

1 cup (240 ml) buttermilk
   (see page 8)

3 large eggs

⅓ cup (64 g) sugar

1 tablespoon cornstarch

1 tablespoon grated lemon zest

2 tablespoons fresh lemon juice

2 teaspoons vanilla extract

Fresh fruit (optional)

1. Preheat the oven to 375°F (190°C). Spray a 10-inch (25 cm) springform pan with cooking spray. Sprinkle the inside of the pan with graham cracker crumbs, then refrigerate.

2. Combine the ricotta, buttermilk, eggs, sugar, cornstarch, lemon zest and juice, and vanilla in a food processor. Process until smooth, scraping down the sides occasionally. Pour the mixture into the springform pan.

3. Place the pan in the oven on the middle oven rack. Place a 13 x 9 x 2-inch (33 x 23 x 5 cm) pan on the bottom rack, below the cake. Fill the pan halfway with hot water to prevent the cheesecake from cracking.

4. Bake for 50 to 60 minutes, until the filling is set. Turn off the oven and leave the cake in the oven with the door slightly ajar 1 inch (2.5 cm) for 1 hour.

5. Remove from the oven and cool in the pan on a wire rack for 1 hour. Cover and refrigerate for at least 4 hours or overnight.

6. To serve, use a sharp knife to loosen the sides of the cake. Remove the sides of the pan, leaving the cake on the bottom. Place the cake on a serving plate. If desired, serve with sliced fresh fruit. Cover and refrigerate leftovers.

Makes one 10-inch (25 cm) cheesecake; 10 servings

Per serving: 179 Calories, 14 g Carbohydrate, 13 g Protein, 8 g Fat,
76 mg Cholesterol, 204 mg Sodium, 0 g Fiber
Exchanges: 1 Starch, 2 Lean Meat (1 Carb Choice)

Chocolate Cheesecake

Prep time: 10 minutes • Bake time: 35 minutes • Cooling time: 1 hour • Chilling time: 3 hours

CRUST

Cooking spray

¾ cup (77 g) graham cracker crumbs

2 tablespoons canola or extra-light olive oil

2 tablespoons sugar

½ teaspoon ground cinnamon

FILLING

2 cups (454 g) reduced-fat ricotta

3 large eggs

⅓ cup (64 g) sugar

⅓ cup (77 g) plain Greek yogurt

¼ cup (20 g) unsweetened cocoa powder, sifted if lumpy

1 teaspoon vanilla extract

1. Preheat the oven to 350°F (180°C). Spray an 8-inch (20 cm) springform pan with cooking spray.

2. **To make the crust,** mix together the graham cracker crumbs, oil, sugar, and cinnamon in a small bowl. Press the mixture onto the bottom and partially up the sides of the prepared pan. Set aside.

3. **To make the filling,** combine the ricotta, eggs, sugar, yogurt, cocoa powder, and vanilla in a food processor or blender. Process, scraping down the sides occasionally, for 1 minute, until smooth. Pour the mixture into the crust.

4. Place the pan in the oven on the middle oven rack. Place a 13 x 9 x 2-inch (33 x 23 x 5 cm) pan on the bottom rack, below the cake. Fill the pan halfway with hot water to prevent the cheesecake from cracking.

5. Bake for 30 to 35 minutes, until the filling is just set (the center will jiggle slightly). Turn off the oven and leave the cake in the oven for 5 minutes longer.

6. Remove from the oven and cool in the pan on a wire rack for about 1 hour. Cover and refrigerate for at least 3 hours before serving.

7. To serve, use a sharp knife to loosen the sides of the cake. Remove the sides of the pan, leaving the cake on the bottom. Place the cake on a serving plate. Cover and refrigerate leftovers.

Makes one 8-inch (20 cm) cheesecake; 8 servings

Per serving (1 slice): 215 Calories, 20 g Carbohydrate, 11 g Protein, 11 g Fat, 84 mg Cholesterol, 160 mg Sodium, 1 g Fiber
Exchanges: 1 Starch, 1½ Lean Meat, 1 Fat (1 Carb Choice)

Berry Buttermilk Cheesecake

Prep time: 10 minutes ◆ Bake time: 7 minutes ◆ Chilling time: 3 hours

CRUST

Cooking spray

1 cup (102 g) graham cracker crumbs

¼ cup (31 g) finely chopped pecans

2 tablespoons canola or extra-light olive oil

1 tablespoon sugar

FILLING

Three 0.25-ounce (7 g) envelopes unflavored gelatin

2 cups (480 ml) buttermilk (see page 8)

¼ cup (48 g) sugar

1 tablespoon grated lemon zest

1 tablespoon fresh lemon juice

2 tablespoons strawberry liqueur or syrup (such as DaVinci, Dekuyper, Giffard, or Torani)

One 16-ounce (454 g) carton nonfat cottage cheese

2 cups (290 g) fresh strawberries, hulled and sliced

1 kiwi, peeled and sliced

½ cup (70 g) fresh blueberries

½ cup (160 g) no-sugar-added strawberry jam

1. Preheat the oven to 350°F (180°C). Spray an 8-inch (20 cm) springform pan with cooking spray.

2. **To make the crust,** mix together the graham cracker crumbs, pecans, oil, and sugar in a small bowl. Press the mixture evenly over the bottom and partially up the sides of the prepared pan. Bake for 7 to 9 minutes until lightly browned. Cool on a wire rack before filling.

3. **To make the filling,** sprinkle the gelatin over 1 cup (240 ml) of the buttermilk in a 2-cup (480 ml) glass measuring cup. Let sit for 1 minute to soften. Microwave on high for 1 to 2 minutes, or until very hot; stir to completely dissolve the gelatin.

4. Combine the gelatin mixture, remaining 1 cup (240 ml) buttermilk, sugar, lemon zest and juice, and strawberry liqueur in food processor or blender. Process until well blended. Add the cottage cheese and process until smooth, scraping down the sides.

5. With the machine running, drop in 1 cup (196 g) of the strawberries and pulse just until small pieces of strawberries remain; scrape down the sides and pour the mixture into the cooled crust.

6. Cover loosely with plastic wrap, then chill for at least 3 hours or overnight until firm.

7. To serve, use a sharp knife to loosen the sides of the cake. Remove the sides of the pan, leaving the cake on the bottom. Place the cake on a serving plate.

8. Arrange the remaining strawberries, kiwi, and blueberries on top of the cake. Heat the jam in the microwave on high for 30 seconds; stir and spoon or drizzle the jam over the fruit. Serve immediately. Cover and refrigerate leftovers.

Makes one 8-inch (20 cm) cheesecake; 8 servings

Per serving (1 slice): 299 Calories, 47 g Carbohydrate, 11 g Protein, 8 g Fat,
5 mg Cholesterol, 327 mg Sodium, 3 g Fiber
Exchanges: 1 Starch, 2 Fruit, 1½ Fat (3 Carb Choices)

Fruity Cheesecake

Prep time: 10 minutes ◆ Bake time: 2 hours ◆ Cooling time: 1 hour ◆ Chilling time: 8 hours

Cooking spray

½ cup (51 g) graham cracker crumbs

One 8-ounce (226 g) package nonfat cream cheese, softened

2 cups (454 g) nonfat ricotta

2 large eggs, at room temperature

¼ cup (48 g) sugar

1 tablespoon cornstarch

1 tablespoon grated lemon zest

1 tablespoon fresh lemon juice

1 teaspoon vanilla extract

1½ cups (368 g) Yogurt Cheese (page 96)

1 cup (150 g) sliced fresh fruit

½ cup (160 g) no-sugar-added jam or ½ cup (85 g) Blueberry Topping (page 93)

1. Preheat the oven to 350°F (180°C). Spray an 8-inch (20 cm) springform pan with cooking spray. Sprinkle the bottom and sides of the pan with graham cracker crumbs. Set aside.

2. Combine the cream cheese, ricotta, eggs, sugar, cornstarch, lemon zest and juice, and vanilla in a food processor or blender and process until smooth, scraping down the sides as needed. Add the yogurt cheese and pulse; scraping down the sides twice, until well blended. Pour the mixture into the crust.

3. Place the pan in the oven on the middle oven rack. Place a 13 x 9 x 2-inch (33 x 23 x 5 cm) pan on the bottom rack, below the cake. Fill the pan halfway with hot water to prevent the cheesecake from cracking.

4. Bake for 55 to 60 minutes, until puffed and lightly browned. Turn off the oven. Leave the cake in the oven with the door slightly ajar about 1 inch (2.5 cm) for 1 hour.

5. Remove from the oven and cool in the pan on a wire rack for 1 hour. Cover and refrigerate for 8 hours or overnight before serving.

6. To serve, use a sharp knife to loosen the sides of the cake. Remove the sides of the pan, leaving the cake on the bottom. Place the cake on a serving plate. Arrange the fruit on top. Microwave the jam on high for 30 seconds; stir, then spoon or drizzle the jam over the fruit or top with Blueberry Topping. Serve immediately. Cover and refrigerate leftovers.

> **Variation:** *This recipe can also be used to make about 60 mini cheesecakes. Pour the batter evenly into paper- or foil-lined mini muffin cups. Bake for 15 to 20 minutes, without a water bath, until puffed and lightly browned. Remove from the oven and cool in the pans on wire racks for at least 30 minutes. Carefully remove the cakes from the pans and cool completely on the racks. Store, covered, in the refrigerator.*

Makes one 8-inch (20 cm) cheesecake; 8 servings

Per serving (1 slice): 250 Calories, 40 g Carbohydrate, 14 g Protein, 4 g Fat, 67 mg Cholesterol, 356 mg Sodium, 1 g Fiber
Exchanges: ½ Starch, 2 Fruit, 2 Lean Meat (2½ Carb Choices)

Pineapple Cheese Pie

Prep time: 10 minutes ◆ *Bake time: 30 minutes* ◆ *Chilling time: 4 hours*

One 20-ounce (567 g) can juice-packed crushed pineapple

One 0.25-ounce (7 g) envelope unflavored gelatin

2 large eggs, separated, at room temperature

2 cups (454 g) reduced-fat ricotta

¼ cup (48 g) sugar

2 teaspoons grated lemon zest

1 teaspoon fresh lemon juice

1 teaspoon vanilla extract

¼ teaspoon salt

Ground cinnamon, for dusting

1. Preheat the oven to 350°F (180°C). Set out a 9-inch (23 cm) pie plate.

2. Drain the pineapple over a 1-cup (240 ml) glass measuring cup to measure ½ cup (120 ml) juice. Set aside the drained pineapple.

3. Sprinkle the gelatin over the juice in a small saucepan. Let stand 1 minute to soften. Place over low heat and stir until the gelatin is completely dissolved, about 3 minutes.

4. Use an electric mixer at high speed to beat the egg whites in a large bowl until the whites form stiff peaks when the beaters are lifted.

5. Combine the egg yolks, drained pineapple, ricotta, and gelatin mixture in a food processor or blender. Process until smooth; scrape down the sides, and add the sugar, lemon zest and juice, vanilla, and salt. Process until blended, scraping down the sides.

6. Use a rubber spatula to gently fold the ricotta mixture into the beaten whites until no white streaks remain. Pour into the pie plate and sprinkle with cinnamon.

7. Bake for 30 to 40 minutes or until the pie is firm and a tester inserted into the center comes out clean.

8. Cool on a wire rack. Refrigerate for at least 4 hours or overnight before serving. Cover and refrigerate leftovers.

Makes one 9-inch (23 cm) pie; 8 servings

Per serving (1 slice): 147 Calories, 18 g Carbohydrate, 9 g Protein, 5 g Fat, 59 mg Cholesterol, 159 mg Sodium, 1 g Fiber
Exchanges: 1 Fruit, 1 Lean Meat (1 Carb Choice)

Pumpkin Swirl Cheesecake

Prep time: 10 minutes ◆ Bake time: 3 hours ◆ Cooling time: 1 hour ◆ Chilling time: 4 hours

One 8-ounce (226 g) package nonfat cream cheese, softened

2 cups (454 g) nonfat ricotta

1 cup (245 g) Yogurt Cheese (page 96)

3 large eggs, at room temperature

¼ cup (48 g) sugar

1 tablespoon cornstarch

1 teaspoon vanilla extract

1 cup (230 g) puréed cooked fresh pumpkin or canned pumpkin

2 teaspoons pumpkin pie spice

1 teaspoon maple extract

1 Oatmeal Crust (page 222), baked in a 10-inch (25 cm) springform pan

1. Preheat the oven to 350°F (180°C).

2. Combine the cream cheese, ricotta, yogurt cheese, eggs, sugar, cornstarch, and vanilla in a food processor or blender and process until smooth, scraping down the sides occasionally. Remove 2 cups (463 g) of the cream cheese mixture and set aside.

3. Add the pumpkin, pumpkin pie spice, and maple extract to the mixture in the food processor and pulse until blended. Scrape down the sides and pour half of the pumpkin mixture onto the oatmeal crust. Spoon half of the reserved cream cheese mixture over the pumpkin mixture in the crust. Repeat the layers, then gently cut through the batter with a table knife to marble. Be sure not to cut into the crust.

4. Place the pan on the middle oven rack. Place a 13 x 9 x 2-inch (33 x 23 x 5 cm) pan on the bottom rack, below the cake. Fill the pan halfway with hot water to prevent the cheesecake from cracking.

5. Bake for 55 to 60 minutes, until the center jiggles slightly, the sides just begin to puff, and the surface is no longer shiny. Turn off the oven and leave the cake in the closed oven for 2 hours.

6. Remove from the oven and cool on a wire rack for 1 hour. Cover and refrigerate for at least 4 hours or overnight.

7. To serve, use a sharp knife to loosen the sides of the cake. Remove the sides of the pan, leaving the cake on the bottom. Place the cake on a serving plate. Cover and refrigerate leftovers.

Makes one 10-inch (25 cm) cheesecake; 10 servings

Per serving (1 slice): 207 Calories, 24 g Carbohydrate, 12 g Protein, 6 g Fat, 67 mg Cholesterol, 249 mg Sodium, 2 g Fiber
Exchanges: 1 Starch, ½ Nonfat Milk, 1 Fat (1½ Carb Choices)

Black and White Cheesecake

Prep time: 10 minutes • Bake time: 1 hour 40 minutes • Cooling time: 1 hour • Chilling time: 4 hours

CRUST

Cooking spray

1 cup (102 g) graham cracker crumbs

3 tablespoons canola or extra-light olive oil

1 tablespoon unsweetened cocoa powder, sifted if lumpy

FILLING

1 cup (227 g) reduced-fat ricotta or cottage cheese

¾ cup (180 ml) nonfat milk

⅓ cup (60 g) sugar

2 teaspoons cornstarch

3 teaspoons vanilla extract

⅛ teaspoon salt

2 large eggs

¼ cup (20 g) unsweetened cocoa powder, sifted if lumpy

1 teaspoon instant coffee powder

Whipped Topping (page 91) or Easy Fat-Free Topping (page 92), to serve (optional)

1. Preheat the oven to 350°F (180°C). Spray a 9-inch (23 cm) pie plate with cooking spray.

2. **To make the crust,** mix the graham cracker crumbs, oil, and cocoa powder in a medium bowl. Pat into the bottom and partially up the sides of the prepared pie plate; set aside.

3. **To make the filling,** combine the ricotta, milk, 2 tablespoons of the sugar, cornstarch, 1 teaspoon of the vanilla, and the salt in a food processor. Process until smooth, scraping down the sides. Add the eggs and process until smooth.

4. Pour 1 cup (212 g) of the mixture into the crust. Bake for 20 minutes or until firm.

5. Add the cocoa powder, remaining 3 tablespoons sugar, remaining 2 teaspoons vanilla, and instant coffee to the remaining ricotta mixture; process to blend well. Scrape down the sides and pour the chocolate mixture evenly over the baked vanilla layer.

6. Bake for an additional 20 minutes or until set. Turn off the oven and leave the pie in the oven with the door slightly ajar for 1 hour.

7. Cool on a wire rack for about 1 hour. Cover and refrigerate for at least 4 hours or overnight before serving. If desired, serve with Whipped Topping or Easy Fat-Free Topping.

Makes one 9-inch (23 cm) pie; 8 servings

Per serving (1 slice): 194 Calories, 20 g Carbohydrate, 7 g Protein, 10 g Fat,
52 mg Cholesterol, 180 mg Sodium, 2 g Fiber
Exchanges: 1 Starch, 1 Lean Meat, 1 Fat (1 Carb Choice)

Apple Cheesecake

Prep time: 10 minutes ◆ Bake time: 1 hour 40 minutes ◆ Cooling time: 30 minutes ◆ Chilling time: 8 hours

CRUST

Cooking spray

½ cup (51 g) graham cracker crumbs

1 tablespoon canola or extra light olive oil

½ teaspoon ground cinnamon

¼ teaspoon ground nutmeg

FILLING

2½ cups (568 g) nonfat ricotta

One 8-ounce (226 g) package nonfat cream cheese, softened

2 large eggs, at room temperature

½ cup (120 ml) buttermilk (see page 8)

½ cup (96 g) sugar

¼ cup (30 g) all-purpose flour

2 teaspoons vanilla extract

½ teaspoon almond extract

2 teaspoons grated lemon zest

½ teaspoon ground cinnamon

2 medium Rome or Pink Lady apples, peeled, cored, and cut into four wedges each

3 tablespoons sliced almonds

1. Preheat the oven to 325°F (165°C). Spray an 8-inch (20 cm) springform pan with cooking spray.

2. **To make the crust,** mix the graham cracker crumbs, oil, cinnamon, and nutmeg in a small bowl until well blended. Pat the mixture onto the bottom of the prepared pan; set aside.

3. **To make the filling,** combine the ricotta, cream cheese, eggs, buttermilk, sugar, flour, extracts, lemon zest, and cinnamon in a food processor. Process until smooth, about 1 minute. Scrape down the sides and process for 30 seconds more or until well blended. With the machine running, drop in the apple wedges and process, scraping down the sides, just until small pieces of apple remain. Pour the mixture into the crust.

4. Place the pan in the oven on the middle oven rack. Place a 13 x 9 x 2-inch (33 x 23 x 5 cm) pan on the bottom rack, below the cake. Fill the pan halfway with hot water to prevent the cheesecake from cracking.

5. Bake for 1 hour. Carefully remove the cheesecake from the oven and sprinkle it with the sliced almonds. Return the pan to the oven and bake for an additional 10 minutes. Turn off the oven and leave the cake in the oven with the door slightly ajar for 30 minutes.

6. Remove the cake from the oven and cool on a wire rack for 30 minutes. Cover and refrigerate at least 8 hours before serving.

7. To serve, use a sharp knife to loosen the sides of the cake. Remove the sides of the pan, leaving the cake on the bottom. Place the cake on a serving plate. Cover and refrigerate leftovers.

Makes one 8-inch (20 cm) cheesecake; 8 servings

Per serving (1 slice): 240 Calories, 32 g Carbohydrate, 14 g Protein, 5 g Fat, 60 mg Cholesterol, 366 mg Sodium, 2 g Fiber
Exchanges: 1 Starch, 1 Fruit, 2 Lean Meat (2 Carb Choices)

Light Cheesecake

Prep time: 10 minutes • Bake time: 35 minutes • Cooling time: 1 hour • Chilling time: 4 hours

Cooking spray

1 cup (227 g) reduced-fat cottage cheese

1 cup (227 g) reduced-fat ricotta

2 large eggs, plus 2 large egg whites, at room temperature

¼ cup (17 g) nonfat milk powder

2 tablespoons sugar

2 teaspoons grated lemon zest

1 teaspoon vanilla extract

¼ teaspoon cream of tartar

½ cup (160 g) no-sugar-added jam of your choice (optional)

Fruit, to serve (optional)

1. Preheat the oven to 350°F (180°C). Spray an 8-inch (20 cm) square baking pan with cooking spray.

2. Combine the cottage cheese, ricotta, the 2 whole eggs, 2 tablespoons of the milk powder, sugar, lemon zest, and vanilla in a food processor or blender. Process until smooth, scraping down the sides. Set aside.

3. Use an electric mixer at high speed to beat the egg whites and cream of tartar in a large bowl until frothy. Gradually beat in the remaining 2 tablespoons milk powder, scraping down the sides occasionally. Continue beating until soft peaks form when the beaters are lifted.

4. Pour the cottage cheese mixture into the beaten egg whites. Use a rubber spatula to gently fold the cottage cheese mixture into the egg whites until no white streaks remain. Pour the mixture into the prepared pan.

5. Bake for about 35 minutes or until the top of the cake is brown and a tester inserted into the center comes out clean.

6. Cool in the pan on a wire rack for about 1 hour. If desired, microwave the jam on high for 30 seconds; stir, then spread the jam on top of the cheesecake. Cover and refrigerate for at least 4 hours before cutting into 16 squares. If desired, serve fruit on the side. Cover and refrigerate leftovers.

Makes one 8-inch (20 cm) square cake; 16 servings

Per serving (1 square): 65 Calories, 9 g Carbohydrate, 5 g Protein, 2 g Fat,
26 mg Cholesterol, 69 mg Sodium, 0 mg Fiber
Exchanges: ½ Starch (½ Carb Choice)

Cheesy Jam Squares

Prep time: 15 minutes ◆ Bake time: 35 minutes ◆ Chilling time: 2 hours

CRUST

Cooking spray

2 tablespoons brown sugar

3 tablespoons canola or extra-light olive oil

½ cup (60 g) whole wheat flour

½ cup (45 g) old-fashioned rolled oats

¼ cup (33 g) chopped nuts

FILLING

One 8-ounce (226 g) package reduced-fat cream cheese, softened

2 tablespoons granulated sugar

1 large egg

2 tablespoons nonfat milk

1 tablespoon fresh lemon juice

1 teaspoon vanilla extract

⅓ cup (105 g) no-sugar-added raspberry jam

1. Preheat the oven to 350°F (180°C). Spray an 8-inch (20 cm) square baking pan with cooking spray.

2. **To make the crust,** mix the brown sugar and oil in a medium bowl until well blended; stir in the flour, oats, and nuts until crumbly. Reserve ½ cup (53 g) of the mixture.

3. Press the remaining crust mixture onto the bottom of the prepared pan. Bake for 8 to 10 minutes until set; then set aside to cool.

4. **To make the filling,** combine the cream cheese and granulated sugar in a food processor or blender and process until smooth. Add the egg, milk, lemon juice, and vanilla and process until smooth, scraping down the sides occasionally. Spread the mixture over the baked crust.

5. Microwave the jam on high for about 30 seconds; stir. Drizzle the jam over the cheese mixture, then swirl it in with a table knife. Be careful not to cut into the crust. Sprinkle with the reserved crumb mixture.

6. Bake for 25 minutes or until the cake is firm and a tester inserted into the center comes out clean.

7. Cool on a wire rack. Refrigerate for at least 2 hours before cutting into 16 squares. Cover and refrigerate leftovers.

Makes one 8-inch (20 cm) square cake; 16 servings

Per serving (1 square): 115 Calories, 10 g Carbohydrate, 3 g Protein, 8 g Fat,
23 mg Cholesterol, 52 mg Sodium, 1 g Fiber
Exchanges: ½ Starch, 1½ Fat (½ Carb Choice)

Layered Cheesecake Squares

Prep time: 10 minutes ◆ *Bake time: 30 minutes* ◆ *Cooling time: 1 hour* ◆ *Chilling time: 4 hours*

Cooking spray

2 cups (454 g) reduced-fat cottage cheese

2 large eggs

¼ cup (30 g) whole wheat flour

¼ cup (48 g) sugar

1 tablespoon grated lemon zest

1 tablespoon fresh lemon juice

½ cup (123 g) plain Greek yogurt

¼ cup no-sugar-added jam of your choice, stirred smooth

1. Preheat the oven to 325°F (165°C). Spray an 8-inch (10 cm) square baking pan with cooking spray.

2. Combine the cottage cheese, eggs, flour, sugar, and lemon zest and juice in a food processor or blender. Process until smooth, scraping down the sides occasionally. Pour into the prepared baking pan.

3. Bake for about 25 minutes or until firm.

4. Meanwhile, stir together the yogurt and jam in a small bowl until well blended.

5. Remove the cheesecake from the oven and immediately spread with the yogurt-jam mixture to cover completely. Return the cake to the oven and bake for 5 minutes more.

6. Remove from the oven and cool a on wire rack for 1 hour. Cover and refrigerate for at least 4 hours. If desired, arrange berries on top. Cut into squares and serve. Cover and refrigerate leftovers.

Makes one 8-inch (20 cm) square cake; 16 servings

Per serving (1 square): 62 Calories, 8 g Carbohydrate, 5 g Protein, 2 g Fat,
25 mg Cholesterol, 74 mg Sodium, 0 g Fiber
Exchanges: ½ Starch (½ Carb Choice)

Pineapple Cheesecake Squares

Prep time: 15 minutes • Bake time: 25 minutes • Cooling time: 30 minutes • Chilling time: 4 hours

CRUST

Cooking spray

1½ cups (153 g) graham cracker crumbs

1½ tablespoons canola or extra-light olive oil

2 tablespoons honey

½ teaspoon ground cinnamon

¼ teaspoon ground nutmeg

FILLING

One 8-ounce (226 g) package reduced-fat cream cheese, softened

1 cup (227 g) reduced-fat ricotta

One 6-ounce (177 ml) can unsweetened pineapple juice (about ¾ cup)

4 large eggs, at room temperature

¼ cup (48 g) sugar

1 teaspoon vanilla extract

TOPPING

One 20-ounce (567 g) can juice-packed crushed pineapple

¼ cup (30 g) all-purpose flour

¼ cup (48 g) sugar

1. Preheat the oven to 350°F (180°C). Spray a 13 x 9 x 2-inch (33 x 23 x 5 cm) baking pan with cooking spray.

2. **To make the crust,** use a fork to blend the graham cracker crumbs, oil, honey, cinnamon, and nutmeg in a medium bowl. Press the mixture firmly onto the bottom of the pan; set aside.

3. **To make the filling,** combine the cream cheese, ricotta, pineapple juice, eggs, sugar, and vanilla in a food processor or blender and process until smooth, scraping down the sides. Pour the mixture over the crust.

4. Bake for 25 to 30 minutes or until the center is set. Cool on a wire rack for about 30 minutes.

5. **To make the topping,** drain the juice of the crushed canned pineapple into a 4-cup (960 ml) glass measuring cup and add enough water to measure 1 cup (240 ml); reserve the pineapple.

6. Use a whisk or a fork to mix in the flour and sugar until smooth. Microwave on high for 2 minutes, stir, and microwave for another 2 minutes, stirring after 1 minute, until thickened.

7. Stir in the reserved pineapple. Spread the pineapple mixture over the cooled cheesecake.

8. Cover loosely and refrigerate for about 4 hours or overnight. Cut into 2-inch (5 cm) squares to serve. Cover and refrigerate leftovers.

Makes one 13 x 9-inch (33 x 23 cm) cake; 24 servings

Per serving (1 square): 121 Calories, 16 g Carbohydrate, 3 g Protein, 5 g Fat, 40 mg Cholesterol, 96 mg Sodium, 0 g Fiber
Exchanges: 1 Fruit, 1 Fat (1 Carb Choice)

Coffee
Cakes &
Scones

Tips & Tricks

COFFEE CAKES

» Coffee cakes are wonderful with a cup of coffee or tea, delicious as an addition to breakfast, marvelous with brunch, and they're great as a snack.

» Coffee cakes can be baked and frozen for up to 3 months. Thaw them at room temperature or in the refrigerator.

» The preparation in making these cakes is similar to muffins, scones, and quick breads—DO NOT overmix them or they will be tough. Mix the ingredients just until blended. The cakes can be prepared and baked in an 8- or 9-inch (20 or 23 cm) pan or in an oblong pan, Bundt pan, or tube pan, depending on the recipe.

» If baking a coffee cake in a glass baking dish, lower the oven temperature by 25°F (14°C).

» The coffee cakes in this book are reduced in total fat, sugar, and salt. A small amount of sugar is used in each recipe, along with fruit or fruit juice for flavor, moisture, and natural sweetness.

SCONES

» Scones hail from Scotland and are a variation of a biscuit, with the addition of sugar, fruit, and eggs. Scones are made basically the same way as muffins and quick breads. The batter should not be overmixed or the scones will be tough.

» Most of the scone recipes in this book contain fruit for natural sweetness. If the scones are not sweet enough for you and additional sugar is no problem for your family's diet, increase the amount of sweetener used in the recipe.

» Whole wheat flour is used in each recipe for added fiber, minerals, and vitamins. If you prefer, whole wheat flour or whole wheat pastry flour can be used in the same amount.

» Once the scone dough holds together, gather it into a ball and place it on a lined or sprayed baking sheet. Pat the dough into a circle 8 or 9 inches (20 or 23 cm) in diameter and about ½-inch (1 mm) thick. Use a sharp knife to score the dough into wedges, being careful not to cut all the way through. Bake according to the recipe directions.

» Scones are done when they are golden brown and sound hollow when tapped. When the scones are cool enough to handle, cut them into wedges and serve warm.

» Store in a covered container at room temperature for up to three days. Reheat in a 350°F (180°C) oven for 5 to 10 minutes, until warmed. Or toast in a toaster oven.

» Baked scones can be frozen for up to 3 months. Enjoy them hot from the oven plain, or with a small amount of your favorite buttery spread and/or the no-sugar-added jam of your choice.

Apple Crumb Coffee Cake

Prep time: 10 minutes • Bake time: 30 minutes

CAKE

Cooking spray

¾ cup (90 g) all-purpose flour

¾ cup (90 g) whole wheat flour

¼ cup (48 g) granulated sugar

2 teaspoons grated lemon zest

1 teaspoon baking powder

½ teaspoon baking soda

¼ teaspoon salt

1 medium apple, peeled, cored, and chopped

¾ cup (180 ml) nonfat milk

1 large egg

¼ cup (60 ml) canola or extra-light olive oil

½ teaspoon vanilla extract

TOPPING

¼ cup (33 g) chopped walnuts

1 tablespoon brown sugar

½ teaspoon ground cinnamon

¼ teaspoon ground nutmeg

1. Preheat the oven to 350°F (180°C). Spray a 9-inch (23 cm) round or square baking pan with cooking spray.

2. **To make the cake,** stir together the flours, granulated sugar, lemon zest, baking powder, baking soda, and salt in a medium bowl until blended. Stir in the chopped apple until coated with the flour mixture.

3. Whisk together the milk, egg, oil, and vanilla in another medium bowl. Add the wet ingredients to the apple mixture and stir just until blended; do not overmix. Spread the batter into the prepared pan.

4. **To make the topping,** mix together the walnuts, brown sugar, cinnamon, and nutmeg in a small bowl; sprinkle over the batter.

5. Bake for 30 minutes or until the cake is brown and a tester inserted into the center comes out clean.

6. Cool in the pan for about 10 minutes on a wire rack before serving warm or at room temperature. Store covered. Refrigerate after 2 days. This cake may be frozen for up to 3 months.

Makes one 9-inch (23 cm) round or square cake; 9 servings

Per serving (1 slice): 191 Calories, 25 g Carbohydrate, 4 g Protein, 9 g Fat, 20 mg Cholesterol, 150 mg Sodium, 2 g Fiber
Exchanges: 1½ Starch, 2 Fat (1½ Carb Choices)

Banana-Date Crumb Coffee Cake

Prep time: 10 minutes • Bake time: 20 minutes

CAKE

Cooking spray

1½ cups (180 g) all-purpose flour

1½ cups (180 g) whole wheat flour

2 tablespoons granulated sugar

2 teaspoons baking powder

1 teaspoon baking soda

1 cup (165 g) chopped pitted dates

1 tablespoon grated orange zest

1 cup (240 ml) fresh orange juice

3 large eggs, at room temperature

1 cup (224 g) mashed ripe banana
(2 medium)

½ cup (120 ml) canola or extra-light
olive oil

1 teaspoon vanilla extract

TOPPING

¼ cup (18 g) unsweetened shredded
coconut

¼ cup (33 g) chopped walnuts

1 tablespoon brown sugar

½ teaspoon ground cinnamon

¼ teaspoon ground nutmeg

1. Preheat the oven to 350°F (180°C). Spray a 13 x 9 x 2-inch (33 x 23 x 5 cm) baking pan with cooking spray.

2. **To make the cake,** stir together the flours, granulated sugar, baking powder, and baking soda in a large bowl until blended. Stir in the dates until coated with the flour mixture.

3. Whisk together the orange zest and juice, eggs, banana, oil, and vanilla in a medium bowl until well mixed. Add the wet ingredients to the dry ingredients and stir just until blended; do not overmix. Spoon the batter into the prepared pan.

4. **To make the topping,** mix the coconut, walnuts, brown sugar, cinnamon, and nutmeg in a small bowl. Sprinkle evenly over the batter.

5. Bake for 25 to 30 minutes or until the cake is browned and a tester inserted into the center comes out clean.

6. Cool in the pan on a wire rack for at least 10 minutes before serving warm or at room temperature. Store covered. Refrigerate after 2 days. This cake may be frozen for up to 3 months.

Makes one 13 x 9-inch (33 x 23 cm) cake; 24 servings

Per serving (1 slice): 156 Calories, 22 g Carbohydrate, 3 g Protein, 7 g Fat,
22 mg Cholesterol, 62 mg Sodium, 2 g Fiber
Exchanges: 1 Starch, ½ Fruit, 1 Fat (1½ Carb Choices)

Berry Coffee Cake

Prep time: 10 minutes ◆ Bake time: 30 minutes

Cooking spray

¾ cup (90 g) all-purpose flour

¾ cup (90 g) whole wheat flour

3 tablespoons brown sugar

3 tablespoons nonfat milk powder
or buttermilk powder (see page 8)

1½ teaspoons baking powder

¼ teaspoon salt

3 tablespoons canola or extra-light
olive oil

2 teaspoons grated orange zest

¾ cup (180 ml) fresh orange juice

1 large egg

½ teaspoon vanilla extract

1 cup (145 g) fresh or frozen
raspberries, blueberries, or
blackberries

1 tablespoon granulated sugar

1. Preheat the oven to 350°F (180°C). Spray a 9-inch (23 cm) round or square baking pan with cooking spray.

2. Stir together the flours, brown sugar, milk powder, baking powder, and salt in a large bowl. Use a pastry blender or fork to cut in the oil until the mixture is crumbly.

3. Whisk together the orange zest and juice, egg, and vanilla in a small bowl until blended. Add the wet ingredients to the dry ingredients and stir just until blended; do not overmix. Spoon the batter into the prepared pan.

4. In the same small bowl, combine the berries and granulated sugar until the berries are coated. Sprinkle the berries over the batter.

5. Bake for 30 to 35 minutes or until the cake is browned and a tester inserted into the center comes out clean.

6. Cool in the pan on a wire rack for about 10 minutes before serving warm or at room temperature. Store covered. Refrigerate after 2 days. This cake may be frozen for up to 3 months.

Makes one 9-inch (23 cm) round or square cake; 9 servings

Per serving (1 piece): 161 Calories, 26 g Carbohydrate, 4 g Protein, 5 g Fat,
20 mg Cholesterol, 80 mg Sodium, 2 g Fiber
Exchanges: 1½ Starch, ½ Fruit, 1 Fat (2 Carb Choices)

Buttermilk Spice Coffee Cake

Prep time: 10 minutes • Bake time: 30 minutes

Cooking spray

¾ cup (90 g) all-purpose flour

¾ cup (90 g) whole wheat flour

¼ cup (48 g) sugar

¼ cup (60 ml) canola or extra-light olive oil

¼ cup (43 g) raisins

2 teaspoons ground cinnamon

2 teaspoons unsweetened cocoa powder

1 teaspoon ground nutmeg

¼ teaspoon ground cloves

½ teaspoon baking soda

¼ teaspoon baking powder

1 cup (240 ml) buttermilk (see page 8)

¼ cup (33 g) chopped nuts

1. Preheat the oven to 350°F (180°C). Spray a 9-inch (23 cm) square baking pan with cooking spray.

2. Stir together the flours and sugar in a large bowl. Use a pastry blender or fork to cut in the oil until the mixture is crumbly. Set aside ½ cup (72 g) of the mixture.

3. Add the raisins, cinnamon, cocoa powder, nutmeg, cloves, baking soda, and baking powder to the remaining crumb mixture; mix well. Make a well in the center and add the buttermilk. Use a wooden spoon or rubber spatula to mix the ingredients just until blended; do not overmix. Spoon the batter into the prepared pan.

4. Stir the nuts into the reserved crumb mixture and sprinkle it over the batter.

5. Bake for 30 to 35 minutes or until the cake is browned and a tester inserted into the center comes out clean.

6. Cool in the pan on a wire rack for 10 minutes before serving warm or at room temperature. Store covered. Refrigerate after 2 days. This cake can be frozen for up to 3 months.

Makes one 9-inch (23 g) square cake; 9 servings

Per serving (1 slice): 187 Calories, 25 g Carbohydrate, 4 g Protein, 9 g Fat,
1 mg Cholesterol, 123 mg Sodium, 2 g Fiber
Exchanges: 1½ Starch, 2 Fat (1½ Carb Choices)

Nutty Raspberry Coffee Cake

Prep time: 10 minutes • Bake time: 40 minutes

Cooking spray

1 cup (125 g) fresh raspberries

1 tablespoon brown sugar

½ cup (60 g) all-purpose flour

½ cup (60 g) whole wheat flour

¼ cup (48 g) granulated sugar

½ teaspoon baking powder

¼ teaspoon baking soda

½ cup (123 g) plain Greek yogurt

1 large egg

2 tablespoons canola or extra-light olive oil

1 teaspoon vanilla extract

3 tablespoons sliced almonds

Confectioners' sugar (optional)

1. Preheat the oven to 350°F (180°C). Spray a 9-inch (23 cm) round or square baking pan with cooking spray.

2. Combine the raspberries with the brown sugar in a small bowl; set aside.

3. Stir together the flours, granulated sugar, baking powder, and baking soda in a large bowl.

4. Whisk together the yogurt, egg, oil, and vanilla in another small bowl. Add the wet ingredients to the dry ingredients and stir just until blended; do not overmix. Set aside about ½ cup (110 g) of the batter.

5. Spoon the remaining batter into the pan; spread it evenly. Sprinkle the sugared raspberries evenly over the batter. Spoon the reserved batter on top, spreading it to cover the tops of the raspberries; sprinkle with the almonds.

6. Bake for 40 minutes or until the cake is browned and a tester inserted into the center comes out clean.

7. Cool in the pan on a wire rack for 10 minutes before serving warm or at room temperature. If desired, sprinkle with confectioners' sugar before serving. Store covered. Refrigerate after 2 days. This cake can be frozen for up to 3 months.

Makes one 9-inch (23 cm) round or square cake; 9 servings

Per serving (1 slice): 136 Calories, 19 g Carbohydrate, 4 g Protein, 6 g Fat, 24 mg Cholesterol, 48 mg Sodium, 1 g Fiber
Exchanges: 1 Starch, 1 Fat (1 Carb Choice)

Streusel Coffee Cake

Prep time: 10 minutes • Bake time: 55 minutes

Cooking spray

STREUSEL

½ cup (85 g) raisins

¼ cup (48 g) packed brown sugar

1 tablespoon butter, melted

1 teaspoon ground cinnamon

CAKE

1½ cups (180 g) all-purpose flour

1½ cups (180 g) whole wheat flour

⅓ cup (64 g) granulated sugar

2 teaspoons baking powder

¾ teaspoon baking soda

¼ cup (40 g) chopped dried apricots

1½ cups (368 g) plain Greek yogurt

3 large eggs, at room temperature

¼ cup (60 ml) canola or extra-light olive oil

2 tablespoons grated lemon zest

1 teaspoon vanilla extract

Confectioners' sugar

1. Preheat the oven to 350°F (180°C). Spray a 10-inch (25 cm) Bundt pan with cooking spray.

2. **To make the streusel,** mix together the raisins, brown sugar, butter, and cinnamon in a small bowl; set aside.

3. **To make the cake,** stir together the flours, granulated sugar, baking powder, and baking soda in a large bowl. Stir in the apricots until coated with the flour mixture.

4. Whisk together the yogurt, eggs, oil, lemon zest, and vanilla in a medium bowl. Add the wet ingredients to the dry ingredients and stir just until blended; do not overmix.

5. Spoon half of the batter into the prepared pan. Sprinkle with the streusel mixture. Spoon the remaining batter over the streusel.

6. Bake for 55 to 60 minutes or until the cake is browned and a tester inserted into the center comes out clean.

7. Cool in the pan on a wire rack for 10 minutes. Use a knife to loosen the cake and invert it onto a serving plate. Place the plate on the rack and cool completely. Sprinkle with confectioners' sugar before serving. Store covered. Refrigerate after 2 days. This cake can be frozen for up to 3 months.

Makes one 10-inch (25 cm) Bundt cake; 20 servings

Per serving (1 slice): 156 Calories, 22 g Carbohydrate, 4 g Protein, 6 g Fat, 33 mg Cholesterol, 70 mg Sodium, 2 g Fiber
Exchanges: 1½ Starch, 1 Fat (1½ Carb Choices)

Pineapple Coffee Cake

Prep time: 10 minutes ◆ Bake time: 25 minutes

Cooking spray

1¼ cups (150 g) all-purpose flour

1 cup (120 g) whole wheat flour

2 tablespoons granulated sugar

2 teaspoons baking powder

¼ teaspoon salt

1 large egg

One 20-ounce (567 g) can juice-packed crushed pineapple, drained, juice reserved

¼ cup (60 ml) plus 2 tablespoons canola or extra-light olive oil

¼ cup (48 g) packed brown sugar

1. Preheat the oven to 400°F (200°C). Spray an 11 x 7-inch (28 x 18 cm) baking pan* with cooking spray.

2. Stir together 1 cup (120 g) of the all-purpose flour, the whole wheat flour, granulated sugar, baking powder, and salt in a large bowl.

3. Fork-whisk the egg, ⅓ cup (80 ml) of the reserved pineapple juice, and ¼ cup (60 ml) of the oil in a small bowl. Stir the mixture into the dry ingredients until well mixed. Press the thick batter into the prepared baking pan.

4. Use a fork to blend the remaining 2 tablespoons oil, brown sugar, and the remaining ¼ cup (30 g) flour in a medium bowl until crumbly. Stir in the pineapple and mix well. Spoon over the batter in the pan.

5. Bake for 25 to 30 minutes or until the cake is browned and a tester inserted into the center comes out clean.

6. Cool in the pan on a wire rack for 10 minutes before serving warm or at room temperature. Store covered. Refrigerate after 2 days. This cake can be frozen for up to 3 months.

*If using a glass baking dish, reduce the oven temperature to 375°F (190°C). Bake for 30 minutes or until the cake is browned and a tester inserted into the center comes out clean.

Makes one 11 x 17-inch (28 x 18 cm) cake; 12 servings

Per serving (1 slice): 112 Calories, 17 g Carbohydrate, 2 g Protein, 4 g Fat,
8 mg Cholesterol, 31 mg Sodium, 1 g Fiber
Exchanges: 1 Starch, 1 Fat (1 Carb Choice)

Speedy Chocolate Coffee Cake

Prep time: 10 minutes ◆ Bake time: 35 minutes

Cooking spray

¾ cup (90 g) all-purpose flour

¾ cup (90 g) whole wheat flour

¼ cup (48 g) granulated sugar

¼ cup (20 g) unsweetened cocoa powder, sifted if lumpy

2 tablespoons brown sugar

2 teaspoons baking powder

¼ teaspoon salt

1 cup (245 g) plain Greek yogurt

2 large eggs

¼ cup (60 ml) canola or extra-light olive oil

1 teaspoon vanilla

¼ cup (33 g) chopped nuts

1. Preheat the oven to 350°F (180°C). Spray a 9-inch (23 cm) square baking pan with cooking spray.

2. Stir together the flours, granulated sugar, cocoa powder, brown sugar, baking powder, salt, yogurt, eggs, oil, and vanilla in a large bowl. Beat with a wooden spoon or rubber spatula for about 1 minute, until well blended. Spoon the batter into the prepared baking pan and sprinkle with the nuts.

3. Bake for 35 to 40 minutes or until the cake is browned and a tester inserted into the center comes out clean.

4. Cool in the pan on a wire rack for about 10 minutes before serving warm or at room temperature. Store covered. Refrigerate after 2 days. This cake can be frozen for up to 3 months.

Makes one 9-inch (23 cm) square cake; 9 servings

Per serving (1 slice): 228 Calories, 25 g Carbohydrate, 6 g Protein, 12 g Fat, 47 mg Cholesterol, 91 mg Sodium, 3 g Fiber
Exchanges: 1½ Starch, 2 Fat (1½ Carb Choices)

Mixed Berry Coffee Cake

Prep Time: 10 minutes ◆ Bake Time: 50 minutes

CAKE

Cooking spray

¾ cup (90 g) all-purpose flour

¾ cup (90 g) whole wheat flour

2 teaspoons baking powder

½ teaspoon baking soda

⅔ cup (81 g) unsweetened applesauce

2 large eggs

¼ cup (62 g) plain Greek yogurt

2 tablespoons granulated sugar

1 tablespoon grated lemon zest

2 cups (290 g) assorted mixed fresh or frozen berries (blueberries, blackberries, raspberries)

TOPPING

½ cup (60 g) all-purpose flour

2 tablespoons brown sugar

1 tablespoon granulated sugar

2 tablespoons cold butter, cut into pieces

1. Preheat the oven to 350°F (180°C). Spray a 10-inch (25 cm) springform pan with cooking spray.

2. **To make the cake,** stir together the flours, baking powder, and baking soda in a small bowl.

3. Whisk together the applesauce, eggs, yogurt, granulated sugar, and lemon zest in a large bowl. Add the dry ingredients to the wet ingredients and stir just until blended. Spread the batter into the prepared pan. Sprinkle the mixed berries on top of the batter.

4. **To make the topping,** mix the flour and the brown and granulated sugars in the same small bowl. Use a pastry blender or fork to cut in the butter until the mixture is crumbly. Sprinkle the topping evenly over the berries.

5. Bake for 50 to 55 minutes or until a tester inserted into the center of the cake comes out clean.

6. Cool in the pan on a wire rack for 20 minutes before serving warm or at room temperature. Use a knife to loosen the cake. Remove the sides of the pan, leaving the cake on the bottom. Place the cake on a serving plate. Store covered. Refrigerate after 2 days. This cake can be frozen for up to 3 months.

Makes one 10-inch (25 cm) cake; 12 servings

Per serving (1 slice): 144 Calories, 26 g Carbohydrate, 4 g Protein, 3 g Fat, 36 mg Cholesterol, 80 mg Sodium, 2 g Fiber
Exchanges: 1½ Starch, ½ Fruit, ½ Fat (2 Carb Choices)

Blueberry Cornmeal Scones

Prep time: 10 minutes ◆ Baking time: 25 minutes

¾ cup (150 g) cornmeal

¾ cup (90 g) whole wheat flour

½ cup (60 g) all-purpose flour

¼ cup (48 g) sugar

1 teaspoon baking powder

½ teaspoon baking soda

¼ teaspoon salt

3 tablespoons cold butter, cut into
  pieces

1 cup (145 g) fresh or frozen
  blueberries

2 teaspoons grated lemon zest

⅔ cup (160 ml) buttermilk
  (see page 8)

1 teaspoon vanilla extract

1. Preheat the oven to 400°F (200°C). Line a baking sheet with parchment paper.

2. Whisk together the cornmeal, flours, sugar, baking powder, baking soda, and salt in a medium bowl. Use a pastry blender to cut in the butter until the mixture forms coarse crumbs. Use a rubber spatula to stir in the blueberries and lemon zest until the berries are coated with the flour mixture.

3. Mix the buttermilk and vanilla in a 1-cup (240 ml) glass measuring cup. Add the buttermilk mixture to the dry ingredients and stir just until the dough is moistened and forms a ball.

4. Place the dough on the lined baking sheet and pat into a 9-inch (23 cm) circle. Use a sharp knife to mark the dough into 12 wedges, cutting into but not through the dough.

5. Bake for 25 minutes or until golden brown. Cut into wedges and serve warm. Or cool and store covered for up to 3 days. Freeze for up to 3 months.

6. To reheat, bake uncovered at 350°F (180°C) for 5 to 10 minutes or toast in the toaster oven until warm.

Makes one 9-inch (23 cm) round scone; 12 servings

Per serving (1 wedge): 130 Calories, 23 g Carbohydrate, 3 g Protein, 3 g Fat,
8 mg Cholesterol, 150 mg Sodium, 2 g Fiber
Exchanges: 1½ Starch, ½ Fat (1½ Carb Choices)

Chocolate Chip Scones

Prep time: 10 minutes • Baking time: 20 minutes

1 cup (120 g) all-purpose flour

1 cup (120 g) whole wheat flour

2 tablespoons granulated sugar

2 tablespoons brown sugar

2 teaspoons baking powder

½ teaspoon baking soda

¼ teaspoon salt

3 tablespoons cold butter, cut into pieces

½ cup (123 g) plain Greek yogurt

1 teaspoon vanilla extract

⅓ cup (53 g) mini semisweet or dark chocolate morsels

1. Preheat the oven to 400°F (200°C). Line a baking sheet with parchment paper.

2. Whisk together the flours, sugars, baking powder, baking soda, and salt in a medium bowl. Use a pastry blender to cut in the butter until the mixture forms coarse crumbs. Use a rubber spatula to stir in the yogurt, vanilla, and chocolate morsels until the dough is moistened and forms a ball.

3. Place the dough on the lined baking sheet and pat into a 9-inch (23 cm) circle. Use a sharp knife to mark the dough into 12 wedges, cutting into but not through dough.

4. Bake for 20 minutes or until golden brown. Cut into wedges and serve warm. Or cool and store covered for up to 3 days. Freeze for up to 3 months.

5. To reheat, bake uncovered at 350°F (180°C) for 5 to 10 minutes or toast in the toaster oven until warm.

Makes one 9-inch (23 cm) round scone; 12 servings

Per serving (1 wedge): 146 Calories, 22 g Carbohydrate, 3 g Protein, 5 g Fat,
11 mg Cholesterol, 129 mg Sodium, 2 g Fiber
Exchanges: 1½ Starch, 1 Fat (1½ Carb Choices)

Date Scones

Prep time: 10 minutes • Bake time: 25 minutes

1 cup (120 g) all-purpose flour, plus more for dusting

1 cup (120 g) whole wheat flour

¼ cup (15 g) wheat bran

2 tablespoons brown sugar

2 teaspoons ground cinnamon

1½ teaspoons baking powder

1½ teaspoons baking soda

¼ teaspoon salt

3 tablespoons cold butter, cut into pieces

½ cup (83 g) chopped pitted dates

⅔ cup (162 g) plain Greek yogurt

1 large egg

1 teaspoon vanilla extract

1. Preheat the oven to 350°F (180°C). Line a baking sheet with parchment paper.

2. Whisk together the flours, bran, brown sugar, cinnamon, baking powder, baking soda, and salt in a medium bowl. Use a pastry blender to cut in the butter until the mixture forms coarse crumbs. Stir in the dates until coated with the flour mixture.

3. Fork-whisk the yogurt, egg, and vanilla in a small bowl. Add the yogurt mixture to the dry ingredients and stir just until the dough is moistened and forms a ball.

4. Place the dough on the lined baking sheet. Sprinkle a little flour on the dough and pat it into a 9-inch (23 cm) circle. Use a sharp knife to mark the dough into 12 wedges, cutting into but not all the way through the dough.

5. Bake for 25 to 28 minutes or until browned. Cut into wedges and serve warm. Or cool and store covered for up to 3 days. Freeze for up to 3 months.

6. To reheat, bake uncovered at 350°F (180°C) for 5 to 10 minutes or toast in the toaster oven until warm.

Makes one 9-inch (23 cm) round scone; 12 servings

Per serving (1 wedge): 152 Calories, 24 g Carbohydrate, 4 g Protein, 5 g Fat,
26 mg Cholesterol, 240 mg Sodium, 3 g Fiber
Exchanges: 1 Starch, ½ Fruit, 1 Fat (1½ Carb Choices)

Ginger Scones

Prep time: 10 minutes ◆ Bake time: 20 minutes

1 cup (120 g) all-purpose flour

1 cup (120 g) whole wheat flour

¼ cup (48 g) sugar

1 tablespoon ground ginger

2½ teaspoons baking powder

½ teaspoon baking soda

¼ teaspoon salt

3 tablespoons cold butter, cut into
    pieces

¾ cup (184 g) plain Greek yogurt

1 large egg

2 tablespoons grated orange zest

1 teaspoon vanilla extract

1. Preheat the oven to 400°F (200°C). Line a baking sheet with parchment paper.

2. Whisk together the flours, sugar, ginger, baking powder, baking soda, and salt in a medium bowl. Use a pastry blender to cut in the butter until the mixture forms coarse crumbs.

3. Fork-whisk the yogurt, egg, orange zest, and vanilla in a small bowl. Add the yogurt mixture into the dry ingredients and stir just until the dough is moistened and forms a ball.

4. Place the dough on the lined baking sheet and pat into a 9-inch (23 cm) circle. Use a sharp knife to mark the dough into 12 wedges, cutting into but not through the dough.

5. Bake for 20 minutes or until browned. Cut into wedges and serve warm. Or cool and store covered for up to 3 days. Freeze for up to 3 months.

6. To reheat, bake uncovered at 350°F (180°C) for 5 to 10 minutes or toast in the toaster oven until warm.

Makes one 9-inch (23 cm) round scone; 12 servings

Per serving (1 wedge): 135 Calories, 20 g Carbohydrate, 4 g Protein, 5 g Fat,
27 mg Cholesterol, 137 mg Sodium, 2 g Fiber
Exchanges: 1 Starch, 1 Fat (1 Carb Choice)

Strawberry Scones

Prep time: 10 minutes • Bake time: 20 minutes

1 cup (145 g) fresh strawberries, hulled and cut into ½-inch (13 mm) pieces

3 tablespoons sugar

1 cup (120 g) all-purpose flour, plus more for shaping the dough

1 cup (120 g) whole wheat flour

2 teaspoons baking powder

2 teaspoons grated lemon zest

¼ teaspoon salt

4 tablespoons cold butter, cut into pieces

½ cup (123 g) plain Greek yogurt

1. Toss the strawberries with 1 tablespoon of the sugar; set aside for 15 minutes.

2. Preheat the oven to 400°F (200°C). Line a baking sheet with parchment paper.

3. Whisk together the flours, baking powder, lemon zest, salt, and remaining 2 tablespoons sugar in a large bowl. Use a pastry blender to cut in the butter until the mixture forms coarse crumbs.

4. Add the yogurt and the sweetened strawberries with their liquid. Mix with a rubber spatula until the mixture holds together.

5. With floured hands, shape the dough into a ball. Place the dough on the lined baking sheet and pat into a 9-inch (23 cm) circle. Use a sharp knife to mark the dough into 12 wedges, cutting into but not through the dough.

6. Bake for about 20 minutes or until golden brown. Cut into wedges and serve warm. Or cool and store covered for up to 3 days. Freeze for up to 3 months.

7. To reheat, bake uncovered at 350°F (180°C) for 5 to 10 minutes or toast in the toaster oven until warm.

Makes one 9-inch (23 cm) round scone; 12 servings

Per serving (1 wedge): 144 Calories, 23 g Carbohydrate, 3 g Protein, 5 g Fat, 13 mg Cholesterol, 84 mg Sodium, 2 g Fiber
Exchanges: 1½ Starch, 1 Fat (1½ Carb Choices)

Fruit Desserts

Tips & Tricks

· · · · · · · · · · ·

» There's a wide variety of excellent fruit-based desserts in this section. Some are quick, taking less than 5 minutes to make, while others require more lengthy preparation and cooking time. Look for frozen desserts as well as baked crisps.

» The recipes range from easy to elegant. Speedy Fruit Crisp (page 145) is great for kids, and you can make it with almost any fruit you wish. Apple-Nut Torte (page 142) or Baked Meringue Pears (page 151) are lovely ways to end a dinner party with friends.

» Made ahead, many of these recipes are also perfect for packed lunches and snacks. The Light and Fruity Shake (page 160) is great for breakfast!

Microwave Applesauce

Prep time: 10 minutes ◆ Cook time: 20 minutes

6 Golden Delicious apples, peeled, cored, and sliced (about 8 cups/ 1 kg)

1 tablespoon sugar

2 teaspoons grated lemon zest

2 teaspoons fresh lemon juice

¾ teaspoon ground cinnamon

1. Place the apple slices and ¼ cup (60 ml) water into a 3-quart (3 L) microwave-safe bowl. Cover and microwave on high for 15 minutes, stirring and rotating every 5 minutes, until the apples are tender.

2. Stir in the sugar, lemon zest and juice, and cinnamon. Let stand, covered, for 5 minutes, then mash by hand with a potato masher or purée in a food processor. Serve warm or chilled.

> **Variations:** *To make chunky applesauce, peel and chop 1 apple; mix with 1 tablespoon water in a small microwave-safe bowl. Cover and microwave for 3 minutes, stirring after 1½ minutes or until the apple chunks are tender. Add to the mashed or puréed applesauce.*
>
> *To make raspberry applesauce, add 1 cup (125 g) fresh or frozen raspberries immediately after removing the applesauce from the microwave. Cover and let stand for 5 minutes. Serve warm or chilled.*

Makes 3 cups (949 g); 6 servings

Per serving (½ cup/158 g): 86 Calories, 24 g Carbohydrate, 0 g Protein, 0 g Fat, 0 mg Cholesterol, 0.5 mg Sodium, 4 g Fiber
Exchanges: 1½ Fruit (1½ Carb Choices)

Simple Baked Apples

Prep time: 10 minutes ◆ Bake time: 8 or 25 minutes ◆ Resting time: 10 minutes

Cooking spray

4 medium Honeycrisp or Jonagold apples (Gala and Golden Delicious also work well)

2 tablespoons grated lemon zest

2 teaspoons fresh lemon juice

2 teaspoons ground cinnamon

1 teaspoon ground nutmeg

2 tablespoons raisins (optional)

½ cup (120 ml) unsweetened apple juice or cider

1. Spray a 9-inch (23 cm) square glass baking dish with cooking spray.

2. Remove about 1 inch (2.5 cm) peel from the top of each apple. Using the end of the peeler or a knife, cut around the stem, and remove the stem, and core the apple.

3. Sprinkle the inside and peeled top section of each apple with about ½ tablespoon lemon zest, ½ teaspoon lemon juice, ½ teaspoon cinnamon, and ¼ teaspoon nutmeg. If desired, stuff each apple with ½ tablespoon raisins.

4. Place the apples into the prepared baking dish; pour the apple juice over each apple, making sure that some juice goes into the cavity of each apple.

5. **To microwave:** Cover the apples with a lid or plastic wrap. Microwave on high for 8 to 12 minutes, rotating the apples every 3 minutes and basting with juices, until tender. Let rest for 10 minutes before serving.

6. **To bake:** Preheat the oven to 400°F (200°C). Cover the apples with foil and bake for 25 minutes, basting the apples with juices 2 or 3 times, until tender. Let rest for 10 minutes before serving.

Makes 4 baked apples; 4 servings

Per serving (1 baked apple): 103 Calories, 28 g Carbohydrate, 0 g Protein, 0 g Fat,
0 mg Cholesterol, 3 mg Sodium, 5 g Fiber
Exchanges: 2 Fruit (2 Carb Choices)

Apple-Berry Yogurt Dessert

Prep time: 5 minutes ◆ *Chilling time: 30 minutes*

2 cups (488 g) unsweetened
applesauce

1 cup (245 g) plain Greek yogurt

2 tablespoons honey

1 cup (125 g) fresh or frozen
raspberries

1. Mix together the applesauce, yogurt, and honey in a medium bowl. Gently stir the in raspberries, reserving a few for garnish.

2. Refrigerate for about 30 minutes or until ready to serve. Cover and refrigerate leftovers.

Makes 4 cups (913 g); 8 servings

Per serving (½ cup/114 g): 96 Calories, 17 g Carbohydrate, 2 g Protein, 3 g Fat,
9 mg Cholesterol, 14 mg Sodium, 1 g Fiber
Exchanges: 1 Fruit, ½ Fat (1 Carb Choice)

Apple-Nut Torte

Prep time: 10 minutes ◆ Bake time: 20 minutes

Cooking spray

¼ cup (33 g) chopped nuts

1 large egg, at room temperature

¼ cup (48 g) sugar

¼ cup (30 g) whole wheat flour

1¼ teaspoons baking powder

1½ cups (188 g) peeled, cored, and chopped Fuji or Honeycrisp apple (1 large)

1 teaspoon vanilla extract

Whipped Topping (page 91; optional)

Confectioners' sugar (optional)

1. Preheat the oven to 375°F (190°C). Spray an 8-inch (20 cm) pie plate with cooking spray.

2. Place the nuts in a small baking pan and bake for 3 to 5 minutes until toasted; set aside.

3. Use an electric mixer at medium speed to beat the egg in a medium bowl until light and frothy. Gradually beat in the sugar until thick and lemon colored, about 2 minutes; scrape down the sides of the bowl.

4. Use a rubber spatula to stir in the flour, baking powder, chopped apple, vanilla, and toasted nuts; mix until well blended. Spoon the batter into the prepared pan.

5. Bake for 20 minutes or until the cake is browned and a tester inserted into the center comes out clean.

6. Cool on a wire rack for 10 minutes. Cut into wedges and serve warm with Whipped Topping or lightly sprinkled with confectioners' sugar, if desired. Cover and refrigerate leftovers.

Makes one 8-inch (20 cm) torte; 8 servings

Per serving (1 wedge): 74 Calories, 11 g Carbohydrate, 2 g Protein, 3 g Fat, 22 mg Cholesterol, 8 mg Sodium, 1 g Fiber
Exchanges: ½ Starch, ½ Fruit, ½ Fat (1 Carb Choice)

Fruit with Yogurt Cream

Prep Time: 5 minutes

½ cup (123 g) plain Greek yogurt or Yogurt Cheese (page 96)

2 teaspoons grated orange zest

1 tablespoon fresh orange juice

1 tablespoon almond-flavored syrup (such as Torani or DaVinci)

1 teaspoon brown sugar

½ teaspoon ground cinnamon

¼ teaspoon ground nutmeg

2 cups (300 g) sliced bananas, strawberries, peaches, or a mixture

¼ cup (29 g) toasted sliced almonds (optional)

1. Mix together the yogurt, orange zest and juice, almond syrup, brown sugar, cinnamon, and nutmeg in a medium bowl until smooth and creamy.

2. Stir in the fruit until well coated with the yogurt mixture. If desired, sprinkle with toasted almonds. Cover and refrigerate until ready to serve.

Makes 2 cups (453 g); 4 servings

Per serving (½ cup): 125 Calories, 24 g Carbohydrate, 3 g Protein, 3 g Fat, 9 mg Cholesterol, 15 mg Sodium, 2 g Fiber
Exchanges: ½ Starch, 1 Fruit, ½ Fat (1½ Carb Choices)

Speedy Fruit Crisp

Prep time: 10 minutes ◆ *Bake time: 12 or 30 minutes*

FILLING

Cooking spray

1 pound (454 g) fruit of your choice*

1 tablespoon grated lemon zest

1 tablespoon fresh lemon juice

1 tablespoon granulated sugar

2 teaspoons cornstarch

TOPPING

¼ cup (30 g) whole wheat flour

¼ cup (23 g) old-fashioned rolled oats

¼ cup (33 g) chopped nuts

3 tablespoons canola or extra-light olive oil

1 tablespoon brown sugar

1 teaspoon ground cinnamon

½ teaspoon ground nutmeg

Whipped Topping (page 91) or Easy Fat-Free Topping (page 92), to serve (optional)

1. Spray an 8-inch glass pie plate with cooking spray. Mix the fruit, lemon zest and juice, granulated sugar, and cornstarch in a large bowl; spoon into the prepared pie plate.

2. In the same bowl, mix together the flour, oats, nuts, oil, brown sugar, cinnamon, and nutmeg until well blended; sprinkle over the fruit filling.

3. **To microwave:** Microwave on high for 12 to 15 minutes, rotating every 4 minutes, until the fruit is tender. Let stand for 15 minutes before serving.

4. **To bake:** Preheat the oven to 400°F (200°C). Bake for 30 to 40 minutes, until the top is browned and the fruit is tender.

5. If desired, serve with the topping of choice.

*Suggested Fruits: 3 to 4 apples, peeled, cored and thinly sliced
3 to 4 ripe pears, peeled, cored, and thinly sliced
6 to 8 ripe medium peaches, peeled, pitted, and thinly sliced
2 cups (290 g) strawberries, hulled and sliced, mixed with 2 cups
  (240 g) finely diced trimmed rhubarb
4 medium bananas, peeled and thinly sliced
6 to 8 ripe medium plums, pitted and thinly sliced
6 to 8 ripe medium nectarines, pitted and thinly sliced
Two 16-ounce (454 g) cans juice-packed fruit of your choice, drained

Makes one 8-inch (20 cm) crisp; 8 servings

Per serving (½ cup/162 g): 219 Calories, 38 g Carbohydrate, 2 g Protein, 8 g Fat,
0 mg Cholesterol, 1 mg Sodium, 4 g Fiber
Exchanges: ½ Starch, 2 Fruit, 1½ Fat (2½ Carb Choices)

Blueberry-Nectarine Crisp

Prep time: 10 minutes • Bake time: 20 minutes

FILLING

Cooking spray

2 ripe medium nectarines, pitted
  and sliced

2 cups (290 g) fresh blueberries

TOPPING

¼ cup (30 g) all-purpose flour

¼ cup (30 g) whole wheat flour

¼ cup (23 g) old-fashioned rolled
  oats

½ teaspoon cinnamon

¼ teaspoon nutmeg

3 tablespoons canola or extra-light
  olive oil

2 tablespoons brown sugar

Whipped Topping (page 91) or
  Easy Fat-Free Topping (page 92),
  to serve (optional)

1. Preheat the oven to 400°F (200°C). Spray a 9-inch (23 cm) square glass baking dish with cooking spray.

2. **To make the filling,** place the nectarine slices on the bottom of the prepared baking dish. Cover with the blueberries.

3. **To make the topping,** mix the flours, oats, cinnamon, nutmeg, oil, and brown sugar in a small bowl until well blended. Sprinkle the mixture over the fruits.

4. Bake for 20 to 25 minutes or until browned. Cool on a wire rack for 15 minutes before serving with the topping of your choice, if desired.

Makes one 9-inch (23 cm) square crisp; 8 servings

Per serving (½ cup/92 g): 132 Calories, 20 g Carbohydrate, 2 g Protein, 6 g Fat,
0 mg Cholesterol, 0.6 mg Sodium, 2 g Fiber
Exchanges: ½ Starch, ½ Fruit, 1 Fat (1 Carb Choice)

Peach Snowcaps

Prep time: 10 minutes • Bake time: 15 minutes • Standing time: 5 minutes

Cooking spray

4 canned juice-packed peach halves, drained and patted dry

2 large egg whites, at room temperature

½ teaspoon almond extract

¼ teaspoon cream of tartar

2 tablespoons sugar

2 tablespoons slivered almonds

1. Preheat the oven to 325°F (165°C). Spray a baking sheet with cooking spray.

2. Place the peaches cut side down on the prepared baking sheet.

3. Use an electric mixer at high speed to beat the egg whites, almond extract, and cream of tartar in a medium bowl until soft peaks form. Gradually beat in the sugar, beating until the whites form stiff peaks when the beaters are lifted.

4. Cover each peach half with the meringue, then top evenly with slivered almonds.

5. Bake for 15 to 20 minutes, until the meringue is browned. Let stand for 5 minutes before serving.

Makes 4 snowcaps; 4 servings

Per serving (1 peach half): 90 Calories, 17 g Carbohydrate, 3 g Protein, 2 g Fat,
0 mg Cholesterol, 31 mg Sodium, 2 g Fiber
Exchanges: 1 Fruit (1 Carb Choice)

Peach Melba Parfait

Prep time: 10 minutes ◆ Chilling time: 30 minutes

3 peaches, peeled,* pitted, and thinly sliced**

2 teaspoons fresh lemon juice

2 cups (490 g) plain Greek yogurt

2 tablespoons sugar-free vanilla syrup (such as Torani, DaVinci, or Amoretti)

½ cup (160 g) no-sugar-added raspberry jam

4 small sprigs fresh mint (optional)

1. Gently mix the sliced peaches and lemon juice in a medium bowl.

2. In a small bowl, mix together the yogurt and vanilla syrup. Cover both bowls and refrigerate for at least 30 minutes to allow the flavors to blend.

3. To serve, microwave the jam on high for about 30 seconds; stir. In 8 ramekins or dessert glasses, evenly layer half of the peaches, half of the yogurt mixture, and half of the raspberry jam; repeat the layers, ending with the jam. Garnish with mint sprig, if desired.

*To peel peaches, plunge them into a pot of boiling water for 30 seconds; drain. Cool briefly under cold water. The peel should slide off easily.
**One 16-ounce (454 g) can juice-packed sliced peaches, drained, can be substituted for the fresh peaches. There's no need to mix the canned peaches with lemon juice.

Makes 8 parfaits; 8 servings

Per serving (1 ramekin): 110 Calories, 14 g Carbohydrate, 4 g Protein, 6 g Fat,
19 mg Cholesterol, 28 mg Sodium, 1 g Fiber
Exchanges: ½ Fruit, ½ Nonfat Milk, 1 Fat (1 Carb Choice)

Strawberry-Rhubarb Dessert

Prep time: 10 minutes ◆ Cook time: 6 minutes ◆ Chilling time: 30 minutes

¼ cup (48 g) sugar

½ teaspoon ground cinnamon

2 teaspoons grated lemon zest

1 pound (454 g) fresh rhubarb stalks (4 to 8 stalks), trimmed and cut into 1-inch (2.5 cm) pieces

2 cups (290 g) fresh strawberries, hulled and halved

2 tablespoons no-sugar-added strawberry jam

Whipped Topping (page 91) or Easy Fat-Free Topping (page 92), to serve (optional)

1. Mix the sugar, cinnamon, lemon zest, and ¼ cup (60 ml) water in a 4-cup (960 ml) glass measuring cup. Microwave on high for 1 minute; stir. Microwave for another minute, until the sugar dissolves.

2. Stir in the rhubarb, cover, and microwave on medium-high for 4 to 6 minutes, stirring every 2 minutes, until the rhubarb is soft and tender.

3. Carefully stir the strawberries and jam into the rhubarb mixture until well mixed.

4. Spoon evenly into 8 dessert bowls and refrigerate for about 30 minutes before serving. If desired, serve with the topping of your choice.

Makes 4 cups (387 g); 8 servings

Per serving (½ cup/48 g): 44 Calories, 12 g Carbohydrate, 0.5 g Protein, 0 g Fat, 0 mg Cholesterol, 2 mg Sodium, 2 g Fiber
Exchanges: 1 Fruit (1 Carb Choice)

Baked Meringue Pears

Prep time: 15 minutes • Cook time: 15 minutes • Bake time: 15 minutes

Cooking spray

2 large firm-ripe Anjou pears, peeled, halved lengthwise, and cored

2 teaspoons granulated sugar

2 tablespoons grated lemon zest

¼ cup (60 ml) dry vermouth or white wine

1 large egg white, at room temperature

⅛ teaspoon cream of tartar

2 tablespoons confectioners' sugar

½ teaspoon almond extract

1. Preheat the oven to 350°F (180°C). Spray a baking sheet with cooking spray.

2. Arrange the pears cut-side up in a 9-inch (23 cm) glass pie plate. Sprinkle each half with ½ teaspoon granulated sugar and 1½ teaspoons lemon zest. Pour the vermouth over the pears and microwave on high for 10 to 15 minutes, until the pears are tender, rotating and basting every 5 minutes.

3. Use a slotted spoon to transfer the pear halves, cut side up, to the prepared baking sheet. Reserve the cooking liquid; set aside.

4. Use an electric mixer at high speed to beat the egg white and cream of tartar in a small bowl until soft peaks form. Gradually beat in the confectioners' sugar and almond extract, beating until stiff peaks form when the beaters are lifted.

5. Cover each pear completely with meringue. Bake for 10 to 15 minutes or until the meringue is browned.

6. While the pears are baking, place the reserved liquid in a glass measuring cup and microwave on high for 2 minutes; stir. Microwave on medium-high until syrupy, 1 to 2 more minutes.

7. Place the pear halves on plates and spoon the warm syrup over each; serve warm or at room temperature.

Makes 4 pear halves; 4 servings

Per serving (1 pear half): 121 Calories, 25 g Carbohydrate, 1 g Protein, 0 g Fat, 0 mg Cholesterol, 16 mg Sodium, 4 g Fiber
Exchanges: ½ Starch, 1 Fruit (1½ Carb Choices)

Berry Baked Pears

Prep time: 5 minutes ◆ Bake time: 35 minutes ◆ Resting time: 15 minutes

Cooking spray

4 firm-ripe Anjou pears, peeled, halved lengthwise, and cored

¼ cup (80 g) no-sugar-added raspberry jam

2 teaspoons fresh lemon juice

1 teaspoon vanilla extract

⅓ cup (38 g) sliced almonds

1 tablespoon butter, cut into tiny pieces

1 cup (245 g) vanilla Greek yogurt (optional)

1. Preheat the oven to 325°F (165°C). Spray a 13 x 9 x 2-inch (33 x 23 x 5) glass baking dish with cooking spray.

2. Arrange the pear halves cut side down in the prepared dish.

3. Mix the jam, lemon juice, and vanilla in a small bowl; drizzle over the pears. Sprinkle with the almonds and dot with butter.

4. Bake for 35 to 40 minutes, basting three times, until the pears are tender.

5. Let rest for 15 minutes before serving warm or, if desired, cold with yogurt. Store leftovers covered in the refrigerator.

Makes 8 pear halves; 8 servings

Per serving (1 pear half): 154 Calories, 21 g Carbohydrate, 3 g Protein, 6 g Fat, 13 mg Cholesterol, 27 mg Sodium, 4 g Fiber
Exchanges: 1½ Fruit, 1 Fat (1½ Carb Choices)

Pineapple Sherbet

Prep time: 10 minutes • Freezing time: 2 hours • Standing time: 10 minutes

One 20-ounce (567 g) can juice-packed pineapple chunks, drained, juice reserved

¼ cup (60 ml) nonfat milk

1. Arrange the pineapple chunks in an even layer on a baking sheet. Place the baking sheet in the freezer until the pineapple chunks are frozen, about 1 hour.

2. With the motor running, gradually drop the frozen pineapple chunks into a food processor and process for 1 minute; scrape down the sides. Add the reserved pineapple juice and milk with the motor running. Process for about 30 seconds, scraping down the sides, until smooth.

3. Pour the mixture into a 9-inch (23 cm) square baking dish, cover and freeze for about 1 hour, until very firm.

4. Remove from the freezer and let stand for about 10 minutes. Cut into chunks and process in the food processor until smooth, scraping down the sides occasionally.

5. Serve immediately or spoon into a covered freezer-safe container and freeze for up to 2 weeks. Remove from the freezer about 15 minutes before serving to soften.

> **Variations:** *One 16-ounce (454 g) can juice-packed peaches, apricots, or pears may be substituted. Drain, reserve the juice, and cut the fruit into 1-inch (2.5 cm) chunks. Add half of the reserved juice along with the milk when processing.*
>
> *Two cups of any fresh fruit (peeled, if necessary) may be substituted. Cut the fruit into chunks before freezing on a baking sheet. Add ½ cup (120 ml) fruit juice along with the milk when processing.*

Makes 4 cups (628 g); 8 servings

Per serving (½ cup/79 g): 43 Calories, 10 g Carbohydrate, 0 g Protein, 0 g Fat,
0 mg Cholesterol, 9 mg Sodium, 1 g Fiber
Exchanges: ½ Fruit (½ Carb Choice)

Peachy Ice Cream

Prep time: 70 minutes ◆ Freezing time: 2 hours

2 cups (310 g) peeled,* pitted, and finely chopped peaches (3 to 4 medium)

¼ cup (48 g) sugar

1 tablespoon grated lemon zest

1 tablespoon fresh lemon juice

2 cups (480 ml) fat-free evaporated milk, chilled

1 cup (240 ml) nonfat milk

½ cup (150 g) sweetened condensed milk

½ cup (160 g) no-sugar-added raspberry jam, stirred smooth

*To peel peaches, plunge them into a pot of boiling water for 30 seconds; drain. Cool briefly under cold water. The peel should slide off easily.

1. Mix the peaches, sugar, and lemon zest and juice in a medium bowl. Cover and refrigerate for 1 hour, stirring frequently.

2. Shake the can of evaporated milk and pour it into a large bowl. Add the nonfat milk and sweetened condensed milk. Use an electric mixer at medium speed (or a whisk) to beat the ingredients until well blended, scraping down the sides of the bowl occasionally. Use a rubber spatula to stir in the peach mixture and raspberry jam until well mixed.

3. Churn in an ice cream machine according to the manufacturer's instructions. Transfer to a freezer-safe container; cover and freeze for about 1 hour before serving.

Makes 7½ cups (1,126 g); 10 servings

Per serving (¾ cup/113 g): 97 Calories, 19 g Carbohydrate, 6 g Protein, 0 g Fat, 2 mg Cholesterol, 90 mg Sodium, 1 g Fiber
Exchanges: 1 Nonfat Milk (1 Carb Choice)

Strawberry Sorbet

Prep time: 10 minutes ◆ Freezing time: 2 hours ◆ Standing time: 15 minutes

2 cups (290 g) fresh strawberries, hulled*

1 tablespoon grated orange zest

1 cup (240 ml) fresh orange juice

¼ cup (48 g) sugar

2 tablespoons fresh lemon juice

*If using frozen strawberries, reduce the freezing time to about 1 hour.

1. Place the strawberries, orange zest and juice, and sugar into a food processor. Process until smooth; scrape down the sides. Add the lemon juice and 1 cup (240 ml) water. Pulse twice; scrape down the sides.

2. Pour the mixture into a 9 x 5 x 3-inch (23 x 13 x 8 cm) loaf pan. Cover and freeze until firm, 2 to 3 hours.

3. Remove from the freezer and let stand for 15 minutes. Cut into chunks. With the motor running, gradually drop the chunks into the food processor; process until smooth, scraping down the sides occasionally.

4. Serve immediately or spoon into a covered, freezer-safe container and freeze until firm. Remove from the freezer about 20 minutes before serving to soften.

Makes 4 cups (882 g); 8 servings

Per serving (½ cup/110 g): 87 Calories, 23 g Carbohydrate, 1 g Protein, 0 g Fat, 0 mg Cholesterol, 2 mg Sodium, 2 g Fiber
Exchanges: 1½ Fruit (1½ Carb Choices)

Frozen Yogurt Pops

Prep time: 5 minutes • Freezing time: 2 hours

2 cups (490 g) plain Greek yogurt

2 tablespoons sugar-free vanilla syrup (such as Torani or Amoretti)

⅔ cup (212 g) no-sugar-added strawberry jam

1. Use an electric mixer at medium speed, a blender, or a food processor to blend the ingredients until frothy and well mixed, about 30 seconds.

2. Evenly pour the mixture into a six-piece popsicle mold, or six 3-ounce (90 ml) foil or paper baking cups on a baking sheet. Freeze for about 1 hour until beginning to firm up.

3. Insert wooden sticks into the center of each cup and freeze until the yogurt mixture is firm, about 1 hour. Remove the baking cups before eating.

Makes 6 frozen pops; 6 servings

Per serving (1 frozen pop): 165 Calories, 27 g Carbohydrate, 5 g Protein, 7 g Fat,
25 mg Cholesterol, 38 mg Sodium, 0 g Fiber
Exchanges: 1½ Fruit, ½ Nonfat Milk, 1 Fat (2 Carb Choices)

Light and Fruity Shake

Prep time: 3 minutes

1 cup (240 ml) nonfat milk

1 small ripe banana, thinly sliced

1 tablespoon chocolate extract*

4 or 5 ice cubes

1. Blend the milk, banana, and chocolate extract in a blender or food processor. Scrape down the sides. With the motor running, add the ice cubes one at a time, and blend until smooth.

2. Pour into glasses and serve immediately.

*1 tablespoon strawberry extract may be substituted.

Makes 2 cups (360 g); 2 servings

Per serving (1 cup/180 g): 105 Calories, 18 g Carbohydrate, 5 g Protein, 0 g Fat,
2 mg Cholesterol, 52 mg Sodium, 1 g Fiber
Exchanges: ½ Fruit, ½ Nonfat Milk (1 Carb Choice)

Homemade Dried Fruit

Prep time: 20 minutes Bake time: 4 hours

¼ cup (60 ml) fresh lemon juice

2 tablespoons grated lemon zest

4 large apples or pears, unpeeled, cored, quartered, and cut into ¼-inch (6 mm) slices

1. Preheat the oven to 170°F (75°C) or the lowest temperature setting.

2. Mix 4 cups (960 ml) water and the lemon juice in a large bowl.

3. Drop the fruit slices into the liquid and soak for 3 minutes. Drain and pat dry.

4. Arrange the fruit slices in a single layer on baking sheets, and place in the oven. Leave the door ajar about 1 inch (2.5 cm). If necessary, prop the door open with a wooden spoon.

5. Let dry in the oven for 4 to 6 hours, rotating the baking sheets and turning the slices over every 2 hours until they are leathery and dry to the touch, yet pliable.

6. Cool and store in a tightly covered container.

Makes 3 cups (1,044 g); 6 servings

Per serving (½ cup/174 g): 89 Calories, 24 g Carbohydrate, 1 g Protein, 0 g Fat,
0 mg Cholesterol, 3 mg Sodium, 4 g Fiber
Exchanges: 1½ Fruit (1½ Carb Choices)

Ambrosia Bars

Prep time: 10 minutes ◆ Chilling time: 2 hours

½ cup (65 g) chopped walnuts

One 8-ounce (227 g) can juice-packed crushed pineapple

Three 0.25-ounce (7 g) envelopes unflavored gelatin

½ cup (85 g) raisins

¼ cup (18 g) unsweetened shredded coconut

1. Place the walnuts in an even layer in a glass pie plate. Microwave on high for about 3 minutes, until toasted, stirring every 30 seconds; set aside.

2. Drain the pineapple into a 4-cup (960 ml) glass measuring cup. Add enough water to measure 1 cup (240 ml) liquid. Reserve the crushed pineapple.

3. Sprinkle the gelatin over the liquid and let soften 1 minute. Stir. Microwave on high for about 1 minute; stir until the gelatin is completely dissolved. Let rest for 1 minute.

4. Stir in the reserved crushed pineapple, raisins, toasted walnuts, and coconut. Mix well, then turn into an 8- or 9-inch (20 or 23 cm) square glass baking dish.

5. Refrigerate for about 2 hours or until firm. Cut into 16 bars. Cover and refrigerate leftovers.

Makes 16 bars

Per serving (2 bars): 104 Calories, 13 g Carbohydrate, 2 g Protein, 6 g Fat,
0 mg Cholesterol, 9 mg Sodium, 2 g Fiber
Exchanges: 1 Fruit, 1 Fat (1 Carb Choice)

Muffins

Tips & Tricks

» Muffins are a treat any time of day. We usually associate muffins with breakfast, but they are delectable for lunch or dinner when served with a salad or soup. They're terrific for a quick and healthy snack, since they're filling and easy to bake.

» Muffins fit the bill when you are short on time but want something homemade. They are quick and simple to make with very little fuss. There's no need to take out the electric mixer for these goodies. To prep them in advance, assemble and mix the dry ingredients in one bowl and mix the wet ingredients in another bowl ahead of time. When ready to bake, combine the dry and wet ingredients and promptly bake, unless the recipe states otherwise.

» The muffin recipes in this book use whole wheat flour. Whole wheat flour adds fiber, which is a necessary nutrient. If you prefer lighter muffins, use a mixture of whole wheat pastry flour and all-purpose flour. Whole wheat pastry flour can be found in the baking aisle in most food stores. Some of my recipes call for old-fashioned rolled oats, which is a whole grain and high in soluble fiber that is good for our hearts.

» This section contains nineteen muffin recipes, all low in added sugar and with no artificial sweeteners. Instead, I use a minimal amount of sugar and fruit or fruit juice for added sweetness. I add citrus zest to enhance the flavor and give that "little something extra" in every bite.

» Here are a few suggestions for delicious muffins. Muffins should not be overmixed, because it will make them tough. Liquid ingredients should be added to dry ingredients and mixed just enough to moisten all of the flour. The batter should be rough and lumpy. When adding nuts or fruit, mix them with the flour before adding to the liquids to avoid extra stirring and to keep them from sinking.

» Knobs, peaks, or tunnels in your muffins are caused by overmixing or oven temperatures that are too low or too high. Spray muffin pans with cooking spray or line them with paper baking cups before adding the batter. When filling prepared muffin pans, fill them about two-thirds full. Too much batter will cause the muffins to spill over. Too little batter will result in flat, short muffins.

» Unless the recipe specifies, muffins should be removed from the pan immediately and served right away, or put on wire racks to cool. When cool, store them covered at room temperature or freeze them for up to 3 months.

» Many of my muffin recipes contain fruit for added sweetness; therefore, they can't remain at room temperature for more than 2 days. Fruit added to baked items makes them moister, sweeter, and more flavorful. But if left at room temperature too long, they will spoil. Refrigeration helps them retain their freshness. Just reheat them in the microwave or toaster oven before serving.

Maple Apple Muffins

Prep time: 10 minutes • Bake time: 20 minutes

Cooking spray

¾ cup (90 g) whole wheat flour

½ cup (60 g) all-purpose flour

1 cup (90 g) old-fashioned rolled oats

1 tablespoon baking powder

1 teaspoon ground cinnamon

¼ teaspoon ground nutmeg

¼ teaspoon salt

1 cup (125 g) peeled, cored, and chopped Honeycrisp or Gala apple (1 medium)

1 cup (240 ml) nonfat milk

1 large egg

3 tablespoons brown sugar

3 tablespoons canola or extra-light olive oil

1 teaspoon maple extract

1. Preheat the oven to 400°F (200°C). Spray 12 muffin cups with cooking spray or line them with paper baking cups.

2. Stir together the flours, oats, baking powder, cinnamon, nutmeg, and salt in a large bowl; stir in the apple until coated with the flour mixture.

3. Whisk together the milk, egg, brown sugar, oil, and maple extract in a small bowl. Add the wet ingredients to the dry ingredients and stir just until blended; do not overmix.

4. Spoon the batter into the prepared muffin cups. Bake for 20 to 25 minutes or until the muffins are browned and a tester inserted into the center comes out clean.

5. Immediately remove the muffins from the pan. Serve warm, or cool on a wire rack. Store covered. Refrigerate after 2 days or freeze for up to 3 months.

Makes 12 muffins; 12 servings

Per serving (1 muffin): 136 Calories, 21 g Carbohydrate, 4 g Protein, 5 g Fat,
15 mg Cholesterol, 65 mg Sodium, 2 g Fiber
Exchanges: 1½ Starch, 1 Fat (1½ Carb Choices)

Apple Spice Muffins

Prep time: 10 minutes ◆ Bake time: 20 minutes

Cooking spray

¾ cup (90 g) all-purpose flour

½ cup (60 g) whole wheat flour

¾ cup (68 g) old-fashioned rolled oats

2 tablespoons sugar

1 tablespoon baking powder

½ teaspoon ground cinnamon

¼ teaspoon ground ginger

¼ teaspoon salt

1 medium apple, unpeeled and finely chopped

3 tablespoons raisins

1 large egg

¾ cup (180 ml) nonfat milk

2 tablespoons canola or extra-light olive oil

1 teaspoon vanilla extract

1. Preheat the oven to 400°F (200°C). Spray 12 muffin cups with cooking spray or line them with paper baking cups.

2. Stir together the flours, oats, sugar, baking powder, cinnamon, ginger, and salt in a large bowl. Stir in the apple and raisins until coated with flour mixture.

3. Whisk together the egg, milk, oil, and vanilla in a small bowl. Add the wet ingredients to the dry ingredients and mix just until blended; do not overmix.

4. Spoon the batter into the prepared muffin cups. Bake for 20 minutes or until the muffins are browned and a tester inserted into the center comes out clean.

5. Immediately remove the muffins from the pan. Serve warm or cool on a wire rack. Store covered. Refrigerate after 2 days or freeze for up to 3 months.

Makes 12 muffins; 12 servings

Per serving (1 muffin): 120 Calories, 20 g Carbohydrate, 3 g Protein, 3 g Fat,
15 mg Cholesterol, 62 mg Sodium, 2 g Fiber
Exchanges: 1 Starch, ½ Fat (1 Carb Choice)

Banana–Poppy Seed Muffins

Prep time: 10 minutes ◆ Bake time: 20 minutes

Cooking spray

1 cup (120 g) all-purpose flour

1 cup (120 g) whole wheat flour

2 tablespoons poppy seeds

2 tablespoons sugar

1 tablespoon baking powder

⅛ teaspoon salt

1 cup (240 ml) buttermilk
(see page 8)

½ cup (112 g) mashed ripe banana
(1 medium)

3 tablespoons canola or extra-light
olive oil

1 large egg

1 tablespoon grated lemon zest

12 slices ripe banana (optional)

1. Preheat the oven to 400°F (200°C). Spray 12 muffin cups with cooking spray or line them with paper baking cups.

2. Stir together the flours, poppy seeds, sugar, baking powder, and salt in a large bowl.

3. Whisk together the buttermilk, banana, oil, egg, and lemon zest in a medium bowl. Add the wet ingredients to the dry ingredients and stir just until blended; do not overmix.

4. Spoon the batter into the prepared muffin cups. Top each muffin with a slice of banana, if desired. Bake for 20 minutes or until a tester inserted into the center comes out clean.

5. Immediately remove the muffins from the pan. Serve warm, or cool on a wire rack. Store covered. Refrigerate after 2 days or freeze for up to 3 months.

Makes 12 muffins; 12 servings

Per serving (1 muffin): 138 Calories, 21 g Carbohydrate, 4 g Protein, 5 g Fat,
15 mg Cholesterol, 69 mg Sodium, 2 g Fiber
Exchanges: 1½ Starch, 1 Fat (1½ Carb Choices)

Blueberry Muffins

Prep time: 10 minutes • Bake time: 20 minutes

Cooking spray

1 cup (120 g) all-purpose flour

1 cup (120 g) whole wheat flour

3 tablespoons sugar

1 tablespoon baking powder

½ teaspoon ground nutmeg

¼ teaspoon salt

1 cup (145 g) fresh or frozen
blueberries

1 cup (240 ml) buttermilk
(see page 8)

1 large egg

3 tablespoons canola or extra-light
olive oil

1 tablespoon grated lemon zest

1. Preheat the oven to 400°F (200°C). Spray 12 muffin cups with cooking spray or line them with paper baking cups.

2. Stir together the flours, sugar, baking powder, nutmeg, and salt in a large bowl. Gently stir in the blueberries until coated with the flour mixture.

3. Whisk the buttermilk, egg, oil, and lemon zest in a small bowl. Add the wet ingredients to the dry ingredients and stir just until blended; do not overmix.

4. Spoon the batter into the prepared muffin cups. Bake for 20 to 25 minutes or until the muffins are browned and a tester inserted into the center comes out clean.

5. Immediately remove the muffins from the pan. Serve warm, or cool on a wire rack. Store covered. Refrigerate after 2 days or freeze for up to 3 months.

Makes 12 muffins; 12 servings

Per serving (1 muffin): 132 Calories, 21 g Carbohydrate, 4 g Protein, 4 g Fat,
15 mg Cholesterol, 92 mg Sodium, 2 g Fiber
Exchanges: 1½ Starch, 1 Fat (1½ Carb Choices)

Chocolate Chip Muffins

Prep time: 10 minutes ◆ Bake time: 15 minutes

Cooking spray

1 cup (120 g) all-purpose flour

1 cup (120 g) whole wheat flour

1 tablespoon baking powder

1 tablespoon brown sugar

1 tablespoon granulated sugar

¼ teaspoon salt

⅓ cup (53 g) mini semisweet or dark chocolate morsels

½ cup (120 ml) fresh orange juice

½ cup (120 ml) nonfat milk

1 large egg

3 tablespoons canola or extra-light olive oil

1 teaspoon vanilla extract

1 teaspoon butter extract

1. Preheat the oven to 400°F (200°C). Spray 12 muffin cups with cooking spray or line them with paper baking cups.

2. Stir together the flours, baking powder, sugars, salt, and chocolate morsels in a large bowl.

3. Whisk together the orange juice, milk, egg, oil, and extracts in a medium bowl. Add the wet ingredients to the dry ingredients and stir just until blended; do not overmix.

4. Spoon the batter into the prepared muffin cups. Bake for 15 to 20 minutes or until the muffins are browned and a tester inserted into the center comes out clean.

5. Immediately remove the muffins from the pan. Serve warm, or cool on a wire rack. Store covered. Refrigerate after 2 days or freeze for up to 3 months.

Makes 12 muffins; 12 servings

Per serving (1 muffin): 148 Calories, 22 g Carbohydrate, 3 g Protein, 6 g Fat,
15 mg Cholesterol, 60 mg Sodium, 2 g Fiber
Exchanges: 1½ Starch, 1 Fat (1½ Carb Choices)

Corn Muffins

Prep time: 10 minutes ◆ *Bake time: 20 minutes*

Cooking spray

1 cup (150 g) yellow cornmeal

½ cup (60 g) all-purpose flour

½ cup (60 g) whole wheat flour

3 tablespoons sugar

1 tablespoon baking powder

¼ teaspoon salt

1 cup (240 ml) nonfat milk or
  buttermilk (see page 8)

1 large egg

3 tablespoons (36 g) canola or extra
  light olive oil

1 tablespoon butter extract

1. Preheat the oven to 425°F (220°C). Spray 12 muffin cups with cooking spray or line them with paper baking cups.

2. Stir together the cornmeal, flours, sugar, baking powder, and salt in a large bowl.

3. Whisk together the milk, egg, oil, and butter extract in a medium bowl until well blended. Stir the wet ingredients into the dry ingredients until just blended; do not overmix.

4. Spoon the batter into the prepared muffin cups. Bake for 20 minutes or until the muffins are browned and a tester inserted into the center comes out clean.

5. Immediately remove the muffins from the pan. Serve warm, or cool on a wire rack. Store covered. Refrigerate after 2 days or freeze for up to 3 months.

> **Variations:** *To make cornbread, spray a 9-inch (23 cm) square baking pan with cooking spray. Pour the corn muffin batter into the pan. Bake for 20 to 25 minutes, until the cornbread is browned and a tester inserted into the center comes out clean. Cut into squares and serve warm.*
>
> *To make blueberry corn muffins, add 1 cup (145 g) fresh or frozen blueberries, 1 tablespoon grated lemon zest, and ½ teaspoon nutmeg to the dry ingredients in step 2.*

Makes 12 muffins; 12 servings

Per serving (1 muffin): 131 Calories, 21 g Carbohydrate, 4 g Protein, 4 g Fat,
0 mg Cholesterol, 170 mg Sodium, 2 g Fiber
Exchanges: 1½ Starch, 1 Fat (1½ Carb Choices)

Fruity Bran Muffins

Prep time: 10 minutes ◆ Bake time: 20 minutes

Cooking spray

1 cup (58 g) wheat bran

1 cup (240 ml) unsweetened fruit
juice of choice (orange, mango,
pineapple, apple, prune)

½ cup (60 g) all-purpose flour

½ cup (60 g) whole wheat flour

¼ cup (23 g) old-fashioned rolled
oats

3 tablespoons sugar

1 tablespoon baking powder

½ teaspoon ground cinnamon

¼ teaspoon ground nutmeg

3 tablespoons raisins or chopped
pitted dates

1 large egg

3 tablespoons canola or extra-light
olive oil

½ cup (112 g) mashed ripe banana
(1 medium)

1. Preheat the oven to 400°F (200°C). Spray 12
   muffin cups with cooking spray or line them with
   paper baking cups.

2. Stir the wheat bran and fruit juice in a small
   bowl; let rest for 5 minutes to soften.

3. Stir together the flours, oats, sugar, baking
   powder, cinnamon, and nutmeg in a large
   bowl. Stir in the raisins and the bran–fruit juice
   mixture.

4. In the same bowl used to combine the bran
   and fruit juice, whisk the egg and oil; stir in the
   mashed banana. Add the wet ingredients to the
   flour mixture and stir just until blended; do not
   overmix.

5. Spoon the batter into the prepared muffin cups.
   Bake for 20 to 25 minutes or until the muffins
   are golden brown and a tester inserted into the
   center comes out clean.

6. Immediately remove the muffins from the pan.
   Serve warm, or cool on a wire rack. Store covered.
   Refrigerate after 2 days or freeze for up to 3
   months.

Makes 12 muffins; 12 servings

Per serving (1 muffin): 130 Calories, 21 g Carbohydrate, 3 g Protein, 4 g Fat,
15 mg Cholesterol, 7 mg Sodium, 3 g Fiber
Exchanges: 1 Starch, ½ Fruit, 1 Fat (1½ Carb Choices)

Cranberry Muffins

Prep time: 10 minutes ◆ Bake time: 15 minutes

Cooking spray

¼ cup (33 g) chopped nuts

¾ cup (90 g) all-purpose flour

¾ cup (90 g) whole wheat flour

¼ cup (48 g) sugar

1 tablespoon baking powder

½ teaspoon baking soda

½ teaspoon ground nutmeg

¼ teaspoon salt

1 cup (100 g) fresh or frozen
   cranberries

2 tablespoons grated orange zest

1 cup (240 m) fresh orange juice

1 large egg

3 tablespoons canola or extra-light
   olive oil

1. Preheat the oven to 400°F (200°C). Spray 12 muffin cups with cooking spray or line them with paper baking cups.

2. Place the nuts in a small baking pan and bake for 3 to 5 minutes, until toasted; set aside.

3. Stir together the flours, sugar, baking powder, baking soda, nutmeg, and salt in a large bowl. Stir in the toasted nuts and cranberries.

4. Whisk together the orange zest and juice, egg, and oil in a medium bowl. Add the wet ingredients to the dry ingredients and stir just until blended; do not overmix.

5. Spoon the batter into the prepared muffin cups. Bake for 15 to 18 minutes or until the muffins are golden brown and a tester inserted into the center comes out clean.

6. Immediately remove the muffins from the pan. Serve warm, or cool on a wire rack. Store covered. Refrigerate after 2 days or freeze for up to 3 months.

Makes 12 muffins; 12 servings

Per serving (1 muffin): 175 Calories, 29 g Carbohydrate, 3 g Protein, 6 g Fat,
15 mg Cholesterol, 107 mg Sodium, 2 g Fiber
Exchanges: 1 Starch, 1 Fruit, 1 Fat (2 Carb Choices)

Honey Bran Muffins

Prep time: 10 minutes ◆ Bake time: 18 minutes

Cooking spray

1¼ cups (72 g) wheat bran

¾ cup (90 g) all-purpose flour

½ cup (60 g) whole wheat flour

2 teaspoons baking powder

¼ teaspoon salt

1 cup (240 ml) nonfat milk

¼ cup (80 g) honey

¼ cup (60 ml) canola or extra-light olive oil

1 large egg

1. Preheat the oven to 375°F (190°C). Spray 12 muffin cups with cooking spray or line them with paper baking cups.

2. Stir together the wheat bran, flours, baking powder, and salt in a large bowl.

3. Whisk together the milk, honey, oil, and egg in a medium bowl. Add the wet ingredients to the dry ingredients and stir just until blended; do not overmix.

4. Spoon the batter into the prepared muffin cups. Bake for 18 to 24 minutes or until the muffins are brown and a tester inserted into the center comes out clean.

5. Immediately remove the muffins from the pan. Serve warm, or cool on a wire rack. Store covered. Refrigerate after 2 days or freeze for up to 3 months.

Makes 12 muffins; 12 servings

Per serving (1 muffin): 142 Calories, 21 g Carbohydrate, 3 g Protein, 5 g Fat, 15 mg Cholesterol, 64 mg Sodium, 3 g Fiber
Exchanges: 1½ Starch, 1 Fat (1½ Carb Choices)

Pineapple-Orange Muffins

Prep time: 10 minutes • Bake time: 15 minutes

Cooking spray

1 cup (120 g) all-purpose flour

1 cup (120 g) whole wheat flour

3 tablespoons (36 g) sugar

1 tablespoon baking powder

¼ teaspoon salt

1 tablespoon grated orange zest

½ cup (120 ml) fresh orange juice

1 large egg

3 tablespoons canola or extra-light olive oil

One 8-ounce (227 g) can juice-packed crushed pineapple

1. Preheat the oven to 400°F (200°C). Spray 12 muffin cups with cooking spray or line them with paper baking cups.

2. Stir together the flours, sugar, baking powder, and salt in a large bowl

3. Whisk together the orange zest and juice, egg, and oil in a medium bowl. Blend in the crushed pineapple with its juice. Add the wet ingredients to the dry ingredients and stir just until blended; do not overmix.

4. Spoon the batter into the prepared muffin cups. Bake for 15 to 18 minutes or until the muffins are golden brown and a tester inserted into the center comes out clean.

5. Immediately remove the muffins from the pan. Serve warm, or cool on a wire rack. Store covered. Refrigerate after 2 days or freeze for up to 3 months.

Makes 12 muffins; 12 servings

Per serving (1 muffin): 131 Calories, 23 g Carbohydrate, 3 g Protein, 4 g Fat, 15 mg Cholesterol, 90 mg Sodium, 2 g Fiber
Exchanges: 1 Starch, ½ Fruit, 1 Fat (1½ Carb Choices)

Raspberry Muffins

Prep time: 10 minutes • Bake time: 15 minutes

Cooking spray

¼ cup (33 g) chopped nuts (optional)

1 cup (120 g) all-purpose flour

1 cup (120 g) whole wheat flour

¼ cup (17 g) nonfat milk powder

3 tablespoons sugar

1 tablespoon baking powder

½ teaspoon baking soda

2 cups (250 g) fresh or frozen raspberries

¼ cup (12 g) bran flakes

1 tablespoon grated orange zest

1 cup (240 ml) fresh orange juice

1 large egg

3 tablespoons canola or extra-light olive oil

1. Preheat the oven to 400°F (200°C). Spray 12 muffin cups with cooking spray or line them with paper baking cups.

2. If using nuts, place them in a small baking pan and bake for 3 to 5 minutes, until toasted; set aside.

3. Stir together the flours, milk powder, sugar, baking powder, and baking soda in a large bowl. Use a rubber spatula to gently stir the raspberries, bran flakes, and toasted nuts, if using, into the dry ingredients.

4. Whisk the orange zest and juice, egg, and oil in a medium bowl. Use a rubber spatula to gently stir the wet ingredients into the raspberry mixture just until blended; do not overmix.

5. Spoon the batter into the prepared muffin cups. Bake for 15 to 18 minutes or until the muffins are golden brown and a tester inserted into the center comes out clean.

6. Immediately remove the muffins from the pan. Serve warm, or cool on a wire rack. Store covered. Refrigerate after 2 days or freeze for up to 3 months.

Makes 12 muffins; 12 servings

Per serving (1 muffin): 159 Calories, 25 g Carbohydrate, 4 g Protein, 6 g Fat,
15 mg Cholesterol, 71 mg Sodium, 2 g Fiber
Exchanges: 1 Starch, ½ Fruit, 1 Fat (1½ Carb Choices)

Maple Nut Muffins

Prep time: 10 minutes • Bake time: 20 minutes

Cooking spray

¼ cup (31 g) chopped pecans

1 cup (120 g) all-purpose flour

1 cup (120 g) whole wheat flour

1 tablespoon baking powder

1 cup (240 ml) nonfat milk

¼ cup (60 ml) pure maple syrup

1 large egg

3 tablespoons canola or extra-light olive oil

2 teaspoons maple extract

1. Preheat the oven to 400°F (200°C). Spray 12 muffin cups with cooking spray or line them with paper baking cups.

2. Place the pecans in a small baking pan and bake for 3 to 5 minutes, until lightly toasted; set aside.

3. Stir together the flours and baking powder in a large bowl; stir in the toasted pecans.

4. Whisk together the milk, maple syrup, egg, oil, and maple extract in a medium bowl. Add the wet ingredients to the dry ingredients and stir just until blended; do not overmix.

5. Spoon the batter into the prepared muffin cups. Bake for 20 to 25 minutes or until the muffins are golden brown and a tester inserted into the center comes out clean.

6. Immediately remove the muffins from the pan. Serve warm, or cool completely on a wire rack. Store covered. Refrigerate after 2 days or freeze for up to 3 months.

Makes 12 muffins; 12 servings

Per serving (1 muffin): 135 Calories, 18 g Carbohydrate, 4 g Protein, 6 g Fat,
15 mg Cholesterol, 16 mg Sodium, 2 g Fiber
Exchanges: 1 Starch, 1 Fat (1 Carb Choice)

Peanut Butter and Jelly Muffins

Prep time: 10 minutes ◆ Bake time: 15 minutes

Cooking spray

1 cup (120 g) all-purpose flour

½ cup (75 g) yellow cornmeal

½ cup (60 g) whole wheat flour

1 tablespoon baking powder

1 tablespoon brown sugar

1 tablespoon granulated sugar

¼ teaspoon salt

1 cup (240 ml) nonfat milk

½ cup (120 ml) fresh orange juice

½ cup (255 g) natural peanut butter

2 large eggs

3 tablespoons canola or extra-light olive oil

2 tablespoons no-sugar-added jelly or jam of your choice

1. Preheat the oven to 425°F (220°C). Spray 12 muffin cups with cooking spray or line them with paper baking cups.

2. Stir together the all-purpose flour, cornmeal, whole wheat flour, baking powder, sugars, and salt in a large bowl.

3. Whisk together the milk, orange juice, peanut butter, eggs, and oil in a medium bowl. Add the wet ingredients to the dry ingredients and stir just until blended; do not overmix.

4. Spoon the batter into the prepared muffin cups. Drop about ½ teaspoon jelly into the center of each muffin, pressing the jelly in slightly with the back of a teaspoon.

5. Bake for 15 to 20 minutes or until the muffins are golden brown and a tester inserted into the center comes out clean.

6. Immediately remove the muffins from the pan. Serve warm or cool on a wire rack. Store covered. Refrigerate after 2 days or freeze for up to 3 months.

Makes 12 muffins; 12 servings

Per serving: 207 Calories, 23 g Carbohydrate, 6 g Protein, 10 g Fat,
30 mg Cholesterol, 88 mg Sodium, 2 g Fiber
Exchanges: 1½ Starch, 2 Fat (1½ Carb Choices)

Pumpkin Muffins

Prep time: 10 minutes ◆ Bake time: 20 minutes

Cooking spray

¼ cup (31 g) chopped pecans

¾ cup (90 g) whole wheat flour

½ cup (60 g) all-purpose flour

½ cup (56 g) wheat germ

2 teaspoons baking powder

1 teaspoon baking soda

1 teaspoon ground cinnamon

½ teaspoon ground nutmeg

¼ teaspoon salt

1 cup (230 g) puréed cooked fresh pumpkin or canned pumpkin

¼ cup (60 ml) canola or extra-light olive oil

¼ cup (60 ml) fresh orange juice

1 large egg

2 tablespoons honey

2 tablespoons molasses

1. Preheat the oven to 375°F (190°C). Spray 12 muffin cups with cooking spray or line them with paper baking cups.

2. Place the pecans in a small baking pan and bake for 3 to 5 minutes, until toasted; set aside.

3. Stir together the flours, wheat germ, baking powder, baking soda, cinnamon, nutmeg, and salt in a large bowl; stir in the toasted pecans.

4. Whisk together the pumpkin, oil, orange juice, egg, honey, and molasses in a medium bowl. Add the wet ingredients to the dry ingredients and stir just until blended; do not overmix.

5. Spoon the batter into the prepared muffin cups. Bake for 20 minutes or until the muffins are lightly browned and a tester inserted into the center comes out clean.

6. Cool the muffins in the pan on a wire rack for 5 minutes. Remove the muffins from the pan and serve warm, or cool completely on the rack. Store covered. Refrigerate after 2 days or freeze for up to 3 months.

Makes 12 muffins; 12 servings

Per serving (1 muffin): 156 Calories, 20 g Carbohydrate, 4 g Protein, 7 g Fat,
15 mg Cholesterol, 194 mg Sodium, 3 g Fiber
Exchanges: 1 Starch, 1 Fat (1 Carb Choice)

Raspberry Jam Muffins

Prep time: 15 minutes ◆ Bake time: 20 minutes

Cooking spray

¾ cup (90 g) all-purpose flour

¾ cup (90 g) whole wheat flour

¼ cup (48 g) sugar

2½ tablespoons nonfat milk powder
or buttermilk powder (see page 8)

2½ teaspoons baking powder

1 teaspoon ground cinnamon

¼ teaspoon salt

¾ cup (180 ml) fresh orange juice

1 large egg

¼ cup (60 ml) canola or extra-light
olive oil

3 tablespoons no-sugar-added
raspberry jam or preserves

1. Preheat the oven to 400°F (200°C). Spray 12 muffin cups with cooking spray or line them with paper baking cups.

2. Stir together the flours, sugar, milk powder, baking powder, cinnamon, and salt in a large bowl.

3. Whisk together the orange juice, egg, and oil in a medium bowl. Pour the wet ingredients into the dry ingredients and stir just until blended; do not overmix.

4. Spoon 1 heaping tablespoon of the batter into each of the prepared muffin cups. Drop about ½ teaspoon of raspberry jam into the center of each; do not spread. Top each with another tablespoon of batter, using all the batter evenly.

5. Bake for 20 minutes or until the muffins are golden brown and the tops spring back when lightly touched in the center.

6. Immediately remove the muffins from the pan. Serve warm, or cool on a wire rack. Store covered or freeze for up to 3 months.

Makes 12 muffins; 12 servings

Per serving (1 muffin): 125 Calories, 18 g Carbohydrate, 3 g Protein, 5 g Fat,
15 mg Cholesterol, 59 mg Sodium, 1 g Fiber
Exchanges: 1 Starch, 1 Fat (1 Carb Choice)

Strawberry Muffins

Prep time: 10 minutes ◆ Bake time: 20 minutes

Cooking spray

1 cup (120 g) all-purpose flour

1 cup (120 g) whole wheat flour

3 tablespoons sugar

1 tablespoon baking powder

½ teaspoon ground cinnamon

1 cup (151 g) coarsely chopped fresh or slightly thawed frozen strawberries

1 cup (240 ml) buttermilk (see page 8)

1 large egg

2 tablespoons canola or extra-light olive oil

1 tablespoon grated orange zest

2 tablespoons fresh orange juice

1 teaspoon vanilla extract

1. Preheat the oven to 400°F (200°C). Spray 12 muffin cups with cooking spray or line them with paper baking cups.

2. Stir together the flours, sugar, baking powder, and cinnamon in a large bowl. Add the chopped strawberries to coat with the flour mixture.

3. Whisk together the buttermilk egg, oil, orange zest and juice, and vanilla in a medium bowl. Add the wet ingredients to the dry ingredients and stir just until blended; do not overmix.

4. Spoon the batter into the prepared muffin cups. Bake for 20 minutes or until the muffins are lightly browned and a tester inserted into the center comes out clean. Immediately remove the muffins from the pan. Serve warm, or cool on a wire rack. Store covered. Refrigerate after 2 days or freeze for up to 3 months.

Makes 12 muffins; 12 servings

Per serving (1 muffin): 135 Calories, 24 g Carbohydrate, 4 g Protein, 3 g Fat,
15 mg Cholesterol, 44 mg Sodium, 2 g Fiber
Exchanges: 1½ Starch, ½ Fat (1½ Carb Choices)

Spicy Ginger Muffins

Prep time: 10 minutes ◆ Bake time: 20 minutes

Cooking spray

1 cup (120 g) all-purpose flour

1 cup (120 g) whole wheat flour

1 tablespoon baking powder

1 tablespoon brown sugar

2 teaspoons ground ginger

1 teaspoon ground cinnamon

¼ teaspoon ground cloves

⅛ teaspoon salt

1 cup (240 ml) buttermilk
(see page 8)

¼ cup (80 g) molasses

1 large egg

3 tablespoons canola or extra-light
olive oil

2 tablespoons fresh orange juice

½ teaspoon vanilla extract

1. Preheat the oven to 400°F (200°C). Spray 12 muffin cups with cooking spray or line them with paper baking cups.

2. Stir together the flours, baking powder, brown sugar, ginger, cinnamon, cloves, and salt in a large bowl.

3. Whisk together the buttermilk, molasses, egg, oil, orange juice, and vanilla in a medium bowl. Stir the wet ingredients into the dry ingredients just until moistened; do not overmix.

4. Spoon the batter into the prepared muffin cups. Bake for 20 to 25 minutes or until the muffins are brown and a tester inserted into the center comes out clean.

5. Immediately remove the muffins from the pan. Serve warm or cool on a wire rack. Store covered. Refrigerate after 2 days or freeze for up to 3 months.

Makes 12 muffins; 12 servings

Per serving (1 muffin): 143 Calories, 23 g Carbohydrate, 4 g Protein, 4 g Fat,
15 mg Cholesterol, 72 mg Sodium, 2 g Fiber
Exchanges: 1½ Starch, 1 Fat (1½ Carb Choices)

Zucchini Muffins

Prep time: 10 minutes ◆ Bake time: 20 minutes

Cooking spray

1 cup (120 g) all-purpose flour

1 cup (120 g) whole wheat flour

¼ cup (48 g) sugar

1 tablespoon baking powder

1 teaspoon ground nutmeg

¼ teaspoon salt

¾ cup (180 ml) nonfat milk

3 tablespoons canola or extra-light olive oil

1 large egg

1 tablespoon grated lemon zest

1 cup (127 g) shredded zucchini

1. Preheat the oven to 400°F (200°C). Spray 12 muffin cups with cooking spray or line them with paper baking cups.

2. Stir together the flours, sugar, baking powder, nutmeg, and salt in a large bowl.

3. Whisk together the milk, oil, egg, and lemon zest in a medium bowl. Stir in the zucchini. Add the wet ingredients to the dry ingredients and stir just until blended; do not overmix.

4. Spoon the batter into the prepared muffin cups. Bake for 20 minutes or until the muffins are golden brown and a tester inserted into the center comes out clean.

5. Immediately remove the muffins from the pan. Serve warm, or cool on a wire rack. Store covered. Refrigerate after 2 days or freeze for up to 3 months.

Makes 12 muffins; 12 servings

Per serving (1 muffin): 127 Calories, 20 g Carbohydrate, 3 g Protein, 4 g Fat,
15 mg Cholesterol, 62 mg Sodium, 2 g Fiber
Exchanges: 1 Starch, 1 Fat (1 Carb Choice)

Poppy Seed Muffins

Prep time: 10 minutes • Bake time: 20 minutes

Cooking spray

¼ cup (31 g) chopped pecans

1 cup (120 g) all-purpose flour

1 cup (120 g) whole wheat flour

⅓ cup (48 g) poppy seeds

3 tablespoons sugar

2½ teaspoons baking powder

½ teaspoon ground nutmeg

¼ teaspoon salt

¼ cup (43 g) golden raisins

1 tablespoon grated orange zest

½ cup (120 ml) fresh orange juice

½ cup (120 ml) nonfat milk

¼ cup (60 ml) canola or extra-light olive oil

2 large eggs

1. Preheat the oven to 400°F (200°C). Spray 12 muffin cups with cooking spray or line them with paper baking cups.

2. Place the pecans in a small baking pan and bake for 3 to 5 minutes, until toasted; set aside.

3. Stir together the flours, poppy seeds, sugar, baking powder, nutmeg, and salt in a large bowl. Stir in the raisins and toasted pecans.

4. Whisk together the orange zest and juice, milk, oil, and eggs in a medium bowl. Add the wet ingredients to the dry ingredients and stir just until blended; do not overmix.

5. Spoon the batter into the prepared muffin cups. Bake for about 20 minutes or until a tester inserted into the center comes out clean.

6. Immediately remove the muffins from the pan. Serve warm, or cool on a wire rack. Store covered. Refrigerate after 2 days or freeze for up to 3 months.

Makes 12 muffins; 12 servings

Per serving (1 muffin): 180 Calories, 21 g Carbohydrate, 5 g Protein, 9 g Fat,
29 mg Cholesterol, 66 mg Sodium, 3 g Fiber
Exchanges: 1½ Starch, 2 Fat (1½ Carb Choices)

Pies, Tarts & Cobblers

Tips & Tricks

» Making pies might seem time consuming and too difficult. Most people reserve them for holidays and special occasions. But the recipes in this section prove it's possible to make delicious pies that are both cheaper and healthier than buying one at the store.

» These recipes are designed to be easy. Most of the crusts take less than 25 minutes from start to finish, and that includes baking! The recipes use only small amounts of sugar. Other ingredients help to reduce the total fat, such as yogurt, nonfat milk, and reduced-fat ricotta. Seasonal fruits, like fresh berries, add color, flavor, and fiber.

» This section also includes a few tart and cobbler recipes. Cobblers, which are filled with fruit, generally have a top biscuit-like crust but no bottom crust. Tarts are like pies, but with no top crust, and jam or custard-like fillings.

» Tart crusts are similar to a pastry crust and are made with a little sugar and butter. The pie crusts in this book are made with meringue, phyllo dough, and healthy oils such as canola or olive oil. A few of the pie crusts call for solid vegetable shortening in much smaller amounts than used in traditional pie crusts.

» Look for the tasty, revised version of baklava, a traditional Greek pastry. Traditionally made by layering clarified butter and a sugar syrup with phyllo pastry, my version (page 220) is made by brushing a mixture of butter and oil and a fruit syrup between phyllo layers. The result is a delicious baklava with only 52 calories and 6 grams of carbs per serving.

» The nutrient analyses provided for the pies in this section include both the filling and the crust in the calculation for a single serving.

Creamy Apple Pie

Prep time: 10 minutes • Bake time: 35 minutes • Cooling time: 1 hour

3 large eggs

2 tablespoons all-purpose flour

1 teaspoon ground cinnamon

¼ teaspoon ground nutmeg

¼ teaspoon salt

1 cup (245 g) plain Greek yogurt

¼ cup (60 ml) unsweetened apple juice

¼ teaspoon almond extract

3 cups (375 g) peeled, cored, and diced Golden Delicious apples (3 medium)

½ cup (85 g) raisins or golden raisins

1 Nutty Pie Crust (page 225) or Oatmeal Crust (page 222), pressed into a 9-inch (23 cm) pie plate and baked

1. Preheat the oven to 350°F (180°C).

2. Whisk the eggs in a large bowl until frothy. Add the flour, cinnamon, nutmeg, and salt, whisking until well blended. Scrape down the sides of the bowl. Whisk in the yogurt, apple juice, and almond extract until well mixed.

3. Combine the apples and raisins in a medium bowl. Spoon the apple mixture into the chosen pie crust. Place the pie plate on a baking sheet to prevent spillovers. Pour the egg mixture over the fruit.

4. Bake for 35 to 40 minutes or until a tester inserted into the center of the pie comes out clean. Cool on a wire rack for 1 hour before serving. Cover and refrigerate leftovers.

Makes one 9-inch (23 cm) pie; 8 servings

Per serving (1 slice): 251 Calories, 32 g Carbohydrate, 7 g Protein, 10 g Fat, 75 mg Cholesterol, 192 mg Sodium, 3 g Fiber
Exchanges: 1 Starch, 1 Fruit, 2 Fat (2 Carb Choices)

Poached Apple Streusel Pie

Prep time: 20 minutes • Bake time: 20 minutes

FILLING

4 cups (500 g) peeled, cored, and sliced Golden Delicious or Granny Smith apples (3 to 4 medium)

¼ cup (43 g) golden raisins

1 tablespoon grated lemon zest

2 tablespoons fresh lemon juice, mixed with enough water to measure ⅓ cup (80 ml)

2 tablespoons frozen unsweetened apple juice concentrate, thawed

1 teaspoon ground cinnamon

1 tablespoon cornstarch

1 Easy Pie Crust (page 223), pressed into a 9-inch (23 cm) pie plate and baked

STREUSEL

¼ cup (30 g) whole wheat flour

¼ cup (33 g) chopped nuts

¼ cup (23 g) old-fashioned rolled oats

1 tablespoon brown sugar

1 teaspoon ground cinnamon

½ teaspoon ground nutmeg

3 tablespoons cold butter, thinly sliced

1. Preheat the oven to 350°F (180°C).

2. **To make the filling,** stir together the apples, raisins, lemon zest, lemon water, apple juice concentrate, and cinnamon in a large skillet. Bring to a boil over medium-high heat. Reduce the heat and simmer for 10 minutes or until the apples are tender. Use a slotted spoon to transfer the apple mixture to a medium bowl; let cool slightly.

3. Stir together the cornstarch and 1 teaspoon water to make a thin paste. Add to the liquid remaining in the skillet. Place over medium heat and cook, stirring constantly, until thickened; pour over the apples and stir to mix. Spoon the apple mixture into the baked pie crust. Place the pie plate on a baking sheet to prevent spillovers.

4. **To make the streusel,** mix together the flour, nuts, oats, brown sugar, cinnamon, and nutmeg in a medium bowl. Use a pastry blender or fork to cut in the butter until the mixture is crumbly. Sprinkle the streusel over the pie.

5. Bake for 20 to 25 minutes or until the streusel is browned. If the crust browns too quickly, loosely cover the edges with aluminum foil. Serve warm. Cover and refrigerate leftovers.

Makes one 9-inch (23 cm) pie; 8 servings

Per serving (1 slice): 155 Calories, 23 g Carbohydrate, 2 g Protein, 7 g Fat, 11 mg Cholesterol, 39 mg Sodium, 3 g Fiber
Exchanges: ½ Starch, 1 Fruit, 1 Fat (1½ Carb Choices)

Apple Tart

Prep time: 10 minutes • Bake time: 40 minutes • Cooling time: 15 minutes

Cooking spray

3 Golden Delicious or Granny Smith apples, peeled, cored, and cut into 4 wedges each

4 large eggs

1 cup (240 ml) nonfat milk

¼ cup (60 ml) canola or extra-light olive oil

¼ cup (48 g) sugar

¼ cup (62 g) plain Greek yogurt

1 tablespoon vanilla extract

2 teaspoons almond extract

1 teaspoon fresh lemon juice

½ teaspoon ground cinnamon

¼ teaspoon ground nutmeg

¾ cup (90 g) all-purpose flour

½ cup (60 g) whole wheat flour

2 tablespoons sliced almonds

1. Preheat the oven to 350°F (180°C). Spray a 10-inch (25 cm) pie plate with cooking spray.

2. Use the slicing disk on a food processor to thinly slice the apple wedges. Layer the apple slices (about 3½ cups/438 g) into the prepared pie plate. Place the pie plate on a baking sheet to prevent spillovers.

3. Place the metal blade in the food processor. Add the eggs, milk, oil, sugar, yogurt, extracts, lemon juice, cinnamon, and nutmeg to the bowl of the food processor. Process until smooth, scraping down the sides once or twice.

4. Add the flours and pulse 3 or 4 times, until just incorporated, occasionally scraping down the sides. Do not overmix. Pour the mixture over the apples, then sprinkle with the almonds.*

5. Bake for 40 to 45 minutes or until the pie is puffed and browned and a tester inserted into the center comes out clean.

6. Cool on a wire rack for about 15 minutes before serving. Cover and refrigerate leftovers. Bring to room temperature before serving.

*If you have more filling than fits into the pan, spray 1 or 2 ramekins with cooking spray and fill with the remaining mixture. Bake these along with the pie.

Makes one 10-inch (25 cm) pie; 10 servings

Per serving (1 slice): 199 Calories, 24 g Carbohydrate, 6 Protein, 9 g Fat,
72 mg Cholesterol, 37 mg Sodium, 2 g Fiber
Exchanges: 1 Starch, ½ Fruit, 2 Fat (1½ Carb Choices)

Flaky Apple Turnovers

Prep time: 30 minutes • Bake time: 15 minutes

Butter-flavored cooking spray

2¼ cups (282 g) peeled, cored, and chopped apples, such as Granny Smith or Gala (2 to 3 medium)

1 teaspoon grated lemon zest

2 teaspoons fresh lemon juice

3 tablespoons sugar

1 tablespoon all-purpose flour

½ teaspoon ground cinnamon

¼ teaspoon ground nutmeg

6 sheets phyllo dough, thawed if frozen

1. Preheat the oven to 400°F (200°C). Spray a baking sheet with cooking spray.

2. Combine the chopped apples and lemon zest and juice in a medium bowl; toss gently. Stir in the sugar, flour, cinnamon, and nutmeg; set aside.

3. Working with one phyllo sheet at a time, cut each sheet lengthwise into four 3½-inch (9 cm) wide strips. Lightly spray each strip with cooking spray. Stack 2 strips one on top of the other. Spoon 1 tablespoon of apple mixture onto the left end corner of each strip, leaving a 1-inch (2.5 cm) border at the bottom. Flatten the apple mixture slightly and fold the right bottom corner over the filling, forming a triangle. Keep folding back and forth into a triangle to the end of the strip. Repeat with the remaining pastry and filling.

4. Place the triangles seam side down on the prepared baking sheet. Lightly spray the tops with cooking spray.

5. Bake for 15 minutes or until golden brown. Serve warm. Cover and refrigerate leftovers.

Makes 12 turnovers; 12 servings

Per serving (1 turnover): 39 Calories, 8 g Carbohydrate, 0.5 g Protein, 1 g Fat,
0 mg Cholesterol, 12 mg Sodium, 1 g Fiber
Exchanges: ½ Fruit (½ Carb Choice)

Blueberry Cobbler

Prep time: 10 minutes ◆ Bake time: 40 minutes

Cooking spray

2 cups (290 g) fresh or frozen
   blueberries

⅓ cup (40 g) all-purpose flour

⅓ cup (40 g) whole wheat flour

¼ cup (48 g) sugar

1 tablespoon grated lemon zest

1½ teaspoons baking powder

⅔ cup (160 ml) nonfat milk

2 tablespoons canola or extra-light
   olive oil

1. Preheat the oven to 350°F (180°C). Spray an 8-inch
   (20 cm) square baking dish with cooking spray.
   Place the blueberries into the prepared baking
   dish.

2. Stir together the flours, sugar, lemon zest, and
   baking powder in a medium bowl. Add the milk
   and oil, and stir to mix well. Evenly spoon the
   mixture over the blueberries.

3. Bake for 40 to 45 minutes or until the top is
   browned. Serve warm. Cover and refrigerate
   leftovers.

Makes 6 servings

Per serving (½ cup/102 g): 148 Calories, 25 g Carbohydrate, 3 g Protein, 5 g Fat,
1 mg Cholesterol, 14 mg Sodium, 2 g Fiber
Exchanges: 1 Starch, ½ Fruit, 1 Fat (1½ Carb Choices)

Crustless Berry Pie

Prep time: 10 minutes • Bake time: 45 minutes • Cooling time: 30 minutes • Chilling time: 1 hour

Cooking spray

2 cups (290 g) fresh or frozen berries (strawberries, raspberries, or blueberries)

One 12-ounce (354 ml) can fat-free evaporated milk

¼ cup (30 g) all-purpose flour

¼ cup (30 g) whole wheat flour

¼ cup (48 g) sugar

4 large eggs

¼ cup (60 ml) canola or extra-light olive oil

1 teaspoon butter extract

1 teaspoon vanilla extract

½ teaspoon almond extract

⅓ cup (24 g) unsweetened shredded coconut (optional)

1. Preheat the oven to 350°F (180°C). Spray a 10-inch (25 cm) pie plate with cooking spray. Place the berries in the prepared pie plate and set on a baking sheet to prevent spillovers.

2. Shake the can of evaporated milk and pour it into a food processor or blender. Add the flours, sugar, eggs, oil, butter extract, and vanilla and almond extracts; process until smooth, scraping down the sides. Add the coconut, if desired, and pulse 2 times. Pour the mixture over the berries.

3. Bake for 45 to 50 minutes or until the pie is golden brown and a tester inserted into the center comes out clean.

4. Cool on a wire rack for about 30 minutes. Refrigerate for about 1 hour before serving. Cover and refrigerate leftovers.

Makes one 10-inch (25 cm) pie; 10 servings

Per serving (1 slice): 203 Calories, 25 g Carbohydrate, 6 g Protein, 9 g Fat,
71 mg Cholesterol, 66 mg Sodium, 2 g Fiber
Exchanges: 1½ Starch, 2 Fat (1½ Carb Choices)

Blueberry Meringue Pie

Prep time: 10 minutes ◆ Bake time: 35 minutes ◆ Cooling time: 1 hour

FILLING

2 large egg whites, at room temperature

⅛ teaspoon cream of tartar

2 tablespoons sugar

3 cups (435 g) fresh or frozen blueberries

1 tablespoon grated lemon zest

1 Easy Pie Crust (page 223), pressed into a 9-inch (23 cm) pie plate and baked

TOPPING

¼ cup (30 g) whole wheat flour

¼ cup (23 g) old-fashioned rolled oats

2 tablespoons sugar

½ teaspoon ground cinnamon

¼ teaspoon ground nutmeg

3 tablespoons cold butter, thinly sliced

1. Preheat the oven to 400°F (200°C).

2. **To make the filling,** use an electric mixer at high speed to beat the egg whites in a large bowl until frothy; beat in the cream of tartar until soft peaks form. Gradually beat in the sugar, beating until the whites form stiff peaks when the beaters are lifted.

3. Use a rubber spatula to gently fold the blueberries and lemon zest into the egg whites. Gently spoon the mixture into the baked pie crust. Place the pie plate on a baking sheet to prevent spillovers.

4. **To make the topping,** stir together the flour, oats, sugar, cinnamon, and nutmeg in a medium bowl. Use a pastry blender to cut in the butter until the mixture is crumbly. Sprinkle over the pie.

5. Bake for 20 minutes, then cover the pie loosely with aluminum foil and continue baking for 15 minutes more or until the filling is set.

6. Cool on a wire rack for about 1 hour before serving. Cover and refrigerate leftovers.

Makes one 9-inch (23 cm) pie; 8 servings

Per serving (1 slice): 208 Calories, 29 g Carbohydrate, 4 g Protein, 10 g Fat, 11 mg Cholesterol, 122 mg Sodium, 3 g Fiber
Exchanges: 1½ Starch, ½ Fruit, 2 Fat (2 Carb Choices)

Blueberry-Nectarine Pot Pie

Prep time: 15 minutes ◆ Bake time: 40 minutes ◆ Cooling time: 1 hour

Cooking spray

2 cups (290 g) fresh or frozen
   blueberries

1 large ripe nectarine, chopped

3 tablespoons instant tapioca

3 tablespoons sugar

1 recipe Easy Pie Crust dough (page
   223), not rolled out, refrigerated

Nonfat milk, to glaze

1. Preheat the oven to 400°F (200°C). Spray a 9-inch (23 cm) pie plate with cooking spray.

2. Stir together the blueberries, nectarine, tapioca, and 2 tablespoons of the sugar in a medium bowl. Spoon into the prepared pie plate. Place the pie plate on a baking sheet to prevent spillovers.

3. Roll out the pie crust dough between 2 pieces of wax paper or plastic wrap to a 10-inch (25 cm) round. Remove the top sheet of wax paper and invert the the dough, paper side up, on top of the filling.

4. Gently peel off the paper. Fold the dough edges under. Use the prongs of a fork to crimp the edge to seal. Brush the crust with milk, and sprinkle with the remaining 1 tablespoon sugar.

5. Bake for 40 to 50 minutes or until the crust is browned. If the crust browns too quickly, cover it loosely with aluminum foil.

6. Cool on a wire rack about 1 hour before serving. Cover and refrigerate leftovers.

Makes one 9-inch (23 cm) pie; 8 servings

Per serving (1 slice): 147 Calories, 25 g Carbohydrate, 2 g Protein, 5 g Fat,
0 mg Cholesterol, 73 mg Sodium, 2 g Fiber
Exchanges: 1 Starch, ½ Fruit, 1 Fat (1½ Carb Choices)

Strawberry-Rhubarb Pie

Prep time: 10 minutes • Bake time: 40 minutes

1 Easy Pie Crust (page 223), pressed into a 9-inch (23 cm) pie plate, unbaked

1 egg white, lightly beaten

FILLING

1 pound (454 g) trimmed rhubarb (4 to 8 stalks), cut into 1-inch chunks

2 cups (290 g) fresh strawberries, hulled and sliced

¼ cup (48 g) granulated sugar

1 teaspoon butter extract

1 teaspoon almond extract

½ teaspoon ground cinnamon

¼ teaspoon ground nutmeg

TOPPING

¼ cup (30 g) whole wheat flour

¼ cup (23 g) old-fashioned rolled oats

¼ cup (60 ml) canola or extra-light olive oil

1 tablespoon brown sugar

¼ teaspoon butter extract

¼ teaspoon ground cinnamon

¼ teaspoon ground nutmeg

¼ cup (33 g) chopped nuts (optional)

1. Preheat the oven to 400°F (200°C). Brush the unbaked pie crust with the beaten egg white before filling; let dry for 5 minutes.

2. **To make the filling,** mix the rhubarb, strawberries, granulated sugar, butter extract, almond extract, cinnamon, and nutmeg in a medium bowl. Spoon the mixture into the pie crust. Place the pie plate on a baking sheet to prevent spillovers.

3. **To make the topping,** mix the flour, oats, oil, brown sugar, butter extract, cinnamon, nutmeg, and nuts, if using, in the same bowl. Sprinkle over the filling.

4. Bake for 10 minutes. Reduce the oven temperature to 350°F (180°C) and bake for 30 minutes more or until the topping is browned. If the crust browns too quickly, loosely cover the edges with aluminum foil.

5. Cool on a wire rack for about 30 minutes. Cover and refrigerate leftovers.

Makes one 9-inch (23 cm) pie; 8 servings

Per serving (1 slice): 296 Calories, 40 g Carbohydrate, 4 g Protein, 15 g Fat, 0 mg Cholesterol, 75 mg Sodium, 5 g Fiber
Exchanges: 1½ Starch, 1 Fruit, 3 Fat (2½ Carb Choices)

Peach Harvest Pie

Prep time: 15 minutes • Bake time: 45 minutes • Cooling time: 1 hour

1 Easy Pie Crust (page 223), pressed into a 9-inch (23 cm) pie plate, unbaked

1 large egg white, lightly beaten

FILLING

2 tablespoons instant tapioca

1 tablespoon granulated sugar

½ teaspoon ground cinnamon

¼ teaspoon ground nutmeg

6 cups (930 g) peeled* and thinly sliced fresh peaches (about 8) or three 16-ounce (454 g) cans juice-packed sliced peaches, drained

1 tablespoon fresh lemon juice

½ teaspoon almond extract

TOPPING

¼ cup (30 g) whole wheat flour

¼ cup (23 g) old-fashioned rolled oats

3 tablespoons canola or extra-light olive oil

1 tablespoon brown sugar

1 tablespoon granulated sugar

½ teaspoon ground cinnamon

¼ cup (33 g) chopped nuts (optional)

*To peel peaches, plunge them into a pot of boiling water for 30 seconds; drain. Cool briefly under cold water. The peel should slide off easily.

1. Preheat the oven to 425°F (220°C). Brush the unbaked pie crust with the beaten egg white before filling; let dry for 5 minutes.

2. **To make the filling,** stir together the tapioca, granulated sugar, cinnamon, and nutmeg in a large bowl; add the peaches and mix well. Add the lemon juice and almond extract; stir to combine. Spoon the filling into the crust. Place the pie plate on a baking sheet to prevent spillovers.

3. **To make the topping,** mix the flour, oats, oil, sugars, cinnamon, and nuts, if using, in a small bowl, until crumbly; sprinkle the mixture over the filling.

4. Bake for 15 minutes. Reduce the oven temperature to 350°F (180°C) and bake for 30 to 35 minutes more, until the crust is browned and the filling is tender. If the crust browns too quickly, loosely cover it with aluminum foil.

5. Cool on a wire rack for about 1 hour before serving. Cover and refrigerate leftovers.

Makes one 9-inch (23 cm) pie; 8 servings

Per serving (1 slice): 258 Calories, 34 g Carbohydrate, 4 g Protein, 13 g Fat,
0 mg Cholesterol, 74 mg Sodium, 4 g Fiber
Exchanges: 1½ Starch, ½ Fruit, 2½ Fat (2 Carb Choices)

Summer Fruit Pie

Prep time: 15 minutes • Chilling time: 5 hours

One 8-ounce (227 g) can juice-packed pineapple chunks

One 0.25-ounce (7 g) envelope unflavored gelatin

¼ cup (60 ml) cold water

¼ cup (48 g) sugar

¾ cup (184 g) plain Greek yogurt

1 tablespoon sugar-free vanilla syrup (such as Torani, DaVinci, or Jordan's)

1 Easy Pie Crust (page 223), pressed into a 9-inch (23 cm) pie plate and baked

½ teaspoon ground cinnamon

1 large peach, peeled* and thinly sliced

¾ cup (125 g) sliced fresh strawberries

¾ cup (100 g) fresh blueberries

*To peel peaches, plunge them into a pot of boiling water for 30 seconds; drain. Cool briefly under cold water. The peel should slide off easily.

1. Drain the pineapple juice into a 2-cup (480 ml) measuring cup; reserve the pineapple chunks. Add enough water to the pineapple juice to measure 1 cup (240 ml). Set aside.

2. In a 1-cup (240 ml) glass measuring cup, sprinkle the gelatin over the ¼ cup cold water; let sit for 1 minute to soften. Microwave on high for 1 minute, until heated; stir to completely dissolve the gelatin. Pour the gelatin into the pineapple juice, and stir in the sugar. Refrigerate for about 1 hour or until syrupy.

3. Reserve ¼ cup (60 ml) of the pineapple-gelatin mixture for the glaze. Stir the remainder with the yogurt and vanilla syrup in a small bowl. Spread the yogurt mixture over the bottom of the baked pie crust. Sprinkle with cinnamon.

4. Arrange the pineapple chunks, peach slices, strawberries, and blueberries over the yogurt mixture. Gently brush the fruit with the reserved pineapple-gelatin mixture.

5. Refrigerate, covered, for at least 4 hours or overnight before serving. Cover and refrigerate leftovers.

Makes one 9-inch (23 cm) pie; 8 servings

Per serving (1 slice): 193 Calories, 31 g Carbohydrate, 4 g Protein, 7 g Fat, 3 mg Cholesterol, 87 mg Sodium, 3 g Fiber
Exchanges: 1 Starch, 1 Fruit, 1 Fat (2 Carb Choices)

Creamy Peach Pie

Prep time: 10 minutes • Chilling time: 3 hours

Cooking spray

2 tablespoons graham cracker crumbs, plus more for garnish

¼ cup (60 ml) cold water

One 0.25-ounce (7 g) envelope unflavored gelatin

One 16-ounce (454 g) can juice-packed peaches, plus more for garnish

One 8-ounce (226 g) package reduced-fat cream cheese, cubed

2 tablespoons sugar

1 tablespoon sugar-free almond syrup (such as Torani or DaVinci)

1. Spray an 8-inch (20 cm) pie plate with cooking spray; sprinkle the bottom and sides with graham cracker crumbs. Set aside.

2. Add the cold water to a food processor with the blade removed. Sprinkle the gelatin over the water and let stand for 1 minute.

3. Meanwhile, drain the peaches into a glass measuring cup or a small microwave-safe bowl. Reserve the peaches. Microwave the peach juice on high for 1 to 2 minutes or until very hot.

4. Put blade back into the food processor. With the motor running, pour the hot peach juice into the food processor and process until the gelatin is completely dissolved, 1 to 2 minutes. Scrape down the sides.

5. Add the peaches, cream cheese, sugar, and almond syrup to the food processor. Process until blended, about 1 minute, scraping down the sides occasionally.

6. Pour the mixture into the crumbed pie plate and refrigerate for 3 hours or until firm. If desired, garnish with additional peach slices and a light sprinkling of graham cracker crumbs. Cover and refrigerate leftovers.

Makes one 8-inch (20 cm) pie; 8 servings

Per serving (1 slice): 121 Calories, 13 g Carbohydrate, 2 g Protein, 7 g Fat,
24 mg Cholesterol, 108 mg Sodium, 1 g Fiber
Exchanges: 1 Starch, 1 Fat (1 Carb Choice)

Peach-Raspberry Cobbler

Prep time: 20 minutes ◆ *Bake time: 20 minutes*

FILLING

Cooking spray

2 tablespoons sugar

1 tablespoon cornstarch

4 cups (620 g) peeled* and sliced fresh peaches (5 or 6 medium)

1 tablespoon grated lemon zest

1 teaspoon fresh lemon juice

2 cups (250 g) fresh or frozen raspberries

TOPPING

½ cup (60 g) all-purpose flour

½ cup (60 g) whole wheat flour

2 tablespoons sugar

1 teaspoon baking powder

½ teaspoon ground cinnamon

3 tablespoons cold butter, sliced

1 large egg

3 tablespoons nonfat milk

Whipped Topping (page 91; optional)

*To peel peaches, plunge them into a pot of boiling water for 30 seconds; drain. Cool briefly under cold water. The peel should slide off easily.

1. Preheat the oven to 400°F (200°C). Spray a 9-inch (23 cm) square baking dish with cooking spray.

2. **To make the filling,** stir together the sugar and cornstarch in a large microwave-safe bowl. Add 2 tablespoons water and mix well. Stir in the peach slices and the lemon zest and juice.

3. Microwave on high for 6 to 7 minutes, until thickened and bubbly, stirring every 3 minutes. Gently fold in the raspberries. Microwave for 1½ minutes more, stir gently, and microwave for another minute. Spoon the mixture into the prepared baking dish.

4. While the fruit is cooking, **prepare the topping.** Stir together the flours, sugar, baking powder, and cinnamon in a medium bowl. Cut in the butter with a pastry blender until the mixture forms coarse crumbs.

5. Fork-whisk the egg and milk in a small bowl and add to the flour mixture, stirring just until blended. Do not overmix.

6. Immediately drop the dough onto the hot fruit mixture in 6 mounds. Bake in the oven for 20 to 25 minutes or until a tester inserted into the topping comes out clean.

7. Serve warm with Whipped Topping, if desired. Cover and refrigerate leftovers.

Makes one 9-inch (23 cm) cobbler; 8 servings

Per serving (½ cup/148 g): 165 Calories, 29 g Carbohydrate, 4 g Protein, 5 g Fat, 33 mg Cholesterol, 45 mg Sodium, 2 g Fiber
Exchanges: 1 Starch, 1 Fruit, 1 Fat (2 Carb Choices)

Old-Fashioned Peach Cobbler

Prep time: 15 minutes ◆ Bake time: 40 minutes

Cooking spray

2 tablespoons brown sugar

1 tablespoon grated lemon zest

1 tablespoon fresh lemon juice

1 teaspoon ground cinnamon

4 cups (620 g) peeled* and sliced fresh peaches (5 or 6 medium), or two 16-ounce (454 g) cans juice-packed sliced peaches, drained

¾ cup (90 g) all-purpose flour

½ cup (60 g) whole wheat flour

1 tablespoon baking powder

4 tablespoons butter, softened

2 tablespoons granulated sugar

1 large egg, at room temperature

½ cup (120 ml) nonfat milk

½ teaspoon vanilla extract

*To peel peaches, plunge them into a pot of boiling water for 30 seconds; drain. Cool briefly under cold water. The peel should slide off easily.

1. Preheat the oven to 375°F (190°C). Spray an 8-inch (20 cm) square baking pan with cooking spray.

2. Stir together the brown sugar, lemon zest and juice, and cinnamon in a large bowl. Add the peaches (if using canned, drain well and discard the juice); toss to mix.

3. Transfer the peaches to the prepared baking pan and bake for 10 minutes.

4. Meanwhile, stir together the flours and baking powder in a small bowl.

5. Use an electric mixer at medium speed to cream the butter and granulated sugar in a medium bowl, until light and fluffy. Beat in the egg until blended; scrape down the sides of the bowl. Mix the milk and vanilla in a separate small bowl.

6. Use a rubber spatula to mix the dry ingredients into the butter-sugar mixture alternately with the milk mixture, until blended, beginning and ending with the dry ingredients. Do not overmix.

7. Remove the peaches from the oven. Drop spoonfuls of the batter over the peach mixture; spread gently. Bake for 25 to 30 minutes or until the top is golden brown. Serve warm. Cover and refrigerate leftovers.

Makes one 8-inch (20 cm) square cobbler; 8 servings

Per serving (1 square): 185 Calories, 29 g Carbohydrate, 4 g Protein, 7 g Fat, 37 mg Cholesterol, 62 mg Sodium, 3 g Fiber
Exchanges: 1½ Starch, ½ Fruit, 1 Fat (2 Carb Choices)

Italian Plum Tart

Prep time: 10 minutes ◆ Bake time: 40 minutes ◆ Cooling time: 1 hour

3 cups (1 pound/454 g) Italian prune-plums* (12 to 14), halved, pitted, and thinly sliced

⅔ cup (160 ml) fat-free evaporated milk (shake before measuring)

1 Tart Shell (page 226), pressed into a 9-inch (23 cm) tart pan and baked

2 large eggs

2 tablespoons sugar

1 teaspoon almond extract

*If Italian prune-plums are not available, use 3 cups (360 g) fruit of your choice.

1. Preheat the oven to 350°F (180°C).

2. Arrange the plums in the baked tart shell, slightly overlapping, to cover the bottom. Place the tart on a rimmed baking sheet to catch any overflow.

3. Whisk together the evaporated milk, eggs, sugar, and almond extract in a 4-cup (960 ml) glass measuring cup until well blended. Place the baking sheet with the tart in the oven and carefully pour the milk mixture over the plums.

4. Bake for 40 to 45 minutes or until the custard is set and the plums are tender.

5. Cool on a wire rack for about 1 hour before serving. Remove the tart pan rim to serve. Cover and refrigerate leftovers.

Makes one 9-inch (23 cm) tart; 8 servings

Per serving (1 slice): 184 Calories, 25 g Carbohydrate, 5 g Protein, 7 g Fat, 60 mg Cholesterol, 84 mg Sodium, 2 g Fiber
Exchanges: 1 Starch, ½ Fruit, 1 Fat (1½ Carb Choices)

Date Chiffon Pie

Prep time: 10 minutes • Chilling time: 3 hours

1¼ cups (300 ml) cold orange juice

One 0.25-ounce (7 g) envelope unflavored gelatin

3 tablespoons sweetened condensed milk

2 tablespoons sugar

1 cup (165 g) finely chopped pitted dates

1 cup (245 g) plain Greek yogurt

2 tablespoons grated orange zest

¼ cup (43 g) instant meringue mix or 1 tablespoon plus 1 teaspoon dried egg whites

¼ cup (60 ml) cold water, or ¼ cup (60 ml) warm water if using dried egg whites

½ teaspoon ground cinnamon

½ teaspoon ground allspice

⅛ teaspoon salt

1 Oatmeal Crust (page 222), Easy Pie Crust (page 223), Flaky Pie Crust (page 224), or Nutty Pie Crust page 225), pressed into a 9-inch (23 cm) pie plate and baked

1. Put the orange juice in a 4-cup (960 ml) glass measure. Sprinkle the gelatin over the juice and let stand 1 minute to soften. Whisk in the sweetened condensed milk and the sugar. Microwave on medium-high for 4 to 6 minutes, stirring every 2 minutes, until slightly thickened. Transfer to a large bowl.

2. Use a rubber spatula to stir in the dates, yogurt, and orange zest; mix well. Refrigerate for about 1 hour or until the mixture begins to set.

3. Use an electric mixer at high speed to beat the meringue mix and water in a medium bowl until foamy. Add the cinnamon, allspice, and salt and beat until stiff peaks form when the beaters are lifted.

4. Use a rubber spatula to gently fold the meringue mixture into the gelatin mixture until no white streaks remain.

5. Spoon the mixture into the baked pie crust. Refrigerate for at least 2 hours or until firm. Refrigerate leftovers.

Makes one 9-inch (23 cm) pie; 8 servings

Per serving (1 slice): 244 Calories, 40 g Carbohydrate, 6 g Protein, 8 g Fat,
55 mg Cholesterol, 68 mg Sodium, 4 g Fiber
Exchanges: 1½ Starch, 1 Fruit, 1½ Fat (2½ Carb Choices)

Lemon Chiffon Pie

Prep time: 15 minutes ◆ *Chilling time: 7 hours*

CRUST

1 cup (102 g) graham cracker
crumbs

3 tablespoons canola or extra-light
olive oil

FILLING

¼ cup (60 ml) cold water

One 0.25-ounce (7 g) envelope
unflavored gelatin

1 cup (240 ml) nonfat milk

¼ cup (75 g) sweetened condensed
milk

¼ cup (48 g) sugar

2 tablespoons grated lemon zest

¼ cup (60 ml) fresh lemon juice

¼ cup (66 g) plus 2 tablespoons
instant meringue mix or
2 tablespoons dried egg whites

⅓ cup (80 ml) cold water, or ⅓ cup
(80 ml) warm water if using dried
egg whites

1. **To make the crust,** mix the graham cracker crumbs and oil in a small bowl; press firmly onto the bottom and partially up the sides of a 9-inch (23 cm) pie plate; refrigerate for about 1 hour.

2. **To make the filling,** put the ¼ cup (60 ml) cold water in a small saucepan. Sprinkle the gelatin over the water and let stand 1 minute to soften. Stir over low heat until the gelatin is completely dissolved, about 3 minutes.

3. Whisk together the nonfat milk, sweetened condensed milk, 2 tablespoons of the sugar, lemon zest and juice, and the dissolved gelatin in a large bowl.

4. Refrigerate for about 1 hour, stirring occasionally, until the mixture mounds when dropped from a spoon.

5. Use an electric mixer at high speed to beat the meringue mix and water in a medium bowl until soft peaks form. Gradually beat in the remaining 2 tablespoons sugar, beating until stiff peaks form when the batter is lifted. Use a rubber spatula to gently fold the meringue into the lemon mixture until no white streaks remain.

6. Spoon the mixture into the crumb crust. Refrigerate until firm, 6 hours or overnight. Cover and refrigerate leftovers.

Makes one 9-inch (23 cm) pie; 8 servings

Per serving (1 slice): 159 Calories, 18 g Carbohydrate, 4 g Protein, 8 g Fat,
70 mg Cholesterol, 129 mg Sodium, 1 g Fiber
Exchanges: 1 Starch, 1½ Fat (1 Carb Choice)

Strawberry Yogurt Pie

Prep time: 10 minutes ◆ Chilling time: 2 to 4 hours

2 tablespoons frozen unsweetened apple juice concentrate, thawed

2 tablespoons cold water

One 0.25-ounce (7 g) envelope unflavored gelatin

⅓ cup (80 ml) boiling water

1 ripe medium banana, sliced

¾ cup (184 g) plain Greek yogurt

1 tablespoon sugar

1 tablespoon sugar-free vanilla syrup (such as Torani, DaVinci, or Jordan's)

2 cups (290 g) fresh or frozen strawberries, hulled and halved

1 Meringue Crust (page 221) or Fat-Free Pie Crust (page 227), pressed into a 9-inch pie plate and baked

1. Mix the apple juice concentrate and cold water in a 1-cup (240 ml) glass measuring cup. Sprinkle in the gelatin and let stand for 1 minute, until softened; stir. Add the boiling water, and stir to completely dissolve the gelatin.

2. Put the gelatin mixture, banana, yogurt, sugar, and vanilla syrup in a food processor and process until smooth, scraping down the sides occasionally.

3. With the machine running, add the strawberries, a few at a time, and process until the strawberries are puréed and mixture is smooth, about 1 minute. Scrape down the sides occasionally.

4. Pour the mixture into a medium bowl; cover and refrigerate for 1 to 3 hours, until thickened and firm.

5. About an hour before serving, stir the thickened strawberry mixture and pour it into the chosen baked pie crust.

6. Refrigerate for about 1 hour before serving. This pie is best served on the same day it's made. Cover and refrigerate leftovers.

Makes one 9-inch (23 cm) pie; 8 servings

Per serving (1 slice): 132 Calories, 28 g Carbohydrate, 3 g Protein, 2 g Fat,
7 mg Cholesterol, 106 mg Sodium, 2 g Fiber
Exchanges: 1½ Starch, ½ Fruit (2 Carb Choices)

Crustless Pumpkin Pie

Prep time: 5 minutes ◆ Bake time: 35 minutes ◆ Cooling time: 30 minutes ◆ Chilling time: 2 hours

Cooking spray

One 16-ounce (454 g) can pumpkin or 2 cups (460 g) puréed cooked fresh pumpkin

One 12-ounce (354 ml) can fat-free evaporated milk, shaken

½ cup (120 ml) reduced-fat buttermilk baking mix (preferably whole wheat)

2 large eggs

¼ cup (48 g) packed brown sugar

1 teaspoon ground cinnamon

½ teaspoon ground ginger

½ teaspoon ground nutmeg

¼ teaspoon ground allspice

¼ teaspoon ground cloves

½ teaspoon maple extract

Whipped Topping (page 91) or Easy Fat-Free Topping (page 92, to serve

1. Preheat the oven to 400°F (200°C). Spray a 10-inch (25 cm) pie plate with cooking spray.

2. Combine the pumpkin, evaporated milk, baking mix, eggs, brown sugar, cinnamon, ginger, nutmeg, allspice, cloves, and maple extract in a food processor. Process until smooth, scraping down the sides occasionally. Pour into the prepared pie plate. Place the pie plate on a baking sheet to prevent spillovers. Use sprayed ramekins or custard cups to hold any extra filling, and bake them with the pie.

3. Bake for 35 to 40 minutes or until the pie is set and a tester inserted into the center comes out clean. Do not overbake.

4. Cool on a wire rack for about 30 minutes, then refrigerate for about 2 hours or overnight before serving. Serve with the topping of choice. Cover and refrigerate leftovers.

Makes one 10-inch (25 cm) pie; 10 servings

Per serving (1 slice): 101 Calories, 17 g Carbohydrate, 5 g Protein, 1 g Fat,
36 mg Cholesterol, 128 mg Sodium, 1 g Fiber
Exchanges: 1 Starch (1 Carb Choice)

Pumpkin-Apple Pie

Prep time: 15 minutes ◆ Bake time: 45 minutes ◆ Cooling time: 30 minutes

CRUST

1 Oatmeal Crust (page 222) or Easy
Pie Crust (page 223), pressed into
a 9-inch pie plate, unbaked

1 egg white, beaten

FILLING

2 cups (220 g) peeled, cored, and
thinly sliced Golden Delicious or
Granny Smith apples
(2 medium)

2 tablespoons all-purpose flour

2 tablespoons brown sugar

½ teaspoon ground cinnamon

One 16-ounce (454 g) can pumpkin
or 2 cups puréed cooked fresh
pumpkin

⅔ cup (160 ml) fat-free evaporated
milk

1 large egg

1 teaspoon ground ginger

¼ teaspoon ground cloves

1. Preheat the oven to 425°F (220°C). Brush the chosen pie crust with a thin layer of beaten egg white. Reserve the remaining egg white. Let the crust dry while preparing the filling.

2. **To make the filling,** stir together the apples, flour, brown sugar, and cinnamon in a large bowl until well blended. Spoon the mixture into the pie crust. Place the pie plate on a baking sheet to prevent spillovers.

3. In the same bowl, whisk together the pumpkin, evaporated milk, egg, reserved egg white, ginger, and cloves until well mixed. Pour the pumpkin mixture over the apples in the crust.

4. Bake for 15 minutes. Reduce the oven temperature to 350°F (180°C) and bake for 30 to 35 minutes more or until a tester inserted into the center of the pie comes out clean.

5. Cool on a wire rack for about 30 minutes before serving. Store, covered, in the refrigerator.

Makes one 9-inch (23 cm) pie; 8 servings

Per serving (1 slice): 180 Calories, 27 g Carbohydrate, 5 g Protein, 6 g Fat,
23 mg Cholesterol, 114 mg Sodium, 3 g Fiber
Exchanges: 1½ Starch, ½ Fruit, 1 Fat (2 Carb Choices)

Chocolate Pudding Pie

Prep time: 10 minutes ◆ Chilling time: 1 hour

2 ripe medium bananas, thinly
   sliced

1 tablespoon fresh orange juice

1 Fat-Free Pie Crust (page 227)
   or Meringue Crust (page 221,
   pressed into a 9-inch pie plate
   and baked

Chocolate Pudding (page 230)

Mix the sliced bananas and orange juice in a small
bowl. Arrange the bananas over the chosen baked
pie crust, then pour the pudding over the bananas.
Chill for at least one hour before serving. Cover and
refrigerate leftovers.

Variation: *Use Simple Vanilla Pudding (page 234) for the pie.*

Makes one 9-inch (23 cm) pie; 6 servings

Per serving (1 slice): 131 Calories, 28 g Carbohydrate, 5 g Protein, 0 g Fat,
2 mg Cholesterol, 160 mg Sodium, 2 g Fiber
Exchanges: 2 Starch (2 Carb Choices)

Chocolate Meringue Pie

Prep time: 20 minutes ◆ Cook time: 35 minutes ◆ Cooling time: 30 minutes ◆ Chilling time: 3 hours

⅓ cup (27 g) unsweetened cocoa powder

¼ cup (48 g) plus 2 tablespoons sugar

4 tablespoons cornstarch

2 cups (480 ml) nonfat milk

2 tablespoons sweetened condensed milk

2 teaspoons vanilla extract

¼ cup (66 g) plus 2 tablespoons instant meringue mix or 2 tablespoons dried egg whites

⅓ cup (80 ml) cold water, or ⅓ cup (80 ml) warm water if using dried egg whites

¼ teaspoon cream of tartar

1 Flaky Pie Crust (page 224), pressed into a 9-inch pie plate and baked

1. Mix the cocoa powder, ¼ cup (48 g) of the sugar, and 3 tablespoons of the cornstarch in a 4-cup (960 ml) glass measuring cup; gradually whisk in the nonfat milk until well blended. Microwave for 5 to 6 minutes at medium-high, stirring every 2 minutes, until the mixture boils.

2. Remove the cocoa mixture from the microwave and whisk in the sweetened condensed milk and the vanilla until blended. Cover the mixture with plastic wrap and set aside.

3. Preheat the oven to 325°F (165°C).

4. Use an electric mixer at high speed to beat the meringue mix, water, remaining 1 tablespoon cornstarch, and cream of tartar in medium bowl until foamy. Gradually beat in the remaining 2 tablespoons sugar, beating until stiff peaks form when the beaters are lifted.

5. Remove the plastic wrap from the chocolate filling and stir; pour it into the baked pie crust. Place the pie plate on a baking sheet to prevent spillovers. Gently spread the meringue evenly over the filling, sealing it to the edge of the crust.

6. Bake for 25 minutes or until the meringue is lightly browned. Cool on a rack for 30 minutes, then refrigerate for 3 hours, or until set, before serving. Cover and refrigerate leftovers.

Makes one 9-inch (23 cm) pie; 8 servings

Per serving (1 slice): 178 Calories, 27 g Carbohydrate, 6 g Protein, 6 g Fat, 23 mg Cholesterol, 124 mg Sodium, 2 g Fiber
Exchanges: 2 Starch, 1 Fat (2 Carb Choices)

Banana Cream Tart

Prep time: 10 minutes • Chilling time: 1 hour

2 ripe medium bananas, thinly
   sliced

1 recipe Simple Vanilla Pudding
   (page 234), cooled, or 2 cups
   (210 g) store-bought sugar-free
   vanilla pudding

1 Tart Shell (page 226), Meringue
   Crust (page 221), or Fat-Free Pie
   Crust (page 227), pressed into a
   9-inch (23 cm) tart pan and baked

Whipped Topping (page 91;
   optional)

Reserve a few banana slices for garnish, if desired; set aside. Stir the remaining banana slices into the pudding in a medium bowl. Spoon the pudding into the chosen baked pie crust, then chill for at least 1 hour or until firm. Remove the sides of the tart pan; leave the tart on the bottom, and place it on a plate to serve. Top with Whipped Topping and the reserved banana slices, if desired. Cover and refrigerate leftovers.

Makes one 9-inch (23 cm) tart; 8 servings

Per serving (1 slice): 182 Calories, 29 g Carbohydrate, 4 g Protein, 6 g Fat,
17 mg Cholesterol, 78 mg Sodium, 2 g Fiber
Exchanges: 1 Starch, 1 Fruit, 1 Fat (2 Carb Choices)

Baklava

Prep time: 15 minutes • Bake time: 30 minutes • Cooling time: 30 minutes

1 medium apple, peeled, cored, and chopped

½ cup (85 g) golden raisins

2 teaspoons grated lemon zest

1 tablespoon fresh lemon juice

1 teaspoon ground cinnamon

Cooking spray

3 tablespoons butter, melted

3 tablespoons canola or extra-light olive oil

6 sheets phyllo dough, thawed if frozen

Butter-flavored cooking spray (optional)

1. Mix 1 cup (240 ml) water, the apple, raisins, lemon zest and juice, and cinnamon in a 4-cup (960 ml) glass measuring cup. Microwave on high for 5 minutes; stir. Microwave on medium-high for 5 minutes; stir. Let rest for 1 minute. Use a slotted spoon to transfer the fruit to a small bowl. Set the fruit aside.

2. Microwave the remaining liquid on medium-high for 3 minutes; stir. Microwave on medium-high for 2 to 3 minutes more or until reduced to a thin syrup. Reserve the syrup.

3. Preheat the oven to 375°F (190°C). Spray a 13 x 9 x 2-inch (33 x 23 x 5 cm) baking pan with cooking spray.

4. Combine the melted butter and oil in a small bowl.

5. Place 1 sheet of phyllo in the prepared baking pan; brush it lightly with the butter-oil mixture. Place another sheet on top and brush with the mixture. Lay a third sheet on top, but do not brush.

6. Spoon the fruit over the phyllo and spread evenly. Repeat step 5, layering the remaining phyllo and brushing lightly with the butter/oil mixture.

7. Use a knife to push the edges of the phyllo down along the sides of the pan; score the top into diamonds. Brush again with the butter/oil mixture. If desired, spray butter-flavored cooking spray over the baklava.

8. Bake for 30 minutes or until lightly browned. Remove the pan from the oven and, while the baklava is still hot, cut all the way through the score marks in the top layer with a large, thin knife. Pour over the syrup, allowing it to coat the top and spill into the cuts you've just made. Cool to room temperature on a wire rack, then serve.

9. Store in a covered container or freeze for up to 3 months.

Makes 2 dozen baklava; 24 servings

Per serving (1 baklava): 52 Calories, 6 g Carbohydrate, 0 g Protein, 3 g Fat,
4 mg Cholesterol, 21 mg Sodium, 0.5 g Fiber
Exchanges: ½ Fruit, ½ Fat (½ Carb Choice)

Meringue Crust

Prep time: 10 minutes • Bake time: 3 hours

3 large egg whites, at room
   temperature*

½ teaspoon almond extract

¼ teaspoon cream of tartar

¼ teaspoon salt

¼ cup (48 g) sugar

*Use ¼ cup (66 g) instant meringue
mix, or 2 tablespoons dried egg
whites, in place of the fresh egg
whites. Add ⅓ cup (80 ml) cold
water, or ⅓ cup (80 ml) warm water
for dried egg whites.

1. Preheat the oven to 300°F (150°C).

2. Use an electric mixer at high speed to beat the
   egg whites, almond extract, cream of tartar,
   and salt in a large bowl until soft peaks form.
   Gradually beat in the sugar, 1 tablespoon at a
   time, beating until the whites form stiff peaks
   when the beaters are lifted.

3. Spread the mixture into a 9-inch (23 cm) pie
   plate, spreading it over the bottom and up the
   sides of the pie plate.

4. Bake for 1 hour. Turn the oven off, leave the oven
   door closed, and cool the crust in the oven for 2
   hours or until dry.

5. Spoon the filling of your choice into the crust just
   before serving. This crust can be prepared up to
   two days ahead and stored, loosely covered, at
   room temperature.

Note: *This pie shell is delicious filled with a mixture of
2 cups (290 g) berries (such as a combination of fresh
strawberries, blueberries, and raspberries), ½ cup (123 g)
plain Greek yogurt, 2 teaspoons sugar, 1 tablespoon sugar-
free vanilla syrup or liqueur, and 1 tablespoon sugar-free
almond syrup. Don't make this on a wet or humid day since
the meringue tends to draw moisture from the air, and the
crust will be soggy.*

Makes one 9-inch (23 cm) pie crust; 8 servings

Per serving (1 slice): 33 Calories, 6 g Carbohydrate, 1 g Protein, 0 g Fat,
0 mg Cholesterol, 93 mg Sodium, 0 g Fiber
Exchanges: ½ Starch (½ Carb Choice)

Oatmeal Crust

Prep time: 5 minutes ◆ *Bake time: 8 minutes*

½ cup (60 g) whole wheat flour

½ cup (45 g) old-fashioned rolled oats

2 tablespoons brown sugar

½ teaspoon ground cinnamon

2 tablespoons canola or extra-light olive oil

1 tablespoon warm water

1. Preheat the oven to 350°F (180°C).

2. Mix together the flour, oats, brown sugar, and cinnamon in a medium bowl. Add the oil and water; mix well with a fork until crumbly.

3. Pat the crust onto the bottom and partially up sides of a 9-inch (23 cm) springform pan or a 9-inch (23 cm) pie plate.

4. Bake for 8 to 10 minutes or until golden brown. Cool on a wire rack before filling.

Makes one 9- or 10-inch (23 cm) crust; 8 servings

Per serving (1 slice): 90 Calories, 13 g Carbohydrate, 2 g Protein, 4 g Fat,
0 mg Cholesterol, 1 mg Sodium, 2 g Fiber
Exchanges: 1 Starch, 1 Fat (1 Carb Choice)

Easy Pie Crust

Prep time: 10 minutes ◆ Chilling time: 1 hour ◆ Bake time: 10 minutes

½ cup (60 g) all-purpose flour

½ cup (60 g) whole wheat flour

¼ teaspoon salt

3 tablespoons solid vegetable shortening

2 tablespoons ice water

1. Mix the flours and salt in a medium bowl. Use a pastry blender to cut in the shortening until the mixture is crumbly. Use a wooden spoon or rubber spatula to stir in the water until the mixture forms a ball. Or pulse the flours, salt, and shortening in a food processor until crumbly (3 or 4 times). Add the water and pulse until a ball forms. Wrap in plastic wrap; press to flatten slightly. Refrigerate for about 1 hour for easier rolling.

2. Unwrap the dough and place it between two pieces of wax paper or plastic wrap and roll it out into a 10- or 11-inch (25 or 28 cm) circle. Peel off one piece of paper and invert the dough, paper-side up, into an 8- or 9-inch (20 or 23 cm) pie plate. Press the dough into the bottom and up sides of the pie plate; fold the edges under and flute.

3. To bake the crust, prick the bottom and sides with a fork. Bake at 400°F (200°C) for 10 minutes or until lightly browned. Cool on a wire rack before filling.

4. For an unbaked crust, do not prick the dough. Spoon in the filling and bake as directed.

Note: If filling the crust with a fruit filling, brush the unbaked pie crust with a beaten egg white. Let the egg white dry for 5 minutes before filling. If the recipe for a fruit-filled pie calls for a baked crust, before baking, brush it with beaten egg white and bake as directed; cool.

Makes one 8- or 9-inch (20 or 23 cm) pie crust; 8 servings

Per serving (1 slice): 94 Calories, 11 g Carbohydrate, 2 g Protein, 5 g Fat,
0 mg Cholesterol, 73 mg Sodium, 1 g Fiber
Exchanges: 1 Starch, 1 Fat (1 Carb Choice)

Flaky Pie Crust

Prep time: 10 minutes ◆ *Bake time: 14 minutes*

Cooking spray

½ cup (60 g) all-purpose flour

½ cup (60 g) whole wheat flour

¼ teaspoon salt

3 tablespoons solid vegetable shortening

3 tablespoons ice water

1 teaspoon fresh lemon juice

1. Preheat the oven to 425°F (220°C). Spray a 9-inch (23 cm) pie plate with cooking spray.

2. Stir together the flours and salt in a medium bowl. Use a pastry blender to cut in the shortening until the mixture is crumbly.

3. Mix the water and lemon juice. Sprinkle the lemon water, 1 tablespoon at a time, over the surface of the flour mixture. Toss with a fork until the dry ingredients are moistened.

4. Gently press the dough into a 4-inch (10 cm) disk on a sheet of plastic wrap. Cover with another sheet of plastic wrap and roll the dough into an 11-inch (28 cm) circle. Place the dough in the freezer for 5 minutes or until the plastic wrap can easily be removed.

5. Remove the plastic wrap and fit the dough into the prepared pie plate. Fold the edges under and flute; prick the bottom and sides of the dough with a fork.

6. Bake for 14 minutes or until lightly browned; cool on a wire rack before filling.

Note: To prevent a soggy crust for a fruit-filled pie, brush the unbaked pie crust with a beaten egg white. Let dry for about 5 minutes before proceeding with the recipe.

Makes one 9-inch (23 cm) pie crust, 8 servings

Per serving (1 slice): 94 Calories, 11 g Carbohydrate, 2 g Protein, 5 g Fat,
0 mg Cholesterol, 73 mg Sodium, 1 g Fiber
Exchanges: 1 Starch, 1 Fat (1 Carb Choice)

Nutty Pie Crust

Prep time: 15 minutes ◆ Chilling time: 30 minutes ◆ Bake time: 5 minutes

½ cup (60 g) all-purpose flour

½ cup (60 g) whole wheat flour

2 tablespoons finely chopped nuts

¼ teaspoon salt

3 tablespoons solid vegetable shortening

2 to 3 tablespoons unsweetened apple juice

1 egg white, beaten

1. Stir together the flours, nuts, and salt in a medium bowl. Use a pastry blender to cut in the shortening until the mixture is crumbly. Sprinkle with 2 tablespoons of the apple juice and gently stir with a fork until the mixture forms a ball. If necessary, add the remaining apple juice. Cover with plastic wrap and flatten slightly; refrigerate for 30 minutes.

2. Preheat the oven to 425°F (220°C).

3. Unwrap the dough. Place the dough between two pieces of wax paper or plastic wrap and roll out to an 11-inch (28 cm) circle. Peel off 1 piece of paper and invert the dough, paper-side up, into a 9-inch (23 cm) pie plate. Gently remove the paper and press the dough into the pie plate. Fold the edges under and flute; prick the bottom and sides of the dough with a fork.

4. Brush the dough with a small amount of beaten egg white. Let dry for 5 minutes. Bake for 5 minutes or until golden brown. Cool on a wire rack before filling.

Makes one 9-inch (23 cm) pie crust; 8 servings

Per serving (1 slice): 111 Calories, 12 g Carbohydrate, 2 g Protein, 6 g Fat,
0 mg Cholesterol, 80 mg Sodium, 1 g Fiber
Exchanges: 1 Starch, 1 Fat (1 Carb Choice)

Tart Shell

Prep time: 15 minutes • Chilling time: 1 hour • Bake time: 10 minutes

½ cup (60 g) all-purpose flour

½ cup (60 g) whole wheat flour

2 tablespoons sugar

4 tablespoons cold butter, cut into pieces

1 to 2 tablespoons ice water

1. Stir together the flours and sugar in a medium bowl. Use a pastry blender to cut in the butter until the mixture is crumbly. Sprinkle with 1 tablespoon of the ice water and stir with a fork until the mixture clumps together to form a dough. Add the remaining tablespoon ice water, if necessary.

2. Press the dough over the bottom and up the sides of a 9-inch (23 cm) tart pan. Prick the bottom all over with a fork. Cover with plastic wrap and refrigerate for 1 hour.

3. Preheat the oven to 425°F (220°C). Place the tart pan on a baking sheet. Bake for 10 to 12 minutes or until golden brown. Cool on a wire rack before filling.

Note: *Use this tart shell for the Italian Plum Tart (page 208) and Banana Cream Tart (page 218).*

Makes one 9-inch (23 cm) tart shell; 8 servings

Per serving (1 slice): 111 Calories, 14 g Carbohydrate, 2 g Protein, 6 g Fat,
15 mg Cholesterol, 46 mg Sodium, 1 g Fiber
Exchanges: 1 Starch, 1 Fat (1 Carb Choice)

Fat-Free Pie Crust

Prep time: 5 minutes • Bake time: 15 minutes • Chilling time: 1 hour

Butter-flavored cooking spray

6 sheets phyllo dough, thawed if frozen

1. Preheat the oven to 350°F (180°C).

2. Spray an 8-, 9-, or 10-inch (20, 23, or 25 cm) pie plate with butter-flavored cooking spray. Lay three sheets of phyllo dough across the pie plate, with the dough hanging over the pie plate on two sides; gently press the dough into the pie plate with your fingers.

3. Lay the remaining 3 sheets of dough in the opposite direction across the pie plate; gently press down the dough with your fingers.

4. Use kitchen shears or a very sharp knife to trim the dough about 2 inches (5 cm) beyond the rim of the pie plate. Gently turn the dough under, leaving a ridge around the rim of the pie plate. Pierce the bottom and sides of the dough with a fork. Spray the pie crust with butter-flavored cooking spray.

5. If desired, form the dough trimmings into decorative shapes, place on a baking sheet, and spray with cooking spray. Bake the crust and shapes for 15 minutes or until golden brown; cool on a wire rack before filling.

6. Fill the cooled pie crust with pudding and/or fruit of your choice. Refrigerate for at least 1 hour or until set; garnish with the decorative shapes.

Note: *This pie crust is best made and served the same day.*

Makes 1 pie crust; 8 servings

Per serving (1 slice): 27 Calories, 6 g Carbohydrate, 1 g Protein, 0 g Fat,
0 mg Cholesterol, 25 mg Sodium, 0 g Fiber
Exchanges: ½ Starch (½ Carb Choice)

Puddings

Tips & Tricks

» Creamy and cool, each of the pudding recipes in this section contains fewer than 170 calories per serving, with 5 grams of total fat or less. Puddings are very versatile and fun to make. Add fruit, and puddings offer an even greater variety of flavors.

» These pudding recipes can be served any time of the day. Try Creamy Rice Pudding (page 235) or Bread Pudding (page 242) for breakfast; or send any of the puddings along in a packed lunch for a comforting meal while away from home. Blueberry Tapioca Pudding (page 240) makes a very classy dessert when served in parfait glasses.

» Some of these puddings are tried and true basics, such as Chocolate Pudding (page 230) and Simple Vanilla Pudding (page 234). Apple-Raisin Noodle Pudding (page 234) is homey and wonderful. For an elegant dessert, serve Orange Soufflé (page 243) or Orange-Honey Custard (page 245).

» We live in a time of convenience when puddings can be made from a box and whipped instantly. But with the pudding recipes here, the investment in longer cooking times is well worth it. Not only are the flavors more intense, but these puddings are more filling while remaining low in sugar and total fat. The recipes use nonfat milk, but you can use skim, 1%, or 2%, choosing the milk that best appeals to you and your family. Other healthful ingredients include fresh fruit, fiber-rich whole wheat noodles, and brown rice.

» I believe you and your guests will find these recipes tasty, filling, and satisfying.

Chocolate Pudding

Prep time: 10 minutes ◆ Cook time: 6 minutes ◆ Chilling time: 1 hour

2 cups (480 ml) nonfat milk

3 tablespoons sugar

2½ tablespoons cornstarch

2 tablespoons unsweetened cocoa powder

2 teaspoons vanilla extract

1. Measure 1½ cups (360 ml) of the milk in a 4-cup (960 ml) glass measuring cup. Microwave on high for 2 to 3 minutes, until the milk is hot and small bubbles appear along the edge.

2. Meanwhile, whisk together the sugar, cornstarch, and cocoa powder in a small bowl. Whisk in the remaining ½ cup (60 ml) milk until smooth.

3. Whisk the cocoa mixture into the hot milk until well blended. Microwave on high for 2 minutes; stir. Microwave for another 2 to 3 minutes, until mixture has thickened.

4. Let rest for 1 minute, then stir in the vanilla. Spoon the pudding into 4 dessert dishes. Refrigerate for about 1 hour before serving.

Makes 2 cups (560 g); 4 servings

Per serving (½ cup/140 g): 99 Calories, 20 g Carbohydrate, 5 g Protein, 0 g Fat,
3 mg Cholesterol, 64 mg Sodium, 1 g Fiber
Exchanges: ½ Starch, ½ Nonfat Milk (1 Carb Choice)

Strawberry Pudding

Prep time: 10 minutes ◆ Chilling time: 1 hour

½ cup (120 ml) cold water

Two 0.25-ounce (7 g) envelopes
  unflavored gelatin

1 cup (240 ml) nonfat milk

3 tablespoons sugar

1 teaspoon almond extract

4 cups (580 g) fresh or frozen
  strawberries, hulled and halved

1. Add the cold water to a food processor with the blade removed. Sprinkle the gelatin over the water. Let stand for 1 minute to soften.

2. Meanwhile, heat the milk in the microwave on high for 1 to 2 minutes, or in a small pot, until almost boiling. Put the blade back in the food processor; add the hot milk and process until the gelatin is completely dissolved, scraping down the sides once.

3. Add the sugar and almond extract. With the motor running, drop in the strawberries a few at a time, processing until they are puréed and incorporated into the mixture; scrape down the sides occasionally.

4. Pour the pudding into 8 dessert dishes. Refrigerate for about 1 hour or until set. Store leftovers, covered, in the refrigerator.

Makes 4 cups (1,408 g); 8 servings

Per serving (½ cup/176 g): 49 Calories, 11 g Carbohydrate, 1 g Protein, 0 g Fat,
1 mg Cholesterol, 17 mg Sodium, 1 g Fiber
Exchanges: 1 Fruit (1 Carb Choice)

Pumpkin Pudding

Prep time: 10 minutes

¼ cup (60 ml) cold water

One 0.25-ounce (7 g) envelope unflavored gelatin

¼ cup (60 ml) boiling water

1 cup (230 g) puréed cooked fresh pumpkin or canned pumpkin

⅔ cup (45 g) nonfat milk powder

3 tablespoons sugar

½ teaspoon pumpkin pie spice

¼ teaspoon maple extract

8 ice cubes (1½ cups/227 g)

1. Add the cold water to a food processor with the blade removed. Sprinkle the gelatin over the water. Let stand for 1 minute to soften. Put the blade back in the food processor, add the boiling water and process until the gelatin is completely dissolved, scraping down the sides once.

2. Add the pumpkin, milk powder, sugar, pumpkin pie spice, and maple extract; process until smooth; scrape down the sides. With the motor running, drop in the ice cubes, one at a time, and process until the cubes are incorporated and the mixture is smooth, scraping down the sides occasionally.

3. Pour the pudding into 6 dessert dishes. Serve immediately or refrigerate until ready to serve. Store leftovers, covered, in the refrigerator.

Makes 3 cups (324 g); 6 servings

Per serving (½ cup/54 g): 60 Calories, 12 g Carbohydrate, 3 g Protein, 0 g Fat,
1 mg Cholesterol, 45 mg Sodium, 1 g Fiber
Exchanges: ½ Starch, ½ Nonfat Milk (1 Carb Choice)

Apple-Raisin Noodle Pudding

Prep time: 10 minutes ◆ *Bake time: 40 minutes*

Cooking spray

2 cups (220 g) peeled, cored, and thinly sliced Gala apples (2 medium apples)

2 cups (280 g) wide whole wheat noodles, cooked and drained

1 cup (245 g) plain Greek yogurt

¼ cup (43 g) golden raisins

2 tablespoons brown sugar

2 tablespoons fresh lemon juice

1 teaspoon vanilla extract

½ teaspoon ground cinnamon

1. Preheat the oven to 350°F (180°C). Spray a 9-inch (23 cm) square baking dish with cooking spray.

2. Mix the apples, noodles, yogurt, raisins, brown sugar, lemon juice, vanilla, and cinnamon in a large bowl. Spoon the mixture into the prepared baking dish.

3. Bake for 35 to 40 minutes or until the top is lightly browned. Serve warm or at room temperature. Store leftovers, covered, in the refrigerator.

Makes 4 cups (952 g); 8 servings

Per serving (½ cup/119 g): 145 Calories, 26 g Carbohydrate, 5 g Protein, 3 g Fat,
9 mg Cholesterol, 109 mg Sodium, 1 g Fiber
Exchanges: 1½ Starch, ½ Fruit, ½ Fat (2 Carb Choices)

Simple Vanilla Pudding

Prep time: 10 minutes ◆ *Chilling time: 1 hour*

2 cups (480 ml) nonfat milk

3 tablespoons cornstarch

2 tablespoons sugar

2 teaspoons vanilla extract

1. Add 1½ cups (360 ml) of the milk to a 4-cup (960 ml) glass measuring cup. Microwave on high for 2 to 3 minutes, until the milk is hot and small bubbles appear along the edge.

2. Meanwhile, whisk together the cornstarch and sugar in a small bowl. Whisk in the remaining ½ cup (120 ml) milk until smooth.

3. Whisk the cornstarch mixture into the hot milk until well blended. Microwave on high for 1½ to 2 minutes, until thickened.

4. Let the pudding rest for 1 minute, then stir in the vanilla. Spoon the pudding into 4 dessert dishes.

5. Refrigerate for at least 1 hour or until the pudding is firm before serving. Serve chilled. Store leftovers, covered, in the refrigerator.

Makes 2 cups (540 g); 4 servings

Per serving (½ cup/135 g): 89 Calories, 17 g Carbohydrate, 4 g Protein, 0 g Fat,
3 mg Cholesterol, 63 mg Sodium, 0 g Fiber
Exchanges: 1 Nonfat Milk (1 Carb Choice)

Creamy Rice Pudding

Prep time: 15 minutes ◆ *Cook time: 45 minutes*

One 12-ounce (354 ml) can fat-free evaporated milk

2½ cups (600 ml) nonfat milk

⅔ cup (119 g) long-grain brown rice

⅓ cup (56 g) raisins

¼ cup (48 g) sugar

2 large eggs

2 teaspoons vanilla extract

1 teaspoon ground cinnamon

½ teaspoon ground nutmeg

1. Shake the can of evaporated milk and pour it into a 4-cup (960 ml) glass measuring cup. Add enough nonfat milk (about 1½ cups/360 ml) to measure 4 cups (960 ml).

2. Bring the milks to a boil in a heavy medium saucepan over medium-high heat. Stir in the rice, raisins, and sugar; cover and cook over medium-low heat, stirring frequently, for 40 to 45 minutes, until the rice is tender.

3. In the same measuring cup, whisk together the remaining 1 cup (240 ml) milk, eggs, vanilla, cinnamon, and nutmeg until well blended.

4. Raise the heat under the rice to medium and gradually pour the egg mixture into the cooked rice mixture. Cook, stirring constantly, until the pudding is slightly thickened but still loose and creamy, about 3 minutes.

5. Remove from the heat and spoon the pudding into 10 dessert dishes. Store leftovers, covered, in the refrigerator. This pudding can be served warm or chilled.

Variation: *For extra-creamy rice pudding, whisk ½ cup (114 g) nonfat ricotta in the measuring cup along with the milk, eggs, vanilla, cinnamon, and nutmeg.*

Makes 5 cups (940 g); 10 servings

Per serving (½ cup/94 g): 107 Calories, 18 g Carbohydrate, 6 g Protein, 1 g Fat, 38 mg Cholesterol, 78 mg Sodium, 1 g Fiber
Exchanges: ½ Starch, ½ Nonfat Milk (1 Carb Choice)

Raspberry Pudding

Prep time: 20 minutes ◆ Chilling time: 3 hours

½ cup (120 ml) cold water

Two 0.25-ounce (7 g) envelopes unflavored gelatin

4 cups (600 g) fresh or frozen raspberries

¼ cup (80 g) no-sugar-added raspberry jam

¼ cup (48 g) sugar

1 cup (244 g) unsweetened applesauce

1 cup (227 g) reduced-fat ricotta

½ cup (86 g) instant meringue mix or 2 tablespoons plus 2 teaspoons dried egg whites

½ cup (120 ml) cold water, or ½ cup (120 ml) warm water if using dried egg whites

½ teaspoon cream of tartar

Additional fresh raspberries and mint leaves for garnish (optional)

1. Add ½ cup (120 ml) cold water to a small bowl. Sprinkle the gelation over the water. Let stand for 1 minute to soften.

2. Mix the raspberries, jam, and 2 tablespoons of the sugar in a 4-cup (960 ml) glass measuring cup. Microwave on high for 4 minutes, stirring after 2 minutes, until the mixture comes to a boil. Stir in the gelatin mixture until the gelatin is completely dissolved; cool 5 minutes.

3. Press the mixture through a strainer into a large bowl; discard the seeds. You should have about 3 cups (476 g) of the mixture. Stir in the applesauce.

4. Refrigerate for at least 1 hour, stirring 3 times, until the mixture thickens to the consistency of unbeaten egg whites and mounds when dropped from a spoon.

5. Process the ricotta in a food processor until smooth and creamy. Stir into the thickened fruit mixture.

6. Use an electric mixer at high speed to beat the meringue mix, water, and cream of tartar in a large bowl until foamy. Gradually beat in the remaining 2 tablespoons sugar, beating until stiff peaks form when the beaters are lifted.

7. Use a rubber spatula to gently fold the meringue into the fruit mixture until no white streaks remain. Spoon the pudding into 8 dessert dishes. Refrigerate for 3 hours or until set. Garnish each serving with raspberries and mint, if desired. Store leftovers, covered, in the refrigerator.

Makes 4 cups (1,112 g); 8 servings

Per serving (½ cup/139 g): 115 Calories, 20 g Carbohydrate, 6 g Protein, 2 g Fat, 8 mg Cholesterol, 60 mg Sodium, 4 g Fiber
Exchanges: 1 Fruit (1 Carb Choice)

Pineapple Rice Pudding

Prep time: 15 minutes • Cook time: 5 minutes • Chilling time: 4 hours

One 8-ounce (227 g) can juice-packed crushed pineapple

3 tablespoons sugar

1 tablespoon plus 1 teaspoon cornstarch

½ cup (120 ml) nonfat milk

3 tablespoons sweetened condensed milk

½ teaspoon vanilla extract

¼ cup (43 g) instant meringue mix or 1 tablespoon plus 1 teaspoon dried egg whites

¼ cup (60 ml) cold water, or ¼ cup (60 ml) warm water if using dried egg whites

⅛ teaspoon cream of tartar

1½ cups (227 g) cooked brown rice

¼ cup (40 g) maraschino cherries or pitted fresh cherries, chopped

1. Drain the pineapple juice into a 4-cup (960 ml) glass measuring cup; set the pineapple aside. Whisk 1 tablespoon of the sugar and the cornstarch into the juice, then blend in the nonfat milk and sweetened condensed milk. Microwave on high for 4 to 5 minutes, stirring after 2 minutes, until thickened. Transfer to a large bowl, stir in the vanilla, and set aside to cool.

2. Use an electric mixer at high speed to beat the meringue mix, water, and cream of tartar in a medium bowl until foamy. Gradually beat in the remaining 2 tablespoons sugar, beating until stiff peaks form when the beaters are lifted.

3. Use a rubber spatula to gently fold the meringue into the thickened pineapple juice mixture until no white streaks remains. Gently fold in the pineapple, cooked rice, and chopped cherries. Cover and refrigerate for about 4 hours before serving. Serve chilled. Store leftovers, covered, in the refrigerator.

Makes 4 cups (472 g); 8 servings

Per serving (½ cup/59 g): 109 Calories, 22 g Carbohydrate, 3 g Protein, 2 g Fat, 46 mg Cholesterol, 94 mg Sodium, 1 g Fiber
Exchanges: 1 Starch, ½ Fruit (1½ Carb Choices)

Pineapple Tapioca Pudding

Prep time: 15 minutes ◆ Cook time: 30 minutes ◆ Chilling time: 30 minutes

1½ cups (360 ml) nonfat milk

3 tablespoons quick-cooking tapioca

2 tablespoons sweetened condensed milk

1 tablespoon sugar

One 8-ounce (227 g) can juice-packed crushed pineapple

½ teaspoon vanilla extract

2 tablespoons instant meringue mix or 2 teaspoons dried egg whites

2 tablespoons cold water, or 2 tablespoons warm water if using dried egg whites

1. In a 4-cup (960 ml) glass measuring cup, whisk together the nonfat milk, tapioca, sweetened condensed milk, and sugar. Let stand for 5 minutes; stir. Microwave on high for 4 to 5 minutes, stirring after 3 minutes, until the mixture boils and thickens. Stir in the pineapple with its juice and the vanilla.

2. Use an electric mixer at high speed to beat the meringue mix and water in a medium bowl until soft peaks form when the beaters are lifted. Gently fold the meringue into the pineapple mixture until no white streaks remains.

3. Spoon the pudding into 4 dessert dishes; refrigerate for about 30 minutes. Serve chilled. Store leftovers, covered, in the refrigerator.

Makes 2 cups (652 g); 4 servings

Per serving (½ cup/163 g): 117 Calories, 22 g Carbohydrate, 5 g Protein, 1 g Fat, 48 mg Cholesterol, 52 mg Sodium, 1 g Fiber
Exchanges: 1½ Fruit, ½ Nonfat Milk (2 Carb Choices)

Blueberry Tapioca Pudding

Prep time: 20 minutes ◆ Cook time: 1 hour ◆ Chilling time: 1 hour

3 tablespoons quick-cooking tapioca

3 tablespoons sugar

3 tablespoons sweetened condensed milk

2½ cups (600 ml) nonfat milk

2 teaspoons grated orange zest

1 teaspoon vanilla extract

¼ cup (43 g) instant meringue mix or 1 tablespoon plus 1 teaspoon dried egg whites

¼ cup (60 ml) cold water, or ¼ cup (60 ml) warm water if using dried egg whites

2 cups (290 g) fresh blueberries

1. Mix the tapioca, 2 tablespoons of the sugar, and the sweetened condensed milk in a 4-cup (960 ml) glass measuring cup. Gradually stir in the nonfat milk. Let stand for 5 minutes; stir.

2. Microwave on high for 4 to 5 minutes, stirring after 3 minutes, until the mixture boils and thickens. Transfer to a large bowl to cool. Stir in the orange zest and vanilla.

3. Use an electric mixer at high speed to beat the meringue mix and water in a medium bowl until soft peaks form. Gradually beat in the remaining 1 tablespoon sugar, beating until stiff peaks form when the beaters are lifted.

4. Gently fold the meringue into the tapioca mixture until no white streaks remain. Stir in the blueberries.

5. Spoon the pudding into 8 dessert dishes. Refrigerate for about 1 hour before serving. Serve chilled. Store leftovers, covered, in the refrigerator.

Makes 4 cups (424 g); 8 servings

Per serving (½ cup/53 g): 101 Calories, 17 g Carbohydrate, 6 g Protein, 1 g Fat,
48 mg Cholesterol, 69 mg Sodium, 1 g Fiber
Exchanges: 1 Fruit (1 Carb Choice)

Bread Pudding

Prep time: 20 minutes • Cook time: 10 or 45 minutes • Cooling time: 15 minutes

Cooking spray

1½ cups (341 g) reduced-fat ricotta

¾ cup (180 ml) nonfat milk

2 large eggs

2 tablespoons sugar

1 teaspoon ground cinnamon

1 teaspoon butter extract

1 teaspoon vanilla extract

4 slices whole wheat bread, cut into ½-inch (13 mm) cubes

¼ cup (42 g) chopped pitted dates

1. Preheat the oven to 350°F (180°C). Spray an 8-inch (20 cm) square baking dish with cooking spray.

2. Combine the ricotta, milk, eggs, sugar, cinnamon, butter extract, and vanilla in a food processor or blender and process until smooth. Scrape down the sides and blend again. Pour the mixture into the prepared baking dish. Add the bread cubes and dates and stir to moisten. Let stand for 15 minutes. Stir again.

3. Place a 13 x 9 x 2-inch (33 x 23 x 5 cm) pan on the middle oven rack. Set the baking dish into the larger pan in the oven. Pour boiling water into the larger pan to reach about 1 inch (2.5 cm) up the sides of the baking dish. Bake for 45 minutes or until a tester inserted into the center comes out clean. Remove the baking dish from the water bath

4. Place the pudding on a wire rack and cool for 15 minutes. Serve warm or cold. Store leftovers, covered, in the refrigerator.

5. **To microwave:** Use a microwave-safe baking dish. Microwave the pudding on high for 2 minutes; rotate. Microwave on medium for 8 to 10 minutes, rotating every 2 minutes, until the pudding is almost set. The center will be slightly soft. Let it rest on a wire rack for at least 15 minutes before serving warm.

> **Variation:** *Substitute 4 slices of whole wheat cinnamon-raisin bread for the whole wheat bread and dates.*

Makes 3 cups (840 g); 6 servings

Per serving (½ cup/140 g): 169 Calories, 20 g Carbohydrate, 11 g Protein, 5 g Fat, 16 mg Cholesterol, 203 mg Sodium, 2 g Fiber
Exchanges: 1 Starch, 1 Fat (1 Carb Choice)

Orange Soufflé

Prep time: 10 minutes ◆ Bake time: 25 minutes

Cooking spray

2 tablespoons cornstarch

2 tablespoons sugar

¾ cup (180 ml) fat-free evaporated milk

3 tablespoons frozen no-sugar-added orange juice concentrate, thawed

2 tablespoons no-sugar-added orange marmalade

1 teaspoon vanilla extract

6 large egg whites, at room temperature

½ teaspoon cream of tartar

1. Preheat the oven to 425°F (220°C). Spray a 2-quart (2 L) soufflé dish with cooking spray.

2. Mix the cornstarch and sugar in a 4-cup (960 ml) glass measuring cup. Whisk in the evaporated milk, orange juice concentrate, marmalade, and vanilla until well blended.

3. Microwave on high for 3 minutes; stir. Microwave for 2 minutes more or until thickened. Transfer to a large bowl. Set aside and let cool.

4. Use an electric mixer at high speed to beat the egg whites and cream of tartar in a large bowl, until the whites form stiff peaks when the beaters are lifted.

5. Use a rubber spatula to stir one-fourth of the beaten whites into the milk mixture to lighten it. Fold in the remaining egg whites until no white streaks remain.

6. Spoon the mixture into the prepared soufflé dish. Bake for 1 minute, then reduce the oven temperature to 375°F (190°C) and bake for 24 minutes more or until puffed and golden. Do not open the oven door during baking. Serve immediately.

Makes one 8-inch (20 cm) soufflé; 8 servings

Per serving (1 slice): 64 Calories, 11 g Carbohydrate, 5 g Protein, 0 g Fat,
1 mg Cholesterol, 69 mg Sodium, 0 g Fiber
Exchanges: 1 Nonfat Milk (1 Carb Choice)

Orange-Honey Custard

Prep time: 10 minutes • Cook time: 11 or 40 minutes • Cooling time: 15 to 30 minutes

Cooking spray

2 cups (480 ml) nonfat milk

½ cup (46 g) nonfat milk powder

2 tablespoons honey

3 large eggs

2 teaspoons grated orange zest

1 tablespoon fresh orange juice

1. Spray an 8-inch (20 cm) baking dish or 6 small (6-ounce) ramekins or custard cups with cooking spray.

2. Add the milk to a 4-cup (960 ml) glass measuring cup and microwave on high for 3 minutes; stir. Microwave for 1 minute more, until the milk hot and small bubbles form around the edge. Whisk in the milk powder and honey until smooth; set aside to cool.

3. Whisk together the eggs, orange zest and juice in a medium bowl. Slowly add to the milk mixture, whisking to blend well.

4. Pour the mixture into the prepared baking dish, ramekins, or custard cups. Place the filled dish or ramekins into a larger microwave-safe dish and fill with ½-inch (13 mm) hot water. Place in the microwave.

5. Microwave on medium for 7 to 12 minutes or until the custard is slightly firm but still soft in the center. Remove the custard-filled dish or ramekins from the water bath. Let the custard cool on a wire rack for 30 minutes before serving. This custard may be served at room temperature or chilled. Store leftovers, covered, in the refrigerator.

6. **To bake the custard:** Preheat the oven to 350°F (180°C). Pour the custard mixture into the prepared baking dish, ramekins, or custard cups, then place the custard-filled dish or ramekins into a 13 x 9 x 2-inch (33 x 23 x 5 cm) baking pan. Place the baking pan with the custard-filled dish or ramekins in the oven, then fill the baking pan with 1-inch (2.5 cm) hot water if using the baking dish, or ¾-inch (2 cm) hot water if using ramekins or custard cups. Bake until the custard is not quite set, about 25 to 35 minutes for the ramekins and 40 to 50 minutes for the baking dish. A tester inserted into the center should come out clean. Remove the custard from the water bath and cool on a wire rack for at least 15 minutes before serving. Store leftovers, covered, in the refrigerator.

Makes 3 cups (732 g); 6 servings

Per serving (½ cup/122 g): 107 Calories, 13 g Carbohydrate, 8 g Protein, 2 g Fat, 90 mg Cholesterol, 96 mg Sodium, 0 g Fiber
Exchanges: 1 Nonfat Milk (1 Carb Choice)

Quick Breads

Tips & Tricks

» Quick breads are aptly named—they are quick and simple to prepare. They're sometimes called tea breads, since they are the perfect accompaniment to a cup of tea or coffee. These breads can be served plain or spread with Yogurt Cheese (page 96), buttery spreads, reduced-fat cream cheese, natural peanut butter, and no-sugar-added jams and jellies. They add a special touch to any meal when used as a sandwich bread or as an addition to soup and salad. They also make terrific snacks, because they are low in sugar, contain "good" fats, and are made with whole grains. When served with fresh fruit, a slice of quick bread is a tasty finale to any meal.

» Some quick breads contain fruit for added flavor and tenderness. Many also contain nuts that are toasted before being added to the recipe, which enhances the flavor.

» As with most of my baked goods recipes, I've used both whole wheat flour and all-purpose flour. Whole wheat pastry flour or white whole wheat flour can be substituted for whole wheat flour. I prefer using whole grains, since many vitamins, minerals, and fiber are not removed in the milling process.

» Similar to making muffins, coffee cakes, and scones, do *not* overmix quick breads. Stir together the dry ingredients, then stir in fruit and/or nuts. Mix the wet ingredients separately from the dry ingredients, then combine the dry and wet ingredients just until blended.

» Many quick breads develop a crack in the center as they bake. This is typical. If the bread contains fruit, don't keep it at room temperature for more than two days, or it can become rancid. After two days, store quick breads in the refrigerator. When ready to serve, slice the bread and either toast or microwave it until warm.

» If you're baking more than one loaf on the same oven rack, make sure there's at least 2 inches (5 cm) between baking pans so that the breads bake evenly. Ovens vary; therefore, I recommend testing the bread for doneness before removing it from the oven.

» If you prefer to bake small loaves instead of one large loaf, three small 5 x 2-inch (13 x 5 cm) loaf pans can be substituted for one 9 x 5-inch (23 x 13 cm) loaf pan. Or one 7½ x 3¾-inch (19 x 10 cm) and one 5 x 3-inch (13 x 8 cm) loaf pan can be substituted for a 9 x 5-inch (23 x 13 cm) loaf pan. If using glass loaf pan(s), lower the oven temperature by 25°F (14°C).

» Many quick breads will be easier to slice if covered and stored for at least 4 hours or overnight after baking. I recommend using a serrated knife to slice them. They can also be sliced and stored in the freezer for several months. Just pop them in the toaster straight from the freezer and enjoy.

Apricot Bread

Prep time: 10 minutes ◆ Bake time: 1 hour

Cooking spray

¼ cup (31 g) chopped pecans or
  walnuts (optional)

1 cup (120 g) all-purpose flour

1 cup (120 g) whole wheat flour

¼ cup (48 g) sugar

2 teaspoons baking powder

¼ teaspoon baking soda

¼ teaspoon salt

½ cup (80 g) chopped dried apricots

1 tablespoon grated orange zest

¾ cup (180 ml) fresh orange juice

1 large egg

2 tablespoons canola or extra-light
  olive oil

1. Preheat the oven to 350°F (180°C). Spray a 9 x 5-inch (23 x 13 cm) loaf pan with cooking spray.

2. If using nuts, place them in a small baking pan and bake for 3 to 5 minutes, until toasted; set aside.

3. Stir together the flours, sugar, baking powder, baking soda, and salt in a large bowl. Stir in the apricots, and toasted nuts, if desired.

4. Whisk together the orange zest and juice, egg, and oil in a small bowl. Add the wet ingredients to the dry ingredients and stir just until blended; do not overmix. Spoon the batter into the prepared loaf pan.

5. Bake for 60 to 65 minutes or until a tester inserted into the center of the bread comes out clean.

6. Cool in the pan on a wire rack for 10 minutes. Use a knife to loosen the bread; turn it out onto the rack to cool completely. Store, covered, for at least 4 hours or overnight for easier slicing. Refrigerate after 2 days. This bread may be frozen for up to 3 months.

Makes one 9 x 5-inch (23 x 13 cm) loaf; 16 servings

Per serving (1 slice): 111 Calories, 18 g Carbohydrate, 2 g Protein, 3 g Fat,
11 mg Cholesterol, 60 mg Sodium, 2 g Fiber
Exchanges: 1 Starch, ½ Fat (1 Carb Choice)

Apple Oatmeal Loaf

Prep time: 10 minutes ◆ Bake time: 1 hour

Cooking spray

¼ cup (33 g) chopped walnuts (optional)

1 cup (90 g) old-fashioned rolled oats

¾ cup (90 g) all-purpose flour

¾ cup (90 g) whole wheat flour

2 teaspoons baking powder

1 teaspoon baking soda

1 teaspoon ground cinnamon

½ teaspoon ground nutmeg

¼ teaspoon salt

1½ cups (188 g) peeled, cored, and diced apple (1 large)

2 large eggs

¼ cup (48 g) packed brown sugar

¼ cup (60 ml) nonfat milk

¼ cup (60 ml) canola or extra-light olive oil

1 tablespoon fresh lemon juice

1. Preheat the oven to 350°F (180°C). Spray a 9 x 5-inch (23 x 13 cm) loaf pan with cooking spray.

2. If using nuts, place them in a small baking pan and bake for 3 to 5 minutes, until toasted; set aside.

3. Stir together the oats, flours, baking powder, baking soda, cinnamon, nutmeg, and salt in a large bowl. Stir in the apple and toasted walnuts, if desired.

4. Whisk together the eggs, brown sugar, milk, oil, and lemon juice in a medium bowl. Add the wet ingredients to the dry ingredients and stir just until blended; do not overmix. Spoon the batter into the prepared loaf pan.

5. Bake for 60 to 65 minutes or until a tester inserted into the center of the bread comes out clean.

6. Cool in the pan on a wire rack for 10 minutes. Use a knife to loosen the bread; turn it out onto the rack to cool completely. Store, covered, for at least 4 hours or overnight for easier slicing. Refrigerate after 2 days. This bread may be frozen for up to 3 months.

Makes one 9 x 5-inch (23 x 13 cm) loaf; 16 servings

Per serving (1 slice): 133 Calories, 18 g Carbohydrate, 3 g Protein, 6 g Fat, 22 mg Cholesterol, 125 mg Sodium, 2 g Fiber
Exchanges: 1 Starch, 1 Fat (1 Carb Choice)

Applesauce Bread

Prep time: 10 minutes ◆ Bake time: 45 minutes ◆ Cooling time: 1 hour

Cooking spray

½ cup (65 g) chopped nuts

1 cup (120 g) all-purpose flour

1 cup (120 g) whole wheat flour

1 teaspoon baking powder

½ teaspoon baking soda

½ teaspoon ground cinnamon

¼ teaspoon ground nutmeg

¼ teaspoon salt

1½ cups (366 g) unsweetened applesauce

¼ cup (80 g) honey

2 large eggs

1. Preheat the oven to 350°F (180°C). Spray a 9 x 5-inch (23 x 13 cm) loaf pan with cooking spray.

2. Place the nuts in a small baking pan and bake for 3 to 5 minutes, until toasted; set aside.

3. Stir together the flours, baking powder, baking soda, cinnamon, nutmeg and salt in a large bowl. Stir in the toasted nuts.

4. Whisk together the applesauce, honey, and eggs in a medium bowl until well mixed. Add the wet ingredients to the dry ingredients and stir just until blended; do not overmix. Spoon the batter into the prepared loaf pan.

5. Bake for 45 to 50 minutes or until a tester inserted into the center of the bread comes out clean.

6. Cool in the pan on a wire rack for 10 minutes. Use a knife to loosen the bread; turn it out onto the rack to cool completely, for 1 hour. Store, covered, for at least 4 hours or overnight, for easier slicing. Refrigerate after 2 days. This bread can be frozen for up to 3 months.

Makes one 9 x 5-inch (23 x 13 cm) loaf; 16 servings

Per serving (1 slice): 112 Calories, 19 g Carbohydrate, 3 g Protein, 3 g Fat,
22 mg Cholesterol, 84 mg Sodium, 2 g Fiber
Exchanges: 1 Starch, ½ Fat (1 Carb Choice)

Banana Nut Bread

Prep time: 10 minutes • Bake time: 1 hour • Cooling time: 1 hour

Cooking spray

¼ cup (31 g) chopped pecans or walnuts

1 cup (120 g) all-purpose flour

1 cup (120 g) whole wheat flour

¼ cup (48 g) sugar

2 teaspoons baking powder

½ teaspoon baking soda

½ teaspoon ground nutmeg

¼ teaspoon salt

1½ cups (336 g) mashed ripe bananas (3 medium or 2 large)

¼ cup (60 ml) canola or extra-light olive oil

1 large egg

2 tablespoons fresh orange juice

½ teaspoon vanilla extract

1. Preheat the oven to 350°F (180°C). Spray a 9 x 5-inch (23 x 13 cm) loaf pan with cooking spray.

2. Place the nuts in a small baking pan and bake for 3 to 5 minutes, until toasted; set aside.

3. Stir together the flours, sugar, baking powder, baking soda, nutmeg, and salt in a large bowl. Stir in the toasted nuts.

4. Whisk together the banana, oil, egg, orange juice, and vanilla in a medium bowl until well blended. Add the wet ingredients to the dry ingredients and stir just until blended; do not overmix. Spoon the batter into the prepared loaf pan.

5. Bake for 60 to 65 minutes or until a tester inserted into the center of the bread comes out clean.

6. Cool in the pan on a wire rack for 10 minutes. Use a knife to loosen the bread; turn it out onto the rack to cool completely, for 1 hour. Store, covered, for at least 4 hours or overnight for easier slicing. Refrigerate after 2 days. This bread can be frozen for up to 3 months.

Makes one 9 x 5-inch (23 x 13 cm) loaf; 16 servings

Per serving (1 slice): 130 Calories, 19 g Carbohydrate, 3 g Protein, 5 g Fat,
11 mg Cholesterol, 80 mg Sodium, 2 g Fiber
Exchanges: 1 Starch, 1 Fat (1 Carb Choice)

Blueberry Bran Bread

Prep time: 10 minutes ◆ Bake time: 50 minutes

Cooking spray

¼ cup (33 g) chopped nuts
   (optional)

1 cup (120 g) all-purpose flour

¾ cup (90 g) whole wheat flour

½ cup (29 g) wheat bran

2 teaspoons baking powder

½ teaspoon baking soda

1 teaspoon ground nutmeg

¼ teaspoon salt

1 cup (145 g) fresh or frozen
   blueberries

¾ cup (180 ml) fresh orange juice

1 large egg

¼ cup (48 g) packed brown sugar

2 tablespoons canola or extra-light
   olive oil

2 tablespoons grated lemon zest

1. Preheat the oven to 350°F (180°C). Spray a 9 x 5-inch (23 x 13 cm) loaf pan with cooking spray.

2. If using nuts, place them in a small baking pan and bake for 3 to 5 minutes, until toasted; set aside.

3. Stir together the flours, bran, baking powder, baking soda, nutmeg, and salt in a large bowl. Stir in the blueberries and toasted nuts, if desired, until coated with the flour mixture.

4. Whisk together the orange juice, egg, brown sugar, oil, and lemon zest in a medium bowl until well mixed. Add the wet ingredients to the dry ingredients and stir just until blended; do not overmix. Spoon the batter into the prepared loaf pan.

5. Bake for 50 to 55 minutes or until a tester inserted into the center of the bread comes out clean.

6. Cool in the pan on a wire rack for 10 minutes. Use a knife to loosen the bread; turn it out onto the rack to cool completely. Store, covered, for at least 4 hours or overnight for easier slicing. Refrigerate after 2 days. This bread can be frozen for up to 3 months.

Makes one 9 x 5-inch (23 x 13 cm) loaf; 16 servings

Per serving (1 slice): 109 Calories, 18 g Carbohydrate, 3 g Protein, 3 g Fat,
11 mg Cholesterol, 80 mg Sodium, 2 g Fiber
Exchanges: 1 Starch, ½ Fat (1 Carb Choice)

Mini Blueberry Loaves

Prep time: 15 minutes ◆ Bake time: 40 minutes ◆ Cooling time: 1 hour

Cooking spray

2 cups (240 g) all-purpose flour

1 cup (120 g) whole wheat flour

¼ cup (48 g) sugar

1 tablespoon baking powder

½ teaspoon baking soda

1 teaspoon ground nutmeg

¼ teaspoon salt

2 cups (290 g) fresh or frozen
  blueberries

1 cup (244 g) unsweetened
  applesauce

2 large eggs

1 tablespoon canola or extra-light
  olive oil

1 tablespoon grated lemon zest

1. Preheat the oven to 350°F (180°C). Spray 3 mini loaf pans (4½ x 2¾-inch/11 x 7 cm) with cooking spray.

2. Stir together the flours, sugar, baking powder, baking soda, nutmeg, and salt in a large bowl. Stir in the blueberries until coated with the flour mixture.

3. Whisk together the applesauce, eggs, oil, and lemon zest in a medium bowl until well mixed. Add the wet ingredients to the dry ingredients and stir just until blended; do not overmix.

4. Spoon the batter into the prepared loaf pans. Bake for 40 to 45 minutes or until a tester inserted into the center of the bread comes out clean.

5. Cool in the pans on wire racks for 10 minutes. Use a knife to loosen the loaves; turn them out onto the racks to cool completely, for 1 hour. Store, covered, for at least 4 hours or overnight for easier slicing. Refrigerate after 2 days. These loaves may be frozen for up to 3 months.

> **Variation:** *These loaves can also be baked in a sprayed 9 x 5-inch (23 x 13 cm) loaf pan. Bake for 55 to 60 minutes or until a tester inserted into the center comes out clean.*

Makes 3 mini loaves; 18 servings

Per serving (1 slice): 120 Calories, 24 g Carbohydrate, 4 g Protein, 2 g Fat,
20 mg Cholesterol, 75 mg Sodium, 2 g Fiber
Exchanges: 1 Starch, 1 Fruit (2 Carb Choices)

Quick Bran Bread

Prep time: 10 minutes ◆ Bake time: 50 minutes ◆ Cooling time: 1 hour

Cooking spray

¼ cup (33 g) chopped walnuts (optional)

1½ cups (360 ml) nonfat milk

1 cup (58 g) wheat bran

¼ cup (80 g) molasses

1 cup (120 g) all-purpose flour

1 cup (120 g) whole wheat flour

2 tablespoons sugar

1 tablespoon baking powder

½ teaspoon baking soda

¼ teaspoon salt

1 large egg

¼ cup (60 ml) canola or extra-light olive oil

1. Preheat the oven to 350°F (180°C). Spray a 9 x 5-inch (23 x 13 cm) loaf pan with cooking spray.

2. If using walnuts, place them in a small baking pan and bake for 3 to 5 minutes, until toasted; set aside.

3. Mix the milk, bran, and molasses in a medium bowl; let stand for 5 minutes or until the bran is soft. Stir and set aside.

4. Stir together the flours, sugar, baking powder, baking soda, and salt in a large bowl. Stir in the toasted walnuts, if desired.

5. Whisk the egg and oil into the bran mixture until well blended. Add the wet ingredients to the dry ingredients and stir just until blended; do not overmix. Spoon the batter into the prepared loaf pan.

6. Bake for 50 to 55 minutes or until a tester inserted into the center of the bread comes out clean.

7. Cool in the pan on a wire rack for 10 minutes. Use a knife to loosen the bread; turn it out onto the rack to cool completely, for 1 hour. Store, covered, for at least 4 hours or overnight for easier slicing. Refrigerate after 2 days. This bread can be frozen for up to 3 months.

Makes one 9 x 5-inch (23 x 13 cm) loaf; 16 servings

Per serving (1 slice): 140 Calories, 20 g Carbohydrate, 4 g Protein, 5 g Fat, 11 mg Cholesterol, 91 mg Sodium, 3 g Fiber
Exchanges: 1 Starch, 1 Fat (1 Carb Choice)

Spicy Carrot Bread

Prep time: 10 minutes • Bake time: 45 minutes • Cooling time: 1 hour

Cooking spray

1 cup (120 g) whole wheat flour

½ cup (60 g) all-purpose flour

2 teaspoons baking powder

½ teaspoon baking soda

1 teaspoon ground cinnamon

½ teaspoon ground ginger

¼ teaspoon salt

1½ cups (165 g) shredded carrots

2 tablespoons golden raisins

¼ cup (33 g) chopped walnuts

⅓ cup (80 ml) nonfat milk

¼ cup (48 g) packed brown sugar

¼ cup (60 ml) canola or extra-light olive oil

1 large egg

1 tablespoon grated orange zest

2 tablespoons fresh orange juice

1 teaspoon vanilla extract

1. Preheat the oven to 375°F (190°C). Spray a 9 x 5-inch (23 x 13 cm) loaf pan with cooking spray.

2. Stir together the flours, baking powder, baking soda, cinnamon, ginger, and salt in a large bowl. Stir in the carrots, raisins, and walnuts until coated with the flour mixture.

3. Whisk together the milk, brown sugar, oil, egg, orange zest and juice, and vanilla in a medium bowl. Add the wet ingredients to the dry ingredients and stir just until blended; do not overmix. Spoon the batter into the prepared loaf pan.

4. Bake for 45 to 50 minutes or until a tester inserted into the center of the bread comes out clean.

5. Cool in the pan on a rack for 10 minutes. Use a knife to loosen the bread; turn it out onto the rack to cool completely, for 1 hour. Store, covered, for at least 4 hours or overnight for easier slicing. Refrigerate after 2 days. This bread can be frozen for up to 3 months.

Makes one 9 x 5-inch (23 x 13 cm) loaf; 16 servings

Per serving (1 slice): 111 Calories, 15 g Carbohydrate, 2 g Protein, 5 g Fat, 11 mg Cholesterol, 90 mg Sodium, 2 g Fiber
Exchanges: 1 Starch, 1 Fat (1 Carb Choice)

Cranberry Nut Bread

Prep time: 10 minutes • Bake time: 40 minutes or 55 minutes • Cooling time: 1 hour

Cooking spray

½ cup (65 g) chopped nuts

1 cup (120 g) all-purpose flour

1 cup (120 g) whole wheat flour

1½ teaspoons baking powder

1 teaspoon baking soda

¼ teaspoon salt

1 cup (100 g) fresh or frozen cranberries

1 tablespoon grated orange zest

¾ cup (180 ml) fresh orange juice

¼ cup (48 g) packed brown sugar

¼ cup (60 ml) canola or extra-light olive oil

1 large egg

1. Preheat the oven to 325°F (165°C). Spray three 5½ x 3-inch (14 x 7.5 cm) mini loaf pans or a 9 x 5-inch (23 x 13 cm) loaf pan with cooking spray.

2. Place the nuts in a small baking pan and bake for 3 to 5 minutes, until toasted; set aside.

3. Stir together the flours, baking powder, baking soda, and salt in a large bowl. Stir in the cranberries and toasted nuts until well mixed.

4. Whisk together the orange zest and juice, brown sugar, oil, and egg in a medium bowl. Add the wet ingredients to the dry ingredients and stir just until blended; do not overmix. Spoon the batter into the prepared loaf pan.

5. Bake for 40 to 45 minutes for the smaller loaves or 55 to 60 minutes for the larger loaf or until a tester inserted into the center of the bread comes out clean.

6. Cool on a wire rack for 10 minutes. Use a knife to loosen the bread; turn out onto the rack to cool completely, for 1 hour. Store, covered, for at least 4 hours or overnight for easier slicing. Refrigerate after 2 days. This bread can be frozen for up to 3 months.

Makes one 9 x 5-inch (23 x 13 cm) loaf; 16 servings

Per serving (1 slice): 167 Calories, 25 g Carbohydrate, 3 g Protein, 6 g Fat,
11 mg Cholesterol, 120 mg Sodium, 2 g Fiber
Exchanges: 1½ Starch, 1 Fat (1½ Carb Choices)

Chocolate Quick Bread

Prep time: 10 minutes ◆ Bake time: 55 minutes ◆ Cooling time: 1 hour

Cooking spray

1¼ cups (150 g) all-purpose flour

1¼ cups (150 g) whole wheat flour

½ cup (96 g) sugar

¼ cup (20 g) unsweetened cocoa
powder, sifted if lumpy

1 tablespoon baking powder

¼ teaspoon salt

1⅓ cups (320 ml) nonfat milk

1 large egg

¼ cup (60 ml) canola or extra-light
olive oil

2 tablespoons fresh orange juice

2 tablespoons chopped nuts

1. Preheat the oven to 350°F (180°C). Spray a 9 x
   5-inch (23 x 13 cm) loaf pan with cooking spray.

2. Stir together the flours, sugar, cocoa powder,
   baking powder, and salt in a large bowl.

3. Whisk together the milk, egg, oil, and orange
   juice in a medium bowl until well blended. Add
   the wet ingredients to the dry ingredients and
   stir just until blended; do not overmix. Spoon the
   batter into the prepared loaf pan. Sprinkle with
   the nuts and lightly press them into the batter.

4. Bake for 55 to 60 minutes or until a tester
   inserted into the center of the bread comes out
   clean.

5. Cool in the pan on a wire rack for 10 minutes. Use
   a knife to loosen the bread; turn it out onto the
   rack to cool completely, for 1 hour. Store, covered,
   for at least 4 hours or overnight for easier slicing.
   Refrigerate after 2 days. This bread can be frozen
   for up to 3 months.

Makes one 9 x 5-inch (23 x 13 cm) loaf; 16 servings

Per serving (1 slice): 134 Calories, 21 g Carbohydrate, 4 g Protein, 5 g Fat,
11 mg Cholesterol, 49 mg Sodium, 2 g Fiber
Exchanges: 1½ Starch, 1 Fat (1½ Carb Choices)

Date Nut Bread

Cooking spray

½ cup (62 g) chopped pecans

1½ cups (360 ml) nonfat milk

¾ cup (124 g) chopped pitted dates

1½ cups (180 g) all-purpose flour

1½ cups (180 g) whole wheat flour

¼ cup (48 g) sugar

1 tablespoon baking powder

½ teaspoon baking soda

¼ teaspoon salt

1 large egg

3 tablespoons canola or extra-light olive oil

3 tablespoons fresh orange juice

1 teaspoon vanilla extract

1. Preheat the oven to 350°F (180°C). Spray a 9 x 5-inch (23 x 13 cm) loaf pan with cooking spray.

2. Place the pecans in a small baking pan and bake for 3 to 5 minutes, until toasted; set aside.

3. Microwave the milk in a 4-cup (960 ml) glass measuring cup on high for 4 minutes. Stir in the dates; let cool.

4. Stir together the flours, sugar, baking powder, baking soda, and salt in a large bowl. Stir in the toasted pecans.

5. Add the egg, oil, orange juice, and vanilla to the cooled milk and whisk to combine. Add the wet ingredients to the dry ingredients and stir just until blended; do not overmix. Spoon the batter into the prepared loaf pan. Let it rest for 20 minutes.

6. Bake for 60 to 70 minutes or until a tester inserted into the center of the bread comes out clean.

7. Cool in the pan on a wire rack for 10 minutes. Use a knife to loosen the bread; turn it out onto a wire rack to cool completely, for 1 hour. Store, covered, for at least 4 hours or overnight for easier slicing. Refrigerate after 2 days. This bread can be frozen for up to 3 months.

Tip: *This bread is great spread with nonfat cream cheese or Yogurt Cheese (page 96).*

Makes one 9 x 5-inch (23 x 13 cm) loaf; 16 servings

Per serving (1 slice): 172 Calories, 27 g Carbohydrate, 4 g Protein, 6 g Fat,
11 mg Cholesterol, 89 mg Sodium, 2 g Fiber
Exchanges: 1½ Starch, ½ Fruit, 1 Fat (2 Carb Choices)

Peanut Butter Bread

Prep time: 10 minutes ◆ Bake time: 45 minutes ◆ Cooling time: 1 hour

Cooking spray

1 cup (120 g) all-purpose flour

1 cup (120 g) whole wheat flour

1 cup (90 g) old-fashioned rolled oats

1 tablespoon baking powder

¼ teaspoon salt

½ cup (85 g) raisins (optional)

1½ cups (360 ml) nonfat milk

2 large eggs

½ cup (128 g) natural chunky peanut butter

¼ cup (80 g) honey

2 tablespoons canola or extra-light olive oil

1. Preheat the oven to 350°F (180°C). Spray a 9 x 5-inch (23 x 13 cm) loaf pan with cooking spray.

2. Stir together the flours, oats, baking powder, and salt in a large bowl. If desired, stir in the raisins.

3. Whisk together the milk, eggs, peanut butter, honey, and oil in a medium bowl. Add the wet ingredients to the dry ingredients and stir just until blended; do not overmix. Spoon the batter into the prepared loaf pan.

4. Bake for 40 to 45 minutes or until a tester inserted into the center of the bread comes out clean.

5. Cool on a wire rack for 10 minutes. Use a knife to loosen the bread; turn it out onto the rack to cool completely, for 1 hour. Store, covered, for at least 4 hours or overnight for easier slicing. Refrigerate after 2 days. This bread can be frozen for up to 3 months.

Makes one 9 x 5-inch (23 x 13 cm) loaf; 16 servings

Per serving (1 slice): 187 Calories, 25 g Carbohydrate, 6 g Protein, 7 g Fat,
22 mg Cholesterol, 77 mg Sodium, 2 g Fiber
Exchanges: 1½ Starch, 1 Fat (1½ Carb Choices)

Poppy Seed Bread

Prep time: 10 minutes • Bake time: 40 minutes • Cooling time: 1 hour

Cooking spray

2 cups (240 g) all-purpose flour

1½ cups (180 g) whole wheat flour

1 tablespoon plus 1 teaspoon
  baking powder

2 tablespoons poppy seeds

1¼ cups (300 ml) nonfat milk

3 large eggs, at room temperature

¼ cup (80 g) honey

¼ cup (60 ml) canola or extra-light
  olive oil

1 tablespoon grated lemon zest

1. Preheat the oven to 350°F (180°C). Spray two 7½ x 3¾-inch (19 x 10 cm) loaf pans with cooking spray.

2. Stir together the flours, baking powder, and poppy seeds in a large bowl.

3. Whisk together the milk, eggs, honey, oil, and lemon zest in a medium bowl until well blended. Add the wet ingredients to the dry ingredients and stir just until blended; do not overmix. Spoon the batter into the prepared loaf pans.

4. Bake for 40 to 45 minutes or until a tester inserted into the center of the bread comes out clean.

5. Cool in the pans on wire racks for 10 minutes. Use a knife to loosen the breads; turn them out onto the racks to cool completely, for 1 hour. Serve warm. Store covered. Refrigerate after 2 days. This bread can be frozen for up to 3 months.

Makes two 7½ x 3¾-inch (19 x 10 cm) loaves; 24 servings

Per serving (1 slice): 111 Calories, 17 g Carbohydrate, 3 g Protein, 3 g Fat,
22 mg Cholesterol, 13 mg Sodium, 1 g Fiber
Exchanges: 1 Starch, ½ Fat (1 Carb Choice)

Pineapple Bread

Prep time: 10 minutes • Bake time: 60 minutes • Cooling time: 1 hour

Cooking spray

¼ cup (33 g) chopped nuts (optional)

1 cup (120 g) all-purpose flour

1 cup (120 g) whole wheat flour

¼ cup (48 g) sugar

1 teaspoon baking powder

1 teaspoon baking soda

¼ teaspoon salt

1 large egg

2 tablespoons canola or extra-light olive oil

1 teaspoon vanilla extract

One 8-ounce (227 g) can juice-packed crushed pineapple

1. Preheat the oven to 350°F (180°C). Spray a 9 x 5-inch (23 x 13 cm) loaf pan with cooking spray.

2. If using nuts, place them in a small baking pan and bake for 3 to 5 minutes, until toasted; set aside.

3. Stir together the flours, sugar, baking powder, baking soda, and salt in a large bowl. Stir in the toasted nuts, if desired.

4. Whisk together the egg, oil, vanilla, and pineapple with its juice in a medium bowl, until well mixed. Add the wet ingredients to the dry ingredients and stir just until blended; do not overmix.

5. Spoon the batter into the prepared loaf pan. Bake for 60 to 65 minutes or until a tester inserted into the center of the bread comes out clean.

6. Cool in the pan on a wire rack for 10 minutes. Use a knife to loosen the bread; turn it out onto the rack to cool completely, for 1 hour. Store, covered, for at least 4 hours or overnight for easier slicing. Refrigerate after 2 days. This bread can be frozen for up to 3 months.

Makes one 9 x 5-inch (23 x 13 cm) loaf; 16 servings

Per serving (1 slice): 102 Calories, 16 g Carbohydrate, 2 g Protein, 3 g Fat, 11 mg Cholesterol, 119 mg Sodium, 1 g Fiber
Exchanges: 1 Starch, ½ Fat (1 Carb Choice)

Raisin Beer Bread

Prep time: 10 minutes • Bake time: 45 minutes • Cooling time: 1 hour

Cooking spray

1½ cups (180 g) all-purpose flour

1½ cups (180 g) whole wheat flour

2½ teaspoons baking powder

1½ teaspoons baking soda

1 teaspoon ground cinnamon

½ teaspoon ground nutmeg

¼ teaspoon ground cloves

½ cup (85 g) raisins

One 12-ounce (355 ml) can light beer

1 tablespoon honey

1. Preheat the oven to 350°F (180°C). Spray a 9 x 5-inch (23 x 13 cm) loaf pan with cooking spray.

2. Stir together the flours, baking powder, baking soda, cinnamon, nutmeg, and cloves in a large bowl. Stir in the raisins until well coated with the flour mixture. Add the beer and honey and stir just until blended; do not overmix. Spoon the batter into the prepared loaf pan.

3. Bake for 45 to 50 minutes or until a tester inserted into the center of the bread comes out clean.

4. Cool in the pan on a wire rack for 10 minutes. Use a knife to loosen the bread; turn it out onto the rack to cool completely, for 1 hour. Store, covered, for at least 4 hours or overnight for easier slicing. Refrigerate after 2 days. This bread can be frozen for up to 3 months.

Makes one 9 x 5-inch (23 x 13 cm) loaf; 16 servings

Per serving (1 slice): 105 Calories, 22 g Carbohydrate, 3 g Protein, 0 g Fat,
0 mg Cholesterol, 120 mg Sodium, 2 g Fiber
Exchanges: 1½ Starch (1½ Carb Choices)

Pumpkin Date Bread

Prep time: 10 minutes ◆ Bake time: 50 minutes ◆ Cooling time: 90 minutes

Cooking spray

¼ cup (33 g) chopped nuts
(optional)

1 cup (120 g) all-purpose flour

1 cup (120 g) whole wheat flour

1 teaspoon baking powder

1 teaspoon baking soda

2 teaspoons pumpkin pie spice

¼ teaspoon salt

½ cup (83 g) chopped pitted dates
or figs

1 cup (230 g) canned pumpkin or
puréed cooked fresh pumpkin

2 large eggs

½ cup (120 ml) fresh orange juice

¼ cup (48 g) packed brown sugar

¼ cup (60 ml) canola or extra-light
olive oil

1. Preheat the oven to 350°F (180°C). Spray a 9 x 5-inch (23 x 13 cm) loaf pan with cooking spray.

2. If using nuts, place them in a small baking pan and bake for 3 to 5 minutes, until toasted; set aside.

3. Stir together the flours, baking powder, baking soda, pumpkin pie spice, and salt in a large bowl. Stir in the dates and toasted nuts, if desired, until coated with the flour mixture.

4. Whisk together the pumpkin, eggs, orange juice, brown sugar, and oil in a medium bowl until well blended. Add the wet ingredients to the dry ingredients and stir just until blended; do not overmix. Spoon the batter into the prepared loaf pan.

5. Bake for 50 to 55 minutes or until a tester inserted into the center of the bread comes out clean.

6. Cool in the pan on a wire rack for 20 minutes. Use a knife to loosen the bread; turn it out onto the rack to cool completely, for 90 minutes. Store, covered, for at least 4 hours or overnight for easier slicing. Refrigerate after 2 days. This bread can be frozen for up to 3 months.

Makes one 9 x 5-inch (23 x 13 cm) loaf; 16 servings

Per serving (1 slice): 142 Calories, 21 g Carbohydrate, 3 g Protein, 5 g Fat,
22 mg Cholesterol, 124 mg Sodium, 2 g Fiber
Exchanges: 1 Starch, ½ Fruit, 1 Fat (1½ Carb Choices)

Raspberry Bread

Prep time: 10 minutes • Bake time: 1 hour • Cooling time: 1 hour

Cooking spray

¼ cup (33 g) chopped nuts
(optional)

1 cup (120 g) all-purpose flour

1 cup (120 g) whole wheat flour

¼ cup (48 g) sugar

2½ teaspoons baking powder

½ teaspoon baking soda

¼ teaspoon salt

2 cups (250 g) fresh or frozen
raspberries

1 tablespoon grated orange zest

¾ cup (180 ml) fresh orange juice

1 large egg

3 tablespoons canola or extra-light
olive oil

1. Preheat the oven to 350°F (180°C). Spray a 9 x 5-inch (23 x 13 cm) loaf pan with cooking spray.

2. If using nuts, place them in a small baking pan and bake for 3 to 5 minutes, until toasted; set aside.

3. Stir together the flours, sugar, baking powder, baking soda, and salt in a large bowl. Gently fold in the raspberries and toasted nuts, if desired, until the raspberries are coated with flour.

4. Whisk the orange zest and juice, egg, and oil in a small bowl. Gently stir the wet ingredients into the dry ingredients just until blended; do not overmix. Spoon the batter into the prepared loaf pan.

5. Bake for 60 to 65 minutes or until a tester inserted into the center of the bread comes out clean.

6. Cool in the pan on a wire rack for 10 minutes. Use a knife to loosen the bread; turn it out onto the rack to cool completely, for 1 hour. Store, covered, for at least 4 hours or overnight for easier slicing. Refrigerate after 2 days. This bread can be frozen for up to 3 months.

Variation: *To make strawberry bread, use 1 cup (151 g) sliced fresh strawberries in place of the raspberries.*

Makes one 9 x 5-inch (23 x 13 cm) loaf; 16 servings

Per serving (1 slice): 113 Calories, 18 g Carbohydrate, 3 g Protein, 4 g Fat,
11 mg Cholesterol, 80 mg Sodium, 1 g Fiber
Exchanges: 1 Starch, 1 Fat (1 Carb Choice)

Soda Bread

Prep time: 10 minutes • Bake time: 55 minutes

1½ cups (180 g) all-purpose flour, plus more for dusting

1½ cups (180 g) whole wheat flour

½ teaspoon baking powder

1 teaspoon baking soda

¼ teaspoon salt

½ cup (85 g) raisins

2 tablespoons caraway seeds

1 cup (240 g) buttermilk (see page 8)

1 large egg

1 tablespoon canola or extra-light olive oil

1. Preheat the oven to 350°F (180°C). Line a baking sheet with parchment paper.

2. Stir together the flours, baking powder, baking soda, and salt in a large bowl. Stir in the raisins and caraway seeds until coated with the flour.

3. Whisk together the buttermilk, egg, and oil in a medium bowl until well mixed. Add the wet ingredients to the dry ingredients and stir well to form a sticky dough.

4. Place the dough on a floured board, sprinkle with flour, and knead two or three times. Shape into a round loaf and place on the lined baking sheet. Flatten to an 8-inch (20 cm) circle about 1½ inches (4 cm) thick. Use a sharp knife to mark a ½-inch (13 mm) deep cross in the top of the bread.

5. Bake for 55 to 60 minutes or until a tester inserted into the center comes out clean. Serve immediately or let cool on a wire rack. Cut into wedges and toast to serve. Store covered. Refrigerate after 2 days. This bread can be frozen for up to 3 months.

Makes 1 round loaf; 16 servings

Per serving (1 wedge): 114 Calories, 22 g Carbohydrate, 4 g Protein, 2 g Fat, 12 mg Cholesterol, 149 mg Sodium, 2 g Fiber
Exchanges: 1½ Starch (1½ Carb Choices)

Sesame Tea Bread

Prep time: 10 minutes • Bake time: 1 hour • Cooling time: 1 hour

Cooking spray

½ cup (64 g) plus 1 tablespoon sesame seeds

1½ cups (180 g) all-purpose flour

1½ cups (180 g) whole wheat flour

¼ cup (48 g) sugar

1 tablespoon baking powder

¼ teaspoon salt

1½ cups (360 ml) nonfat milk

2 large eggs

¼ cup (60 ml) canola or extra-light olive oil

1 tablespoon grated lemon zest

1. Preheat the oven to 325°F (165°C). Spray a 9 x 5-inch (23 x 13 cm) loaf pan with cooking spray.

2. Place ½ cup (64 g) of the sesame seeds in a small baking pan and bake for 3 to 5 minutes, until toasted; set aside.

3. Stir together the flours, sugar, baking powder, salt, and toasted sesame seeds in a large bowl.

4. Whisk together the milk, eggs, oil, and lemon zest in a medium bowl until well blended. Add the wet ingredients to the dry ingredients and stir just until blended; do not overmix. Spoon the batter into the prepared loaf pan and sprinkle with the remaining 1 tablespoon sesame seeds.

5. Bake for 60 to 65 minutes or until a tester inserted into the center of the bread comes out clean.

6. Cool in the pan on a wire rack for 10 minutes. Use a knife to loosen the bread; turn it out onto the rack to cool completely, for 1 hour. Serve warm. Store covered. Refrigerate after 2 days. This bread may be frozen for up to 3 months.

Tip: *This is best served toasted, with your favorite nut butter, buttery spread, or no-sugar-added fruit preserves.*

Makes one 9 x 5-inch (23 x 13 cm) loaf; 16 servings

Per serving (1 slice): 161 Calories, 22 g Carbohydrate, 5 g Protein, 6 g Fat, 22 mg Cholesterol, 56 mg Sodium, 2 g Fiber
Exchanges: 1½ Starch, 1 Fat (1½ Carb Choices)

Whole Wheat Raisin Bread

Prep time: 10 minutes ◆ Bake time: 50 minutes

Cooking spray

½ cup (65 g) chopped walnuts

2 cups (240 g) whole wheat pastry flour

1 teaspoon baking powder

1 teaspoon baking soda

¼ teaspoon salt

1 cup (170 g) raisins

1¾ cups (420 ml) buttermilk (see page 8)

1 large egg

½ cup (160 g) honey

¼ cup (60 ml) canola or extra-light olive oil

1. Preheat the oven to 350°F (180°C). Spray an 8 x 5-inch (20 x 13 cm) loaf pan with cooking spray.

2. Place the walnuts in a small baking pan and bake for 3 to 5 minutes, until toasted; set aside.

3. Mix together the flour, baking powder, baking soda, and salt in a large bowl. Stir in the raisins and toasted walnuts until coated with flour.

4. Whisk together the buttermilk, egg, honey, and oil in a medium bowl until well blended. Add the wet ingredients to the dry ingredients and stir just until blended; do not overmix. Spoon the batter into the prepared loaf pan.

5. Bake for 50 to 55 minutes or until a tester inserted into the center of the bread comes out clean.

6. Cool on a wire rack for 10 minutes. Use a knife to loosen the bread; turn it out onto the rack. Serve warm or cool. Store covered. Refrigerate after 2 days. This bread can be frozen for up to 3 months.

Makes one 8 x 5-inch (20 x 13 cm) loaf; 14 servings

Per serving (1 slice): 211 Calories, 33 g Carbohydrate, 4 g Protein, 7 g Fat, 14 mg Cholesterol, 196 mg Sodium, 3 g Fiber
Exchanges: 1 Starch, 1 Fruit, 1 Fat (2 Carb Choices)

INDEX

ABOUT THE AUTHOR

KATHY KOCHAN was diagnosed with diabetes at five years old. For years, she managed her diabetes using an insulin pump, ate dessert every day, and credited her excellent health to conscientious food preparation. She was a cooking enthusiast, regularly lecturing and teaching healthy cooking classes in her native New Jersey. In 2010, she passed away after a twenty-two-year battle with breast cancer; she was also a proud fifty-six-year survivor of insulin-dependent diabetes. She is survived by her husband, Henry, and her sons, David and Marc.